"This super-personal book lets us in on the magical mind and mission that have given us two of my favorite restaurants—Contramar and Cala. Gabriela Cámara's passion for the lush, fresh, and bold flavors of her home country of Mexico bursts from these pages and her detailed recipes give us all a chance to bring her delicious food into our own homes."

—Suzanne Goin, chef and co-owner of Lucques, a.o.c., and Tavern

"As a fellow female chef and entrepreneur, Gabriela Cámara's culinary career stands out to me as one of great authenticity and passion. Her devotion to her food, staff, and community resonates throughout her restaurants, filling them with an ethos of family that is felt by each and every person who enters."

—Melissa Perello, chef-owner of Frances and Octavia

"Gabriela Cámara brings tradition and innovation together in recipes that are familiar yet original, simple but sophisticated. I can hear her saying 'you must try this!' as I read her recipes and I agree—you must."

—Elisabeth Prueitt, co-founder of Tartine Manufactory and Tartine Bakery

"This book brings me back to the first time I ate at Contramar, and the radical simplicity of Gabriela Cámara's grilled whole fish: superbly fresh, adorned with red and green salsas, and served family-style with a stack of freshly made tortillas. Cámara is a beautifully intuitive cook and keen observer of flavor, but her cooking is about so much more than just tasty and inspiring food. Cámara's restaurants are gathering places that celebrate the deep importance of sustainability as well as the culture, creativity, and diversity of Mexico City. These are the powerful and delicious messages delivered to you with every organic corn tortilla."

—Alice Waters, owner of Chez Panisse and founder of The Edible Schoolyard Project

MY
MEXICO
CITY
KITCHEN

FOR LUCAS

MY MEXICO CITY KITCHEN

RECIPES AND CONVICTIONS

GABRIELA CÁMARA

WITH MALENA WATROUS

Photographs by Marcus Nilsson

LORENA JONES BOOKS
An imprint of **TEN SPEED PRESS**
California | New York

CONTENTS

2

DESAYUNO
Breakfast 92

EVERYTHING CAN
BE A TACO 112

TORTAS 119

3

ANTOJITOS Y PRIMEROS
Finger Food and First Courses 140

CONTRAMAR'S TUNA TOSTADA 178

MASA IN MANY FORMS 190

5

POSTRES
Desserts 306

6

BEBIDAS
Drinks 336

CON LIMÓN 348

NOT YOUR TYPICAL MEXICAN GIRL

learned to make tortillas because I wanted to fit in. I was seven years old, and my family had moved to the small town of Tepoztlán, about an hour outside of Mexico City. My mom was an art history professor and most of the other women in our neighborhood were housewives. While they made fresh tortillas at every meal for their families—which meant standing at a stove, flipping tortillas one after another and serving them hot, only sitting down after everyone else was done eating—my mother had no interest in slaving away while the rest of us ate. Today, as a busy single mom running restaurants in two countries, I get it. But back then, I just wanted us to have fresh tortillas on the table like everyone else.

Of course, our eating habits weren't the only thing that set us apart. We were different, primarily because we were always living in places where we didn't quite belong. My mother is Italian, and she met my Mexican father in Cambridge, Massachusetts, in the 1960s, when they were both in graduate school and members of the same Catholic community. They moved to the slums of the city of Chihuahua when they married, because my father was working in a community center that he had established. They built the home we lived in themselves, and it was an amazing hippie house. My favorite part was a domed ceiling lined with wine bottles, so the light shone through in all different colors. My parents were definitely ahead of their time, with solar ovens and water heaters, and everything that could make our lifestyle more self-sufficient. We always had a vegetable garden, and as far back as I can remember, I would be watering the plants and feeding the chickens and rabbits.

When we settled in Tepoztlán, it was on land that had belonged to my father's cousin Carlos Pellicer Cámara. Known as the Poet of the Americas, Carlos was a powerful and influential figure, and an expert on pre-Hispanic art, who was super-important to Tepoztlán, a town that is very proud of its Aztec background. Among his many accomplishments, Carlos helped

bring a high school to the town and built a museum. He was somewhat of an eccentric, but highly respected because he was an internationally celebrated artist, which made it possible for our family to have deep roots in Tepoztlán upon arrival. We were very different in most every way, from the art we had on display to the massive quantity of books filling our house to the fact that my father made breakfast for our family every morning—and because he spent his days in his study or at a workshop.

In many ways, Tepoztlán was the ideal place to be a kid. Most of its streets were still unpaved, and my brother and I got to ride horses bareback and run free in the fields. We learned to drive on the narrow cobblestone streets while sitting on our dad's lap, long before our feet reached the pedals. But like small towns everywhere, Tepoztlán was a pretty conservative place, and our family was not. Just as in Chihuahua, my parents insisted on growing most of our food themselves, including the vegetables that my mother missed from Italy, such as fennel and arugula. All of our water was rain water, collected in cisterns, then piped into the house; this meant that during the dry season, we had to be very careful with our water use. My brother and I were raised with an understanding that water and food are precious resources, never to be wasted.

I come from a family that has always enjoyed food, and a lot of our family time revolved around cooking and eating. When I was little, everyone was always surprised by how I ate as much as an adult and was willing to try anything. My mother didn't know how to cook Mexican food because it wasn't her culture and my father had lived abroad enough that he didn't cook Mexican food either, but I grew up enjoying Mexican food nevertheless. Victoria, the lady who helped around the house, made the most delicious corn tortillas, which we all loved. In Tepoztlán, when the construction workers came to work on our house, they would share the food that their wives or mothers had packed for their almuerzo, a snack to be eaten at their midmorning break: tamales, stews and tortillas, sopes, and pozole, among other delights. I remember trying my first chile relleno taco and thinking, *This is the best thing I've ever tasted*. Thanks to my endless curiosity and the generosity of Mexicans, who are used to sharing whatever they are eating, I got an early introduction to many of the simple Mexican foods I still love most. In the market, my favorite snacks were a specialty of Tepoztlán, itacates. They are triangles of masa and lard that get cut in half and stuffed with different fillings and then eaten like a sloppy sandwich.

Even though my parents didn't cook much Mexican food, we had plenty of it in our home. Victoria and other ladies in town taught me many of the things I know about Mexican cooking. When I got married, she and a bunch of other ladies prepared a delicious mole for eight hundred people, just

I COME FROM A FAMILY THAT HAS ALWAYS ENJOYED FOOD, AND A LOT OF OUR FAMILY TIME REVOLVED AROUND COOKING AND EATING.

as they do for any big party. Every day, Victoria made a stack of tortillas from the corn that she had taken to the molino (mill) down the street to be ground into masa before lunch. Many times at night we would reheat the tortillas, and they were excellent, but I knew they would have been even better if they had been eaten fresh, right after they came off the comal (the oblong metal pan used for stove-top cooking). I decided that I wanted Victoria to teach me how to make them, as we all loved them so much and I figured any respectable household needed an expert tortilla maker.

Victoria believed that seven-year-olds were too young to make tortillas. She had a point. For a tortilla to cook properly, the comal needs to be hot, and it's easy to get burned. Victoria was very busy and, while she and I adored each other, she didn't have a kind and patient nature. But my parents were firm believers in our capacities from a young age, and they'd always encouraged us to figure out what we wanted to do and go for it. I was annoyingly persistent, so even though Victoria never was that patient with me, I was always around her while she made tortillas and I studied her every move: rolling balls of masa between her palms, squishing each one in a heavy press lined with two halves of a plastic bag, easing the disk onto her palm to give it a couple of extra "slaps," and then carefully dropping it onto the comal, where the edges would start to turn opaque as the tortilla cooked. She'd flip it the first time after about 30 seconds. The second side had to cook a bit longer. Then she'd flip it again, and the tortilla would puff up, as if someone were blowing air into a balloon.

My parents had no objection to letting me stand at the comal, flipping tortillas over the stove, if that's what I wanted to do. My dad, who works in education reform, has always been a firm believer in the "unschooling" movement, convinced that kids do best when allowed to follow their own passions and learn what they are truly interested in. Because I knew how to read and write (my father had taught me) when I started elementary school, they made me skip first grade, so I finished primary school when I was just eleven—a year ahead of my best friend. I wanted to wait for her to catch up so that we could go on to the same secondary school together. That school required good writing and grammar in English, which I wanted to improve, as I had never studied the language formally, so I decided to take a "sabbatical" year and dedicate it to studying English on my own while volunteering at an organization for elderly homeless people and interning for a local veterinarian. It was one of the most extraordinary years of my life. I learned that I could set my own goals and achieve them without teachers telling me what to do, but rather by knowing what I wanted to accomplish.

I probably don't need to tell you that having fresh tortillas at the table didn't suddenly make my family blend in. It did, however, teach me a lot.

I learned to cook with my senses and have continued to cook in an intuitive way, integrating my observations into whatever I am doing, because paying close attention—from the market to the table—is the key step toward making great food. And after I became the family tortilla maker, I learned that even greater than the joy of cooking is the pleasure of serving others, especially people you love, and seeing the delight on their faces when they taste something hot and fresh that's been made just for them.

My grandmothers, on both sides, loved to feed people. I remember my eighty-six-year-old Mexican grandmother fixing a cake for my brother and uncle for San Carlos Day, and my Italian grandmother eternally saying, "Mangia, mangia!" Cooking was their way of showing love to the family. I learned early on that food isn't just what you feed your family. Sharing it is what makes people family.

To this day, my favorite thing is to be in the kitchen with people I love, turning fresh ingredients into a delicious meal that we all get to eat together. That's why good home cooking usually beats restaurant cooking. Not only do you know exactly where the food you're eating came from but that it was chosen and made with love. I always try to bring the perspective of home cooking into my restaurants, Contramar in Mexico City and Cala in San Francisco, which is my home in the United States. Some of the recipes in this cookbook come from Contramar and Cala, but I would and do make all the others at home, because for me there has never been a huge difference between the two. I cook what I love to eat—my own take on Mexican classics, with twists that have more to do with celebrating fresh and local ingredients than with being different for the sake of being different.

This cookbook doesn't represent all of Mexican food, which is a vast cuisine. There are already encyclopedia-length cookbooks for those who want to tour the country gastronomically, trying ten different kinds of mole, for instance, and noting the regional distinctions. I deeply respect that knowledge, but this book isn't about that. What I want is to show you how we cook and eat in Mexico City, or more specifically how I cook and eat in Mexico City. Like all major cities, Mexico City is a melting pot. We've borrowed all kinds of influences from the people of various cultures and backgrounds who've passed through this city and called it home, incorporating their practices into a diet as varied and interesting as the population itself.

In Mexico City, I found a place where I belong. It remains my home base, but I've traveled a lot and learned to create a sense of belonging through cooking. No matter where I am, how stressed or how busy, if I can get access to a kitchen and some fresh and inspiring ingredients, I can ground myself by preparing the recipes I'm sharing in this book. Whether you're new to cooking Mexican food or looking for new interpretations of dishes you already know, I hope that my recipes have the same effect on you, bringing you joy in making, serving, and eating some of my favorite food.

THE EVOLUTION OF MY FOOD IN MEXICO CITY

Growing up, my family kept a close connection to Mexico City, where we'd go grocery shopping, see movies, visit exhibitions, and attend family gatherings and political protests. When I went to university in Mexico City in the 1990s, there was a growing awareness that the capital of our country was a cool place, riding a building wave of international popularity. One sign of this was that the city was becoming a stop on mainstream musicians' concert tours. I remember going to a Rod Stewart concert and thinking, *Now we're like any first-world metropolis!*

These days, Mexico City seems to be on everyone's radar. But that wasn't the case when I opened Contramar, my first restaurant, twenty years ago. Nowadays, the kinds of food we serve—sustainable seafood, lots of ceviches and aguachiles, and fresh organic produce—is super-trendy. But when we first opened in the late 1990s, no one else in Mexico City was really doing that. Back then, Mexico was still very much under the spell of European cuisine, particularly Spanish. Chefs were dazzled by molecular gastronomy. People were excited to be able to get anything from anywhere—foie gras from France, caviar from Russia—at any time. The modern Spanish movement had seeped into the restaurant scene in a big way, bewitching Mexican chefs into treating food like a chemistry experiment. The positive outcome was the refocus on quality ingredients.

Still in my early twenties, I had no culinary training and zero experience in restaurant kitchens. I was living in Mexico City, studying history, and planning to continue studying abroad so I could become a curator of contemporary art at a museum. I still loved to cook and go out to eat, and I found molecular gastronomy amusing and, when well executed, sublime. As in all big cities at that time, an interest in food was spreading across the culture, reflected by

cool restaurants that appealed to more than the middle-age and older elites. It was a time when people of different ages and classes started going out to experience food as a form of entertainment—almost in the same way as they'd take in art—becoming more sophisticated diners as a result of gaining greater exposure to varied foods. To this day, I love the entertainment of "modern food," but a squiggle of foam under a tower of unrecognizable food has never excited me as much as flavorful, market-driven cooking, in which you can taste the freshness of the ingredients shining through.

Although I always loved Mexico City, everyone who lives in a city that size knows that as often as possible, you need a break from the urban grind. My favorite place to go to, besides Tepoztlán, was Zihuatanejo, a beach town on the Pacific Coast, where I'd spent many family vacations. We'd usually eat at two beachfront palapas, La Perla and La Gaviota, where they served delicious fresh seafood, ceviches, and fresh fish tacos that we couldn't get in Mexico City at the time. A palapa is an open-air restaurant with a ceiling of woven palm fronds; feeling the breeze and smelling the sea are as much a part of the experience as the food. When I was twenty-two, I took a trip to Zihuatanejo with some friends, and we started talking about how we wished we could hold on to that feeling of relaxation back in Mexico City. Instead of the stuffy restaurants dominating the urban scene at that time, we wanted someplace to go that was like these palapas, with a modern take on beach food and a chic yet relaxed vibe.

Although back then Mexico City didn't have much in the way of seafood restaurants, other than the more traditional Spanish ones, people in the city sometimes had access to even fresher fish than what we were eating on the beach. You could get super-fresh seafood at stalls in and around the major markets in Mexico City. Because Mexico City is so central, the shuttling of fish from the shore to the city for processing is a practice that dates back to the time of the Aztecs, when Emperor Moctezuma had his racers run a relay from the coast of Veracruz to Mexico City to bring him fresh fish.

There was no reason a restaurant in Mexico City couldn't serve seafood as fresh (or fresher) than what we were having at the beach. We wanted seafood prepared in a similarly unpretentious way and saw no reason we couldn't try to re-create the relaxed atmosphere of the palapas. Even though none of us had ever built a restaurant or worked in a professional kitchen, we were young and cocky enough to think that we could pull off whatever we set our minds to. And somehow, *we should do this* became *let's do this*. By the end of that trip, the wheels were set in motion.

SOBREMESA IS MEXICO CITY'S TIME-OUT—A WAY TO PROLONG A GREAT MEAL WHILE ENJOYING YOUR COMPANY.

We knew what we wanted to create: someplace bistro-y and cool, like the bed-and-breakfasts in the south of France or the trattorias of Italy, where the produce used in the kitchen is grown nearby. I'd been living in Italy when the Slow Food movement began—with Carlo Petrini making pasta in the Piazza di Spagna to protest McDonald's—and that was an inspiration. But, of course, our food would be Mexican—the food we'd enjoyed at the beachside palapas. We thought we'd eventually rely on my family's small farm in Tepoztlán to grow a lot of the organic produce for our restaurant. We also wanted our seafood-focused restaurant to be serving fish caught only in Mexican waters. Back then, in Mexico City, the only fish considered really good in high-end restaurants was white-fleshed fish, so we could buy tuna for 8 pesos per kilo. (Nowadays, it goes for infinitely more.) We found a perfect location in Colonia Roma, a district that was still a little off the beaten path, and we converted a refrigeration warehouse into the space of our dreams, complete with a ceiling of petates (palm mats), which was our low-budget, urban adaptation of the beach palapas. I asked my uncle Carlos to paint something in the space because it was clear we needed color. He painted a huge blue mural of fish on the wall behind what would become the bar, bringing the ocean into the space and establishing the coastal vibe in the restaurant.

We were afraid of that humongous space—we thought we would never be able to fill it up. But almost from the beginning, people were intrigued. Here were these kids, working hard to run a restaurant at a time when there were very few restaurants with young people in charge. Peruvian Nikkei and Mediterranean food were a huge influence, but ours was always a Mexican place. We had lots of raw fish in ceviches and Mexican-inflected sashimi, plus fresh-made salsas and tortillas for our grilled fish. One of the most important decisions we made from the very start was to make our tortillas from fresh masa and serve them hot off the comal, just as was done in the good beach palapas. We wanted the best masa we could source, so we started getting it from molinos in the city that would grind it to order for us. The quality of the corn was as important as the quality of the fish.

Most things were served family-style—and that was such a hit—but there were white tablecloths and waiters in tuxedos, as was the tradition for professional waiters in trustworthy restaurants. It was high-quality food, but it wasn't stuffy. It was Mexican food, but it wasn't like any other restaurant in Mexico City at that time. Contramar became a place everyone liked to eat at, from star artists to grandmas, business people, expats, and tourists. We made a place that could have been located in any modern city, where anyone could feel at home. I remember finding it interesting that on long weekends, while other restaurants were empty, Contramar was packed. I think that's because we succeeded in creating what we'd hoped for: that feeling of being at the beach yet still in the city. It was like a vacation in people's minds.

Contramar was unique when we opened and it remains relevant twenty years later—even more so now that Mexico City is full of food lovers looking for authentic and local food. I am flattered by how many other restaurants are doing what we were doing from the start: raw fish, small bites, and family-style shared plates, with everything made from local and extremely fresh ingredients and elevated flavors served in ways that are not intimidating. We are only open for lunch, but in Mexico City, lunch can stretch on into the night. That's because almost everyone sticks around for a sobremesa, which loosely translates to "over the table" and refers to the period spent lingering over coffee or drinks, after dessert. Sobremesa is Mexico City's time-out—a way to prolong a great meal while enjoying your company.

Even when I'm insanely busy and running behind (which is pretty much all the time), my favorite thing is hanging out at the table, surrounded by the people I love while sharing one last glass together and talking about anything and everything. After two decades in this business, I still consider it a privilege to prepare and serve my favorite dishes to our guests. And I love it when they linger for their own sobremesa.

WHAT IS "MODERN" MEXICAN?

Before moving to San Francisco to open my first restaurant outside of Mexico, I found myself wondering if there was a place in the United States for the kind of cooking that I like to do. I knew that Mexican food was already popular in the US—that tacos in particular had become a kind of comfort food for many people, especially in the western states—and I wondered if I had anything new to offer.

My restaurants in Mexico City were thriving. I was plenty busy. But my business partner was convinced that the moment was right to open a Contramar-inspired restaurant in the United States, where Mexican food was rising in importance. He wanted to live in San Francisco, a city we'd both enjoyed on brief vacations and gastronomic expeditions. While he saw this as a business opportunity, I couldn't stop thinking about the abundance of fresh and gorgeous ingredients I'd have access to in the San Francisco Bay Area, with its mythic farmers' markets. But I barely knew the city. So before taking the plunge, I visited to scout it out.

On that trip, I walked around the city as much as I could, sampling all of the Mexican food I came across. Mainly I ate giant burritos and tacos, usually filled with the same rotation of ingredients (carne asada, pollo asado, carnitas) and often smothered in a blanket of melted cheese, watery guacamole, and faded pico de gallo. Most of the ingredients were not in season but were included because people expected them to be. The food wasn't terrible, but it didn't excite me. And none of it tasted like the Mexican food I like to cook and eat. Rather than feeling discouraged, I started to get excited, because clearly there was a space for me to fill. My cuisine was on the verge of being similar to what people already liked but also different in ways that meant I had something new to bring to the scene. I'd have access to those amazing farmers' markets and could build a menu from the ingredients that inspired me, tweaking it according to the seasons, while cooking traditional Mexican food and bringing my own creativity into the mix.

It took a lot of hard work to get Cala going, but the restaurant has been warmly received, featured in many articles heralding the rise of "modern Mexican." I'm never totally sure what people mean when they describe my cooking that way. I'm not trying to be trendy; I'm just cooking in the way I always have, combining the fanaticism for freshness that I got from my Italian side with the love of flavor that's my Mexican birthright. I never tweak traditions just for the sake of being different. If anything, I'm convinced that most traditions persist because they're the best way to do something. But I'm also not afraid to make interesting substitutions in classic recipes, especially with produce, to take advantage of ingredients that inspire me. If I come across some fabulous wild mushrooms at the farmers' market, even if they're not ones found in Mexico, I'll find a way to use them on a tostada or with a mole. If I have access to a great local chèvre, I'll use that to stuff peppers instead of using a processed cheese with a Mexican name on the label, which tastes like the plastic it's wrapped in. While I respect tradition, I don't worry about authenticity any more than I aspire to be modern. Anything I make is authentic to me, as modern as the moment in which I'm cooking.

That said, modernism and minimalism often go together, and I guess there is a certain minimalism to the way I cook, which is not the same as being austere. I don't cut corners or skimp on ingredients just for the sake of holding back. But I also think carefully about every ingredient I put into a recipe, being careful not to add something that isn't going to enhance to the finished taste of the dish. When you start with great ingredients, you need fewer of them. You want to be able to savor each one. I guess it is that simple.

I often overhear people dining at Cala saying that my cooking tastes lighter and fresher than the Mexican food they're used to. I don't avoid fats. As we all know, fat is flavor (or at least one of the components that brings out flavor). But I don't heap on gratuitous toppings either. The right toppings can be enhancements, but I want you to be able to taste the dish itself, too. In my mussel tamales, I embed the whole bivalves in a masa flecked with fresh herbs, making them so flavorful that they don't need any salsa. While I like good cheese, nothing I serve comes blanketed in the stuff.

Just like my seven-year-old self, I still believe that dinner should be served with hot fresh tortillas. At Cala, they're made continuously throughout the dinner service, from organic corn masa that we have nixtamalized, which is the process of soaking dried corn in a mixture of water and lime that "cooks" the kernels until they're soft enough to mill, and also releases amino acids that turn the corn into a complete protein. Then we grind the kernels right in our kitchen. Ironically, that seems to be one of the hallmarks of "modern" cooking—getting back to the way things were traditionally done, avoiding processed foods, using whole spices, whole grains, and the whole animal. This is really the oldest way of cooking.

WHILE I RESPECT TRADITION, I DON'T WORRY ABOUT AUTHENTICITY ANY MORE THAN I ASPIRE TO BE MODERN.

Once I saw that there was a gap to fill with the kind of Mexican food I like to cook, I realized that the same gap existed for a cookbook. Most Mexican cookbooks available outside of Mexico are either encyclopedic volumes chronicling regional variations of every conceivable Mexican dish, or they're reductively simplistic, focusing on one dish—often tacos. Of course, there are the iconic books by the inimitable Diana Kennedy, the purist who is lauded for faithfully documenting the foodways and recipes of Mexico. Just as I didn't see a lot of Mexican restaurants in the United States serving the kind of food that I most often cook and eat, I didn't see cookbooks teaching people how to make my style of Mexican food.

This book is a collection of my own favorite recipes, including things I serve at my restaurants—like Contramar's tuna tostadas, a dish that has become iconic and reinterpreted at restaurants all over the world. But this is not a restaurant cookbook in the usual sense, as so many restaurant cookbooks seem to be more aspirational than practical, featuring dishes that few people would attempt without having attended culinary school. Maybe it's because I didn't go to culinary school that I don't cook that kind of food. I'm more interested in how food tastes than how it looks. Of course, I want my cooking to be beautiful—but beautiful ingredients don't need much dressing up.

These are the dishes that I make for family and friends at home, both in Mexico City and in San Francisco. A few of these recipes may seem tricky—dishes to cook for a special occasion or a large dinner party—but most are quite simple. They're foods that I put together when I have half an hour to fix dinner for my son and myself and often a few guests. Simple isn't the same as easy. My way of cooking is not difficult, but if you want these dishes to taste as good as they can, you need to be mindful about everything from the ingredients you select to how you cook and serve them. I've included a lot of seafood recipes in this book because that's what I most love to cook and eat. Many people harbor the misbelief that seafood has to be fancy, which isn't true—seafood is part of home cooking in coastal regions. And because more people everywhere now have access to high-quality fish that has been frozen right after it was caught, you don't actually need to live by a coast to cook this food. You just need to make sure you're always getting the best-quality fish and seafood.

My cooking is the result of decades of trial and error in the kitchen and also the product of getting to work with amazing teachers, from my nonna and my aunts in Mexico City and Florence, Italy, to my neighbors in Tepoztlán, to the cooks on the teams at my restaurants, to Diana Kennedy, to whom we owe so much for the extensive research she has done on regional Mexican cooking. It's my privilege to share what I've learned with you, so that you can make this food in your own kitchen, wherever you live.

WELCOME TO MY KITCHEN

My kitchen practices are definitely old-fashioned. Maybe that's because so much of what I learned came from my maternal grandmother. My nonna loved to garden, cook, bake, knit, sew, quilt, carve wood, and make pottery and jewelry. Not only was she gifted manually, she enjoyed doing everything very carefully and extremely well. She was a thwarted artist, prohibited from going to art school because in her day well-raised Italian girls did not pursue careers as artists. She's the one who taught me that the secret to making something good is being careful. Her instructions to me are now the ones I'm passing along to you: Pay attention, take your time, and respect your resources.

Nonna hated waste. She had been pregnant and had a toddler (my mother) at the end of World War II when the people of Florence were starving, and she always remembered the day the US Army flew over her city, dropping parcels of food that included Spam. Although she later shuddered to think of eating tinned meat, she never forgot how it felt to be hungry, and always treated food as a sacred resource. She only let me start cooking with her once I could peel an apple without sacrificing any of the white flesh of the fruit. To this day, I hate to see any kitchen waste, and I cook in a way that minimizes it as much as possible.

It's particularly important not to waste when you're using good ingredients. That's as true in Mexican cooking as in any other cuisine. Maybe it's the Italian in me, but I always start by looking for what's at maximum ripeness, making sure to use up what's going to be the first to go bad. When I'm meal planning, I begin by looking at what I want to use first (either at the farmers' market or that I already have in my own kitchen), and then I design what I want to cook from those ingredients.

I always try to cook with local and sustainable ingredients, both in my restaurants and at home. For some of my recipes, this has required me to find substitutions in the United States, but I enjoy the creative challenge and interesting results. To update my tuna tostada in California using a sustainable local fish, I found a trout farm where they feed the fish pistachio silage from organic pistachios grown nearby. These incredibly fat fish have the most brilliant rainbow scales and are as flavorful as salmon. In the summer, I've started making tostadas to take advantage of ingredients like heirloom tomatoes, laying juicy slices on a base of homemade queso fresco flecked with lemon zest. I love quelites, which are wild bitter greens in the amaranth family that grow abundantly in Mexico. I can't always get the same exact ones in San Francisco, but in dishes that call for these bitter greens I've substituted local greens, which in many cases were considered weeds, with great results.

While I love recipes, and have an extensive cookbook collection, I use them more as templates than rules, and I encourage you to do the same with my recipes. Just as a taco can be anything you want as long as it's served in a folded hot tortilla, a tostada can hold any ingredients you like, as long as the base is a fried or baked tortilla. Sopes can contain any kind of guiso (stew) and salsa as a filling. Think of this as a modular cuisine. Mix and match and don't be afraid to take risks. If you choose your ingredients with care and cook with attention to detail, the results will be better for being uniquely yours.

While cooking well begins with shopping well, it's not enough just to go to a great market. You need to know how to get the best that the market has to offer, no matter where you shop. This is particularly true when shopping for seafood and essential when buying seafood that you intend to use raw. Make sure to buy sashimi-grade, either caught within the last forty-eight hours or frozen immediately after it was caught. Ask the fishmonger (or whoever is working behind the counter) for the best quality they have, and even ask to sniff it before they wrap it. I know common sense is the least common of senses, but use it to guide you. Is the fish free of any discernible fishy smell? Are the eyes clear and does it look beautiful enough to be attractive when served raw? On your next visit, be sure to give the fishmonger feedback about your last purchase to show you are serious about freshness and quality, because then they will always want to give you the best they have. Especially if you keep coming back.

Shopping sustainably is a challenge. Good ingredients do tend to cost more. It costs more to grow organic produce, raise animals without hormones and antibiotics, and fish ethically in ways that don't deplete the already depleted sea—not to mention pay a living wage to the people involved in each of these

I HATE TO SEE ANY KITCHEN WASTE, AND I COOK IN A WAY THAT MINIMIZES IT AS MUCH AS POSSIBLE.

labors. But it's money well spent, because it supports the people who make the effort to cultivate good food without harming the planet and it produces food that we would all prefer to eat. Make sure you shop in a way that isn't wasteful. If you're treating yourself to a beautiful piece of fish, the rest of your meal might be composed of foods such as rice, beans, and corn, none of which is expensive. While the fish in a ceviche might be expensive, all you need is some lime, onion, cilantro, and chile to complete the dish. I'm also a fan of Mexican classics that are really clever ways to use ingredients before they go bad, such as chilaquiles and huevos con migas, both of which repurpose stale tortillas into delicious breakfast staples.

Another way to save a bit of money while maximizing flavor is to cook with the whole animal whenever possible. I realize that this is easier in a restaurant than in a home kitchen (most people aren't going to be roasting whole pigs at home), but there are ways for home cooks to use the whole animal. With chicken, for example, instead of buying bits and pieces (who knows how long those chopped thighs have been sitting on their Styrofoam tray?), buy the whole chicken and have it cut into serving-size pieces. You can then use them to create a savory stock (see page 88) and reserve the poached meat for other dishes that call for it. The same applies to fish. Fish stock (see page 89) is a staple in many of my dishes, and it's so simple to make. When you buy a fish, ask the fishmonger to fillet it but also give you the head, still attached to the spine and tail. If you're buying from a market where the fish were already filleted, they probably still have heads and bones lying around, and will give them to you for free or sell them inexpensively. Similarly, instead of buying shrimp that have already been peeled and deveined, buy them whole and save the heads and shells to use in a shrimp stock. Not only is this stock super-easy to make, but the shrimp will be infinitely tastier than the ones sold already shelled.

I can't stress enough the importance of cooking with your own stock whenever possible. Being able to do this means having stocks available at short notice, so plan ahead and use your freezer. Any meat (or vegetables) cooked in liquid will result in a stock, or the base of a stock. When I braise a tongue, for instance, rather than throw out the water in which the tongue was braised, I freeze it to use later in picadillo, where the rich meaty broth is the perfect complement for the ground beef in which it simmers. I also keep a small container in my freezer with odd bits of vegetables that would add flavor to a stock, such as the green tips of leeks or fresh garlic, excess fresh herbs, or root vegetables that are going soft. That way, when I have a chicken carcass or the bones of a fish, all I have to do is reach into the freezer for these greens or aromatics, put them in a stockpot of water, turn on the heat, and let the whole thing simmer. It's hard to mess up a stock, especially when it's going into a dish to which other flavors will be added. I like to freeze stocks in quart containers. They're easy to thaw, and if I know how much the container holds, I know exactly how much I'm adding to a recipe.

As you work through these dishes, you may note that many of them contain more salt than you are used to cooking with, especially if you don't cook food with a lot of chile. That's because salt tempers heat. The spicier the food, the more salt it will probably need in order to taste balanced. While I have given some guidelines about how much salt I think these recipes require, it's impossible to predict how spicy the chiles you use will be or to know what your personal heat threshold is. So my advice is to salt in increments as you cook, tasting as you go, because you can always add more, but you can't take it out once it's in there. I recommend cooking with sea salt when you prepare these dishes, because that is the kind traditionally used in Mexican cooking, although I also sometimes use a finishing salt such as Maldon or fleur de sel when I want to add that perceptible crunch, especially on raw foods such as salads, ceviche, or aguachile.

Taste your food as you cook, at every step of the process. This way you can get a clear sense of how the food you are making tastes, which allows you to adjust the flavor along the way to ensure that the result is something you will actually like. This gets easier to do with practice, as you get used to gauging taste as it develops, but it's one of every good cook's secrets to making great-tasting food.

In terms of special equipment, there's not a lot that you really need in order to cook the dishes in these pages. A powerful blender is essential, because many of these sauces require you to liquefy chiles, nuts, and other ingredients. If your blender isn't that powerful, you should have a spice grinder. I keep two blender jars—one for savories and one for sweets, so that I never have to worry about my custards having a fiery kick. A couple of fine-mesh strainers are also something you may want to invest in, as you will use them to strain any fibrous bits from moles, salsas, and aguas frescas. If you're going to be making your own tortillas, and I sincerely hope that you do, a tortilla press is essential. They are inexpensive and available at most Mexican markets as well as most cooking stores and online. Without one, it's nearly impossible to press a tortilla to a uniform thinness, unless you are an experienced tortillera, who can make yours by clapping the masa between your hands. A comal is a nice thing to have, but not crucial. But again, a comal is not particularly expensive and definitely works well for the purpose of cooking tortillas as well as for cooking vegetables and chiles. But you can also make do with a pair of cast-iron skillets.

I can't resist giving a pitch for the pressure cooker. The truth is, I don't always plan ahead. My pressure cooker allows me to make up for the times when I don't, enabling me to cook with whole ingredients and make what I want in a fraction of the time. In less than an hour, you can turn a whole chicken into a savory stock, get an octopus cooked and tender, or transform dried beans from hard into soft enough to refry.

Between all that I juggle, I'm often running from one thing to the next. But every time I cook one of these dishes, I feel myself calming down as I focus on each step. Cooking is one of the only activities I do during which I don't multitask. I can see only as far as the onion I'm chopping. I have to pay attention exclusively to the chile I'm roasting to ensure it doesn't burn. By the time I'm done cooking, I always feel happier—a feeling I know comes across in the dishes I serve. Cooking feeds my soul as much as it feeds the people at my table.

Paying attention to every step of the process requires a singularity of focus that I think we all crave, which is one of the reasons cooking with care is a pleasure and not just a means to an end.

1 BASICOS

BASICS

Many Mexican recipes are made from the same basic building blocks: salsas, rice, beans, and masa. But the recipes taste different depending on how the building blocks are used. You can scramble refried beans into eggs or poach eggs in bean soup. The ingredients are almost the same, but one dish is dense and hearty, the other lighter and more delicate. Salsa verde can be used sparingly as a condiment spooned onto tacos or by the cupful as the simmering base of a stew, or you can swirl crema into it to make the rich and tangy sauce for chilaquiles. One thing is for sure: most Mexican meals require more than one building block to play with. That's why this chapter contains so many recipes.

Some of these basic recipes, like the ones for soupy beans and white rice, are so simple that you could learn them by heart without trying. You might be wondering why you need recipes for these things at all. Just because a recipe is easy and simple doesn't mean you shouldn't pay attention to every step of making it. On the contrary, the fewer ingredients and steps a dish has, the more care you should put into preparing it. For instance, my recipe for soupy beans is fairly long, not because it's difficult but because a lot of steps ensure that the beans turn out just right. I'm sure you've had some bad beans, cooked to a disintegrating mush or crunchy and underdone. If you follow my directions, you'll end up with beans that are creamy on the inside with their skins still intact.

Having the basic components that you need to make a great Mexican meal can take advance planning. You need an hour or two to cook dried beans (although it's largely inactive cooking time). Guacamole is quick to prepare but also turns brown quickly, so you need to make it shortly before you sit down to eat. Making your own queso fresco requires that you let the curds drain for several hours so the cheese reaches the right consistency. Crema needs to sour for about 24 hours, but then it keeps for up to 10 days. Salsas also usually keep in the fridge, so if you make those in advance, they're ready at a moment's notice, and beans and tortillas also store and reheat well. You can either make your basic building blocks ahead of time to go into a particular dish you have in mind or look at what you have left in the refrigerator and design a meal from that.

If you're familiar with Mexican food, you'll probably recognize most of these basics as classics. But everyone does things a little differently, and these are my versions. I've tried to share all of the tricks that I've learned over my years of cooking. While I respect traditions, I'm not rigid. Sometimes the desire to use sustainable ingredients prompts me to use something not found in Mexico, such as the raw trout that we put on our tostadas at Cala instead of the classic (but overfished) raw tuna. Where produce is concerned, I am always drawn to the most gorgeous in-season fruits and vegetables. In Mexico, the availability of some produce is more consistent, but when I'm in California or elsewhere, the produce I get can change a lot, and I enjoy incorporating the different ingredients into my Mexican food, even if it means deviating from standard recipes.

Pay attention to the steps I outline for making these basic building blocks, but don't be afraid to improvise, especially if you come across an interesting ingredient you want to substitute. Odds are good that if it's fresh and in season, it will taste great.

ZANAHORIAS CON LIMÓN Y CHILE PIQUÍN
MARINATED CARROTS WITH LIME AND CHILE PIQUÍN

MAKES 4 CUPS / 500G

8 to 10 tender young organic
   carrots
½ cup / 120ml freshly squeezed
   lime juice
1 Tbsp sea salt
1 tsp ground chile piquín

These carrots are the most basic thing, briefly soaked in lime and shaken up with salt and chile piquín. These little nibbles start every meal at Cala, brought to the table in a small wooden bowl for diners to enjoy while studying the menu. The truth is, any kid could throw this together. In fact, when my son, Lucas, learned how to chop, this was the first thing he wanted to make. By the time we return to the table at Cala to take an order, the bowl of carrots is always empty. It's a nice way to ease into a meal, making you hungry for more substantial food.

We use fresh young carrots—slender ones that snap when you bend them in half, so sweet they don't need peeling, just a good scrub. Feel free to substitute (or add) other vegetables, such as jicama, daikon or watermelon radish, celery, and cucumber. You can also briefly marinate fruit, such as watermelon or pineapple, in this same bath of lime, salt, and chile piquín. Just make sure any produce you use is as fresh as it can be. This is always true when you're serving something raw. Because you want the vegetables to be crunchy and still sweet, they are best when marinated for only a couple of hours before you serve them. Softer vegetables or fruit don't need to marinate at all so you can serve them immediately.

You may not be able to find ground chile piquín, but the dried ones—which are about the size of pencil erasers—are widely available at Mexican markets, and you can throw them into a spice grinder. If you go through this step, grind more than you need, since it's a great spice to have on hand to garnish bowls of beans or soups: spicy but not overwhelmingly so.

Remove the carrot tops and scrub the carrots thoroughly. (If they're not very young and tender, you should also peel them.) Cut them in half lengthwise, then into 2- to 3-inch / 5 to 7.5cm pieces. (If you're using other vegetables, just weigh them to be sure that the ratio of vegetables to marinade matches this ratio and slice them in a way that will be attractive on a serving plate.)

Place the carrots in a jar or other container with a lid, add the lime juice, salt, and chile and shake or stir to combine. Place in the refrigerator to chill and absorb the flavors for no less than 15 minutes and up to 2 hours. Serve them cold.

Leftover carrots can be stored in the refrigerator but the lime oxidizes and can take on a metallic taste after a day or two, and the carrots can become rubbery as they lose their crunch, so these are better eaten sooner rather than later.

CEBOLLAS ROJAS ENCURTIDAS PICKLED RED ONIONS

Tangy, pickled red onions add a snap of flavor and a vibrant hit of color to whatever they garnish. They're especially good as a complement to rich things like carnitas (page 124) or cochinita pibil (page 291). This recipe calls for vinegar, but you can also pickle onions in lime juice if you'd like, though they won't last as long. Onions pickled in vinegar can last for a couple of weeks in the refrigerator, but I always finish mine long before that!

MAKES ABOUT 2 ½ CUPS / 450G

1 Tbsp sea salt
⅔ cup / 160ml white vinegar
2 red onions, thinly sliced

———————

Whisk the salt and vinegar in a jar until the salt dissolves. Place the onions in the vinegar and marinate for 1 hour before serving. These onions can be stored in a sealed container in the refrigerator for up to 2 weeks.

SALSAS CLÁSICAS

For the same reasons an Italian cook wouldn't buy a jar of spaghetti sauce—because making your own is easy and tastes one hundred times better—in Mexico, anyone who likes to cook makes their own salsas, usually without glancing at a recipe. We know our favorites by heart and can improvise as we go, making adjustments depending on what's at hand and what we plan to eat it with.

Your own salsa will be infinitely better than any salsa you can buy because you choose your ingredients and fix it to your own taste, and it won't have been sitting in a refrigerator case fading or going fizzy as it nears its expiration date. In Mexico, salads are not a big part of the diet as they are in other cuisines, and I think that's because salsas (and aguas frescas) provide all the greens and vitamins we need.

There are so many Mexican salsas that you could easily fill a cookbook with nothing else. A salsa can be cooked or raw, blended or chunky, made with fresh chiles or with dried ones that you soak and blend. Some salsas are clearly intended for specific dishes, like Salsa Ahogada (page 126), which gets ladled over a torta ahogada (a drowned sandwich). But most are staples that can be mixed and matched with any variety of foods. I like to have at least two salsas in my fridge at all times to use as the mood strikes me, whether poured over eggs, enjoyed with tacos, or spooned into a bowl of beans.

My favorite salsas vary depending on the season, especially in the United States, where produce is so seasonally variable. There is no hiding a mealy pink tomato, and a raw tomato salsa made from out-of-season ingredients always looks a little sad to me. So in the winter, even when I make a cooked tomato salsa, I will sometimes add a spoonful of tomato paste so that the finished product has the dark red color I like. Another of my favorite raw salsas, Salsa Brava (page 45), can be enjoyed in any season, since it's made of just slivered onion and habaneros, marinated in equal parts olive oil and lime juice. It's a great way to get that nice raw crunch, even in the winter.

While a raw salsa is best eaten on the day it's made, cooked salsas last for about a week in the refrigerator, so they're something I like to prepare on a Sunday and then use all week long. Cooked salsas also freeze well, so you can double your recipe and freeze the second half for up to 6 months.

For me, salsa is as much about adding color to food as flavor. Most salsas are either red (tomato-based) or green (tomatillo-based), although I am also so crazy about one yellow salsa, Salsa de Chile Manzano (page 46), that I am never without a jar of it. Whether I'm at the market or searching through my refrigerator to figure out what to cook, I let my eyes guide me. I see what's available, what looks good, or what needs to be used up first, and I build the meal from that. Instead of treating salsa as an afterthought, use it as a starting point.

VERDURAS EN ESCABECHE HOT PICKLED VEGETABLES

1½ tsp olive oil

4 garlic cloves

2 carrots, cut into slices

3 cactus paddles, dethorned and
cut into chunks

5 or 6 jalapeño chiles, halved
lengthwise

1 bunch of scallions, crowns
discarded, cut into 1-inch /
2.5cm pieces

⅔ cup / 160ml white vinegar

6⅓ oz / 180g cauliflower,
cut into chunks

2 tsp sea salt, plus more as needed

2½ oz / 75g zucchini,
cut into slices

Many cultures have their own recipes for pickled vegetables, probably because it's the best way to preserve vegetables to ensure you can keep enjoying them during the winter. In Mexico, that's not the issue, but pickling is also a great way to preserve produce when the temperature is hot and you lack refrigeration. But what may have started as a practical thing has persisted because pickled vegetables add a delicious hit of spice, salt, and acid to whatever they accompany. They are great in tacos, with any grilled meat, or on their own. One of my favorite pickled vegetables is the nopal, or cactus paddle, which already has a tart flavor. At Mexican markets in California, you can buy them in the produce section, and often they have already been shorn of their thorns. If you find them with their thorns still on, use a paring knife to carefully nick them off. If you can't find them at all, just increase the quantity of the other vegetables.

_____

In a large skillet, warm the oil over medium heat. Once it's shimmering, add the garlic and fry until golden brown. Then add the carrots, cactus, chiles, and scallions and continue frying while stirring for 10 minutes, until everything softens.

Add the vinegar to the skillet and bring to a boil. Then add the cauliflower and return to a boil. Season with the salt.

Remove the skillet from the stove and add the zucchini. Let the mixture cool. Taste and add more salt if needed.

Transfer the vegetables to a sealed container with a lid and refrigerate until chilled, about 2 hours. Store in the refrigerator for up to 2 weeks. Serve cold.

SALSA VERDE CRUDA RAW GREEN SALSA

This raw salsa, made from blended tomatillos and avocado, is a good one to make when you need to use up a ripe avocado, even one that may be slightly past its prime, since you won't notice the discoloration once it's whipped with the other ingredients. This is one of the two salsas always available at the communal counter at Tacos Cala, the taco shop adjacent to my sit-down restaurant. I love the contrast of a fresh raw salsa on top of a slow-cooked stew. Don't use this salsa interchangeably with Salsa Verde (page 50). While that one serves as the base for lots of stews, this one shouldn't be heated up because of the raw ingredients. It's very Mexican to dollop two (or more) salsas on a taco or a plate of eggs. One salsa alone just won't do. This green salsa pairs beautifully alongside red Salsa Mexicana (page 49) or Salsa de Chile Cascabel (page 54).

Combine the tomatillos, garlic, shallot, avocado, lime juice, cilantro, lettuce, chiles, and salt in a blender. Blend thoroughly until the salsa is creamy. Taste and add more lime or salt if needed.

Serve the salsa cold. Store in a sealed container in the refrigerator for up to 2 days. After 2 days, the raw ingredients can separate and turn brown.

MAKES 3 CUPS / 720ML

10 tomatillos, papery husks removed and discarded, rinsed, and cut in half
1 large garlic clove
1 shallot, cut into pieces
1 avocado, cut in half, pitted, and peeled
Juice of 1 lime, plus more as needed
3 sprigs cilantro
4 leaves romaine or 1 small head Little Gem lettuce
2 serrano chiles, stemmed, seeded, and veins removed (or not, depending on how spicy you want this to be)
1 tsp sea salt, plus more as needed

PICO DE GALLO CHOPPED FRESH SALSA

MAKES 2 CUPS / 480ML

½ avocado, cut in half, pitted, and diced
½ white onion, diced
3 Roma tomatoes, cored and diced
1 Tbsp minced cilantro leaves
1 serrano chile, stemmed, seeded, veins removed (or not, depending on how spicy you want this to be), and minced, plus more as needed (optional)
Juice of 1 lime
1 Tbsp olive oil
1 tsp sea salt, plus more as needed

A lot of people who haven't been exposed to a wide variety of Mexican foods think of pico de gallo when they think of salsa. This is the chunky one made from chopped raw tomatoes, onion, cilantro, and chile (if you want it spicy). A lot of times, in the United States, pico de gallo comes in sealed plastic tubs where all of the ingredients have faded to a uniform and unappealing pink color. Don't bother. I only make this salsa when there are tomatoes worth eating raw, which in the United States means during the summer. I also only make it on the day I'm going to eat it, as close to the start of that meal as possible. Like a salad, it will wilt by the hour. But also like a salad, the fresher and better the ingredients, the fresher and better it will taste.

You'll notice that white onions show up all the time in Mexican cooking. Why "white" onions? Because that is the kind of onion commonly found across Mexico. They tend to be sharper than the slightly sweeter yellow onions and are also a bit more tender. Different onions can be substituted without great variation in the result, and you may find that the change actually works to the advantage of a recipe and makes it your own. Just note that if you use red onions, they are likely to change the color of a dish. A salsa brava made with red onions, something I often do on purpose, is lovely. But if I have a white-fleshed fish and want to make a ceviche, I wouldn't use a red onion and risk dyeing the fish pink (unless I wanted that result).

———

In a bowl, gently stir the avocado, onion, tomatoes, cilantro, chile, lime juice, oil, and salt. Taste and add more chile or salt if needed. Serve immediately.

SALSA BRAVA "FIERCE" SALSA

The abundant habanero chile infusing slivered onion makes this salsa fiercely hot. Soaked in equal parts olive oil and lime juice, with a good amount of salt and oregano, this all-purpose condiment adds a tangy burst of heat to whatever it touches. Recently, I opened a jar of this salsa that had gone fizzy, turning the contents into a fermented salsa brava, which I knew was safe to eat because it had been kept refrigerated. It was delicious, like a Mexican kimchee. Not a morsel went to waste.

Whenever working with chiles, I strongly encourage you to wear rubber gloves. This is particularly important when handling the potent habaneros. You don't want the oil from the chile to get into cuts on your hands or to accidentally transfer to your eyes when you rub them.

Place the chiles and onion in a jar that can hold them with a little extra headroom. Add the oregano, salt, lime juice, and oil. Shake to combine or use a spoon to push the slices down so that everything is submerged in the liquid. Cover with a lid. Let the mixture sit in the refrigerator for no less than 2 hours and preferably for 1 day before using.

This salsa can be stored in the sealed jar in the refrigerator for about 2 weeks. I like it best after about 1 week, when the onions have fully soaked up the juices and the spice from the habaneros but still retain some crunch.

MAKES 3 CUPS / 720ML

2 habanero chiles, stemmed, seeded, veins removed (or not, depending on how spicy you want this to be), and thinly sliced
1 large white or red onion, thinly sliced
Heaping 1 tsp dried oregano
1 tsp sea salt
¼ cup / 60ml freshly squeezed lime juice
¼ cup / 60ml extra-virgin olive oil

SALSA DE CHILE MANZANO MANZANO CHILE SALSA

MAKES 1 ½ CUPS / 360ML

6 to 8 manzano chiles
2 tsp sea salt, plus more as needed
½ cup / 120ml extra-virgin olive oil,
   plus more as needed

Manzano chiles are not widely known in the United States, and yet I've seen them for sale at Mexican markets, farmers' markets, and even at some well-stocked supermarkets in San Francisco. They are yellow or orange, sometimes with a slight green tinge, and about the size and shape of a crabapple. And like the apple for which they're named, they're a little sweet and a little sour, in addition to packing a ton of heat that nonetheless manages to please (if you like spicy food).

In Mexico, manzano chiles can be more difficult to come by than they are in the United States, since they grow only after the rainy season. That's why I stock up on them when I visit Diana Kennedy in Zitácuaro, Michoacán, in the early fall. Needing to use them up before they spoil, I always roast the peppers and blend them with a generous amount of olive oil and salt. The result is this salsa, which is one of my all-time favorites. The roasted manzano chile pulp has the rich yellow color of egg yolks. It emulsifies with olive oil to form a paste that looks like mustard but has the taste and texture of a very (very!) spicy aioli. I love it as a spread on sandwiches, in quesadillas, and dolloped into soup, where it breaks into fiery little beads that skitter across the surface of the broth. Whenever people taste this, they assume it must be full of ingredients, because it has so much flavor. But it's just the manzano chiles bringing their inherent complexity to this very simple salsa, which also makes a great gift for fellow spicy-food lovers.

If you have heard that you can affect the spiciness of a dish by either keeping or discarding the seeds of a chile, then you have fallen prey to a myth. Lots of us—myself included—grew up hearing that the seeds were the spiciest part of a chile, so leaving out the seeds would result in milder food. The truth, according to pepper researchers, is a bit more complex. It's actually the chile's veins (also known as the placenta, which sounds awfully mammalian) that hold the highest concentration of capsaicin, the compound we have to thank (or blame) for a pepper's heat. That said, two things contribute to the continuance of the myth of the spicy seeds: (1) seeds are often attached to veins, and if you carefully remove the seeds—at the sink, for instance, using your fingernail to scrape them out—then you'll also be removing the truly spicy part of the chile; and (2) the spiciness of chiles varies enormously, not only from one variety to another but also from one chile to another. You can buy a serrano that is fiery hot and another from the same pile that's relatively mild. You never know what you're going to get. So it's possible to remove just the seeds from a mildish chile and persuade yourself that, yes, removing the seeds made your dish less spicy. So, if you want to try to control the spiciness of a dish, remove not only the seeds but also the veins of your chile, cleaning out its insides thoroughly. But remember that there is capsaicin in every part of the chile and, if you happen to get a particularly spicy one, there's no way of ensuring that it's not going to burn at least a little. The safest way to keep your food from being too hot? Leave the chiles out completely. Most of the recipes in this book have enough flavor coming from other ingredients that they will still be delicious without the heat—at least to those who don't like it hot.

———————

Preheat the broiler.

Place the chiles on a baking sheet and broil for 15 to 20 minutes, checking every 5 minutes and rotating the chiles with tongs so they get evenly charred. They should slump, feel completely soft, and be blackened in spots. Alternatively, toast the chiles on a comal or in a skillet on the stove top over medium-high heat, rotating them regularly while keeping watch over them. Both methods produce equally good results, although these chiles are spicy enough that the smoke they produce when charring them on the stove top can make you cough, which is why you might prefer to keep them contained in the oven.

Once roasted, transfer the chiles to a plastic bag or a closed container to "sweat," so the skins loosen and peel away more easily. Once the chiles are cool enough to handle, put on gloves and use your thumbs to slit the chiles open. Remove and discard the stems and clumps of black seeds. Peel the chiles and discard the charred skins.

Transfer the chiles to the blender and, using the most powerful setting, puree until the mixture is as smooth as possible. Add the salt. With the blender running, drizzle in the oil, the slower the better, since this helps the mixture emulsify. Adding too much oil at a time can cause the mixture to separate. When it emulsifies, the chile and oil should be thoroughly combined and have the look and consistency of mustard. Taste and add more salt if needed.

This salsa can be stored in a sealed container in the refrigerator for up to 2 weeks.

SALSA ROJA ASADA CHARRED RED SALSA

MAKES 2 CUPS / 720ML

6 Roma tomatoes, cored and
    cut in half
1 white onion, quartered
2 to 4 serrano chiles, stemmed,
    seeded, and veins removed
    (or not, depending on how
    spicy you want this to be)
1 Tbsp olive oil
2 garlic cloves
1 tsp sea salt, plus more as needed
½ cup / 10g cilantro leaves,
    minced

All of the ingredients in this salsa are roasted before they're blended. You want everything to get blackened, since the black flecks will add visual appeal as well as a smoky taste. Use your comal, if you have one, or a skillet to roast your vegetables on the stove top. People in Mexico use comales to cook on the street, as well as in their own kitchens. Traditionally, they were made of clay, but now metal ones have become more common for practical reasons. When cooking vegetables on a comal, you have to stand over them and tend them quite constantly. But it's pleasing—to me, at least—to stand there, rotating tomatoes, chiles, and onions, watching them turn soft and earn their tasty black skins. I like being able to see (and smell) when they're done.

Place a comal or large skillet over medium heat. When hot, arrange the tomatoes, onion, and chiles, on the pan. Drizzle the vegetables with the oil and cook for about 15 minutes, using tongs to turn them every couple of minutes, until all sides are blackened. While you don't want your vegetables to get thoroughly burned, you do want the skins of everything to be blistered and scorched. Alternatively, if you'd prefer not to stand over the stove, preheat a broiler, toss your vegetables with the oil, and blacken them on a baking sheet under the broiler, periodically turning them with tongs. Add the garlic in the last 5 minutes, letting it get lightly toasted and not blackened.

Once the tomatoes, onion, and chiles are charred on the outside and the garlic is toasted, scrape everything into a blender. Add the salt and enough water to fill the blender jar one-third full. Pulse. It's up to you how chunky you want this salsa. Traditionally, it's made in a molcajete, a Mexican-style mortar and pestle formed of volcanic black rock, which retains more of the texture of the ingredients than processing them in a blender. If you have a molcajete, by all means use it. Once the salsa reaches the consistency you like, add the cilantro. Taste and add more salt if needed.

Refrigerate to chill and serve cold. This salsa can be stored in a sealed container in the refrigerator for up to 5 days.

SALSA MEXICANA MEXICAN-STYLE SALSA

Salsa Mexicana is the little black dress of salsas. It's simple but not boring, goes with just about everything, and can be pulled together with very little effort. Like anything "a la Mexicana," this salsa earns its name because the red, green, and white of the tomatoes, chiles and onion share the colors of the Mexican flag. You can leave out the tomatoes and make an even simpler salsa of just onions and chiles that tastes great on scrambled eggs or paired with Huevos Libaneses (page 108). When you make Salsa Mexicana, be sure to core the tomatoes well—completely removing and discarding the seeds and their surrounding juices—otherwise they'll make the salsa too watery.

———————

Warm the oil in a small heavy-bottom saucepan over medium heat until it's hot but not smoking. Add the onion and chiles and sauté until the onion is translucent but not browned. Add the garlic and tomatoes and cook for about 10 minutes, until the vegetables look stewed. Transfer the vegetables to a blender and blend until completely pureed. Return the mixture to the pan and simmer over low heat for another 10 minutes, until the sauce has reduced by about one-third. Add the cilantro and salt. Taste and add more salt if needed.

This salsa is usually served hot. It can be stored in a sealed container in the refrigerator for up to 5 days. When I make it without tomatoes, I prefer to eat it when it's freshly made.

MAKES 2 CUPS / 480ML

2 Tbsp olive oil
1 white onion, chopped
2 serrano chiles, stemmed, seeded, veins removed (or not, depending on how spicy you want this to be), and chopped
2 garlic cloves, chopped
5 Roma tomatoes, cored, seeds and juices discarded, and chopped
¼ cup / 5g cilantro leaves, minced
1 tsp sea salt, plus more as needed

SALSA VERDE GREEN SALSA

10 small tomatillos, papery husks
    removed and discarded, rinsed,
    and cut in half
2 to 4 serrano chiles, stemmed,
    seeded, and veins removed (or
    not, depending on how spicy
    you want this to be)
1 small white onion, half left intact
    and the other half minced
1 large garlic clove
1 Tbsp sea salt, plus more
    as needed
½ cup / 10g cilantro leaves,
    finely chopped

Salsa Verde is a workhorse salsa. It serves as the base for so many dishes, such as Chilaquiles (page 118), and can also be spooned over just about anything as a tasty condiment. It's nearly impossible to mess up this salsa, since all of the ingredients are simply boiled and then pureed in their cooking juices.

Choose the smallest tomatillos you can find, tightly encased in their papery skins, since they will be the freshest and least bitter. If they're available, the tiny purplish tomatillos—although not traditional—are significantly less sour than the green ones, so use those if you want a less acidic salsa. You can, of course, adjust the recipe to use more or less chile. Just remember that the spicier you make this salsa, the more salt you should add to offset the heat. An aggressively spicy (and salty) salsa verde will be better used as a condiment than as the base for a main dish served to people with varying levels of heat tolerance.

Combine the tomatillos, chiles, intact onion half, garlic, and salt in a medium saucepan. Add water just to cover and bring to a boil over medium-high heat. Decrease the heat to maintain a simmer and cook until the tomatillos become more translucent and the chiles have gone from bright green to a faded khaki color. Pour everything into a blender, including the liquid, and puree. Return the puree to the saucepan and simmer gently over low heat until reduced by about one-third, about 10 minutes. Add the minced onion and cilantro to the cooked salsa and stir to combine. Taste and add more salt if needed.

This salsa is excellent served hot or cold. It can be stored in a sealed container in the refrigerator for up to 1 week.

SALSA DE CHILES SECOS Y TOMATILLOS
SALSA WITH DRIED CHILES AND TOMATILLOS

At Tacos Cala, the taco shop adjacent to my sit-down restaurant, I always like to offer both a green salsa and a red one, but in the winter, I'm so uninspired by the mealy pink tomatoes that I can't bring myself to use them. That's when I make this red salsa instead. It uses tomatillos as a base, but a combination of chiles de árbol and guajillo chiles gives it a dark red color. This is a very piquant and pungent salsa, but you can cut back on the number of chiles de árbol and garlic cloves if you want it less assertive.

_____

Warm an ungreased comal or large skillet over medium heat. When hot, place the tomatillos on it and cook them for about 10 minutes, using tongs to turn them so they cook evenly. Place the tomatillos in a blender.

Dry off the comal or skillet. Return it to the heat, add all the chiles, and toast them lightly, stirring constantly, for about 2 minutes. Don't let them brown or blister at all and remove them from the heat as soon as they start to smell nutty. Add the chiles to the blender. Drop the garlic cloves onto the comal or skillet and cook, stirring or flipping them so they get lightly browned on all sides, then place them in the blender, too, along with the salt. Puree completely. Taste and add more salt if needed.

Serve this salsa at room temperature. It can be stored in a sealed container in the refrigerator for up to 1 week.

MAKES 3 CUPS / 720ML

10 tomatillos, papery husks removed and discarded, rinsed
10 chiles de árbol, stemmed and seeded (or not, depending on how spicy you want this to be)
2 guajillo chiles, stemmed and seeded (or not, depending on how spicy you want this to be)
4 garlic cloves
1 tsp sea salt, plus more as needed

DRIED CHILES

There's a dizzying array of chiles used in Mexican cooking. This is part of what makes it such a complex cuisine. Not only do an enormous variety of chiles grow in Mexico, but we like to coax every possible flavor out of each kind by drying, smoking, pickling, or soaking them in adobo sauce as well as enjoying them fresh and raw. Each treatment changes the taste of the chile. The ancho, for instance, is the dried version of a ripe poblano. The chipotle is a dried and smoked jalapeño, sometimes reconstituted in adobo sauce. I'm not going to give you a comprehensive primer on all the kinds of chiles you could use in each and every form. There are books on the matter. But I will not hold back from recommending a wider variety of chiles than you may be used to using, both fresh and dried. If you've never cooked with dried chiles before, don't be daunted. They're available at Mexican markets as well as at many conventional supermarkets and online. They're inexpensive and easy to use once you get the hang of following a few steps.

Many recipes will call for dried chiles to be reconstituted in some kind of liquid and then blended. Frequently you will also be asked to toast them first, before soaking them. This is a bit misleading, since "toasting" implies that something is turning brown, and you don't actually want that to happen to your chiles, especially not with the thin-skinned red ones, because they taste bitter when they get even slightly burnt. With small red chiles, such as the chile de árbol or chile piquín, you should scatter them whole in a small ungreased comal or skillet over medium heat and be sure to turn them constantly with a spatula or spoon, heating them up for just a minute. Err on the side of caution and take them off the stove just as soon as you can smell them. With larger chiles, such as anchos, you should stem them first and discard the seeds, then tear them into strips before placing on an ungreased comal or in a skillet over medium heat. Again, don't let them brown or blister, and take them off the stove as soon as you smell them. You might wonder if this step is worth the effort when you're toasting them so lightly, but it definitely is. Heating them up coaxes out even more flavor—a simple way to achieve a complex-tasting result.

SALSA DE CHILE CASCABEL CASCABEL CHILE SALSA

MAKES 2 CUPS / 480ML

10 cascabel chiles, stemmed
    and seeded
2 garlic cloves
4 Roma tomatoes, cored and
    cut in half
5 tomatillos, papery husks removed
    and discarded, rinsed
Olive oil (optional)
1 tsp sea salt, plus more as needed

Cascabel means "jingle bell." This chile gets its name from the rattle of the dried seeds when you shake it. It's one of my favorites: mild, smoky, and a little sweet. Salsa de Chile Cascabel can be made with tomatillos or Roma tomatoes or a combination of the two. Even when red tomatoes are in season, I like to add a few tomatillos because their acidity complements this chile. This salsa is good with many things, particularly with eggs, grilled cactus, or grilled meat.

Warm an ungreased comal or skillet over medium heat. Tear the chiles in half, add to the comal, and toast for about 2 minutes while turning them constantly. Don't let the chiles blister or burn, since this will make your salsa bitter. Remove from the heat as soon as they start to smell nutty. Drop the garlic cloves onto the comal or skillet and cook, stirring or flipping them until they get lightly browned on all sides, and remove them from the heat once they smell fragrant.

In a small saucepan over high heat, cover the toasted chiles with water and bring to a boil. Turn off the heat and let them soak and soften in this water for 1 hour, until they're quite soft.

Place an ungreased comal or large skillet over medium heat. When hot, arrange the tomatoes and tomatillos on the pan. Cook for about 15 minutes, using tongs to turn them every couple of minutes, until all sides are blackened. While you don't want your vegetables to get thoroughly burned, you do want the skins to be blistered and scorched. (Alternatively, if you'd prefer not to stand over the stove, preheat the broiler, rub the tomatoes and tomatillos with oil and blacken them on a baking sheet under the broiler, periodically turning them with tongs. Remove the pan from the oven when the tomatillos and tomatoes are slumped, blackened, and sizzling, and let them cool while the chiles finish soaking.)

Remove the soaked chiles from the water, and place in a blender with ½ cup / 120ml of their soaking liquid, the tomatillos, tomatoes, garlic, and salt. Blend to a smooth consistency. Pour the sauce into a saucepan and simmer over medium heat until reduced by one-third. Taste and add more salt if needed.

Serve this salsa hot. It can be stored in a sealed container in the refrigerator for up to 1 week.

SALSA DE CHILE MORITA MORITA CHILE SALSA

A morita chile is a ripe serrano chile that has been dried and lightly smoked. It's always harvested in "the last picking," meaning that it's as ripe as can be. It can easily be confused with the mora chile, which is a dried and smoked ripe jalapeño that's a bit larger and darker in color although it's similar in shape and texture. This sauce can be made with either morita or mora chiles, but I prefer to use moritas. But you can feel confident about using either of them, because both make a deliciously complex sauce. You never know exactly how spicy these chiles (or this salsa) will be, but you can be sure it will be delightfully tart, with an attractive orange-brown color. When you smell this salsa, it will remind you of barbecue, and it does, in fact, taste great on grilled meats and onions and also with eggs.

Many of the recipes in this book instruct you to fry an onion in a bit of lard or oil until it turns translucent but not browned. Once it becomes translucent, it will have lost its crunch and sharpness, but it won't be cooked to the point of mush or take on the caramelized taste that a browned onion begins to acquire. You can ensure you cook onions just until they become translucent by keeping your cooking temperature at medium instead of high heat, monitoring your onions as they cook, and only cooking them for a few minutes.

MAKES 3 CUPS / 720ML

4 Tbsp / 60ml vegetable oil
6 Roma tomatoes, cored and
    coarsely chopped
10 chiles moritas, stemmed and
    seeded (or not, depending on
    how spicy you want this to be)
½ large white onion, coarsely
    chopped
1 garlic clove, coarsely chopped
1 Tbsp dried oregano
1 tsp sea salt, plus more as needed
¼ cup / 60ml extra-virgin olive oil

Place two skillets over medium heat and put 2 Tbsp of the vegetable oil in each. When the oil is hot but not smoking, place the tomatoes in one of the skillets and let them cook, stirring occasionally. Meanwhile, in the other skillet, add the chiles and fry for 1 to 2 minutes. When the chiles have puffed up and browned to a dark chocolate color, add the onion and garlic; they will soak up the chile-infused oil as they sauté. Once the onion is translucent, add the partially cooked tomatoes and let it all cook together for about 15 minutes.

Pour everything into a blender, and add the oregano and salt. Slowly drizzle in the oil while blending to emulsify. Taste and add more salt if needed.

Serve this salsa at room temperature. It can be stored in a sealed container in the refrigerator for up to 1 week.

SALSA NEGRA BLACK SALSA

MAKES 2 CUPS / 480ML

2 cups / 480ml rice bran oil,
    safflower oil, or any vegetable
    oil with a high smoke point
1½ oz / 40g chiles mecos (about
    15 dried smoked chipotle chiles),
    stemmed and seeded
40 garlic cloves (about 2 heads)
1 Tbsp piloncillo, grated, or firmly
    packed 1 Tbsp light brown sugar
1 Tbsp sea salt
Heaping 1 cup / 120g walnuts

This salsa gets its black color (and name) from chiles mecos. The chile meco is a smoked and dried jalapeño. It has a completely desiccated, almost brittle texture, unlike the more leathery, still-red mora. When you fry chiles mecos, they turn from the color of milk chocolate to dark chocolate. After the fried chiles get blended with fried garlic, piloncillo, and toasted walnuts, the resulting salsa is savory with just a hint of sweetness, smoky and spicy in a way that manages to be both intense and mellow. It is oily and thick like a pesto, and a little goes a long way. At Cala, we serve it in a small wooden bowl alongside a whole roasted sweet potato (see page 299). It's also a great rub for Pulpo a las Brasas (page 266). You can sauté greens with 1 tsp of Salsa Negra, toss summer squash with it before roasting, or add a spoonful to Picadillo (page 296).

Make sure you're buying dried chipotles, or chiles mecos, not chipotles canned in adobo, the more common form of chipotle chiles. You can order the dried ones online if you don't have a market nearby with a well-stocked Mexican food section.

Piloncillo is the most minimally processed form of sugar that you can buy: cane juice boiled into a syrup and poured into cone-shaped molds. For small amounts (like this salsa calls for), you can use a grater or a Microplane. For larger quantities, use a butcher knife to cut off chunks that you can weigh. It melts easily and has a subtle caramel taste, with just a hint of smokiness. While you can substitute light brown sugar and this will still taste good, note that piloncillo is naturally brown, unlike American brown sugar, which is just refined white sugar with molasses mixed in. The molasses imparts its own flavor, which isn't one that's part of traditional Mexican cooking.

In a medium heavy-bottom saucepan, heat the oil to 350°F / 180°C. Make sure to use a pan that is big enough to fry your chiles without crowding them. The oil should be 1 to 2 inches / 2.5 to 5cm deep. To test whether the oil is hot enough, place a wooden spoon in the oil and see if tiny bubbles gather around the wood. Once they do, add the dried chiles and fry for 3 to 4 minutes, until they puff up and turn the color of dark chocolate. Once they're done, turn off the heat under the pan, remove the chiles with a slotted spoon, and place them in the bowl of a food processor or in the jar of a very powerful blender.

Immediately drop all of the garlic cloves into the same hot oil used to fry your chiles. Even though the stove is off, the oil should still be very hot, and you will see a commotion of bubbles as the garlic is submerged in it. The cold garlic will begin to lower the temperature of the oil. Let them simmer in it for about 10 minutes, watching to make sure there are always small bubbles rising in the pot but that it's not frying at a raucous boil. You may need to turn your stove back on to the lowest possible heat setting if the bubbles come to a stop. You want the garlic to get super-soft and stay fairly light in color, not turn a dark brown so that you get a custardy, roasted garlic texture and a taste that is not bitter but sweet. To test for doneness, use a slotted spoon to remove one of the fried cloves of garlic from the oil. When you press on it with the back of a spoon, it should mash easily. Once the garlic has reached this texture, use the slotted spoon to remove them from the oil (reserving the oil) and place them in the food processor or blender with the chiles. Add the piloncillo or brown sugar and the salt.

Preheat the oven to 350°F / 180°C.

Place the walnuts on a baking sheet, in a single layer, and lightly toast for 5 minutes. You only want to activate the oils, not darken the walnuts, or they will become bitter.

By the time your walnuts have toasted, the reserved oil will have cooled to a temperature where you can handle it. Add the walnuts to the food processor or blender, then puree while slowly adding between ¾ and 1½ cups / 180 and 360ml of the reserved oil in a thin stream. Blend until it seems as if it can't get any smoother. You want a dark paste that is as uniform as possible. Transfer to a container with a tight-fitting lid and refrigerate overnight or for up to 24 hours before using so that any remaining chile bits soften.

Because the garlic has been confited in oil, this salsa will keep in a sealed container in the refrigerator for up to 3 months. You can also freeze it for up to 6 months.

ADOBO DE CHILES ROJOS RED CHILE RUB

MAKES 2 CUPS / 480ML

4 cascabel chiles, stemmed
   and seeded
1 ancho chile, stemmed and seeded
1 guajillo chile, stemmed and seeded
1 pasilla chile, stemmed and seeded
2 chiles de árbol, stemmed, seeded,
   and veins removed (or not,
   depending on how spicy you
   want this to be)
4 Roma tomatoes, cored
¼ white onion
5 garlic cloves
2 cloves
½ cup / 120ml safflower oil
2 Tbsp freshly squeezed
   orange juice
1 Tbsp freshly squeezed lime juice
1 tsp ground achiote (annatto) seeds
Pinch of ground cumin
Pinch of dried oregano
1½ Tbsp sea salt, plus more
   as needed

This adobo sauce is what flavors the red half of Pescado a la Talla (page 244), Contramar's signature red-and-green fish. It also gives the distinct red color to Pollo o Puerco al Pastor (page 278). Adobos tend to be tart—either from vinegar or citrus juice—and this one is no exception, with freshly squeezed orange and lime juices. But it's got a lot of other flavors, too, with the smoky dried chiles, ample garlic, and spices.

———————

Place the cascabel, ancho, guajillo, and pasilla chiles in a saucepan and cover with 1 cup / 240ml water over low heat. Bring to a simmer and then remove from the heat, cover the pan, and let the chiles soak and soften for 15 minutes.

In the jar of a blender, blend the chiles with their soaking water, the chiles de árbol, tomatoes, onion, garlic, cloves, oil, orange juice, lime juice, achiote seeds, cumin, oregano, and salt, pureeing until smooth. Taste and add more salt if needed.

This sauce can be stored in a sealed container in the refrigerator for up to 1 week or frozen for up to 3 months.

AGUACATES

Avocados are native to Mexico, a popular ingredient going back to the Mayans, and they are just as popular today. And it's no wonder. They are a welcome addition to just about any Mexican dish. You'll see sliced avocado being recommended as a garnish for a lot of recipes in this book, and it could probably garnish the rest, too. The truth is, it is rare to come across someone who objects to finding a few perfect slices of avocado on their plate.

The best-known and most popular variety of avocado is the Hass, which is consistently creamy and tasty, but there are a lot of other varieties as well, all definitely worth trying. In San Francisco, at the Ferry Plaza Farmers Market, we buy most of what we use from the Brokaw Ranch Company, which specializes in sustainably farming a wide range of avocados. In addition to Hass, we buy many varieties that are far less common, including Gwen, Gem, and Carmen avocados. Each has a slightly distinctive taste and texture, so if you ever have access to lesser-known avocado varieties, like the ones you can eat with the skin on, sample whatever you can find.

If you are new to avocado buying, here are a few pointers. You want to cut into an avocado when it's perfectly ripe, not before. When you pinch the fruit, the flesh should indent slightly, the way it would on a perfectly ripe peach. (But as with a ripe peach, it should not be mushy.) If you're buying avocados to use in a few days, buy them slightly hard. They will continue to ripen on your countertop until they're ready. If you need to speed up this process, you can wrap them in newspaper, as we do in Mexico. Once you cut into an avocado, make sure to eat it soon (within the day, if not immediately), since the cut surface will turn brown and the taste will deteriorate.

To cut an avocado, use a sharp knife and slice it lengthwise all the way around the pit. Twist the two sides in opposite directions so the avocado separates neatly into halves. To remove the pit, hack into it with your knife and then pivot the knife slightly from side to side until you can free the pit. You can now cut each half of the avocado into quarters that you can neatly peel and cut into thinner slices.

GUACAMOLE MASHED AVOCADO

MAKES 4 TO 6 SERVINGS AS
A STARTER OR MORE AS A
CONDIMENT

4 avocados, cut in half and pitted

1 tsp sea salt, plus more as needed

Juice of 1 or 2 limes, plus more
as needed

½ white onion, minced

1 Roma tomato, cored and
finely chopped

1 serrano chile, stemmed,
seeded, veins removed (or not,
depending on how spicy you
want this to be), and minced,
plus more if desired

¼ cup / 5g cilantro leaves, minced

1 tsp extra-virgin olive oil, plus
more as needed (optional)

Some purists insist that guacamole should be just mashed avocado and salt. But the truth is, people across Mexico put all kinds of things in it. When I was young, my friend's mom served a guacamole that tasted different from anything I'd ever had. I watched while she mashed up the next batch and saw her spoon Knorr seasoning powder from a jar into the molcajete. Loaded with MSG, that bouillon was giving the guacamole an artificial injection of umami, which is why it was so tasty. However, you can get a complex and addictive flavor naturally from a blend of salt, lime, onion, tomato, chile, cilantro, and oil, which is how I make mine.

The real secret to guacamole is using perfectly ripe avocados. But sometimes, when you cut into what seems like the perfect avocado, the flesh beneath the skin can be disappointing—rotten in spots, stringy, or unevenly ripe. If only some parts of your avocados are good, don't despair. Just cut out and discard the rotten bits and then add a teaspoon of olive oil to the mixing bowl. This will enhance the naturally silky texture of the avocado. Make sure to prepare guacamole right before serving it, if possible. Adding a bit of lime will also help stop it from turning brown.

Spoon the avocado flesh into a medium bowl. With a fork, mash the avocado to the texture you prefer. (I like my guacamole a little lumpy.) Add the salt, lime juice, onion, tomato, chile, and cilantro. Drizzle in the oil and mix well. Then taste and add, just before serving, more lime juice, salt, chile, and oil if needed.

MAYONESA CON CHIPOTLE CHIPOTLE MAYONNAISE

MAKES 1 CUP / 240G

1 egg
1 Tbsp freshly squeezed lime juice
½ tsp sea salt
1 canned chipotle chile in adobo,
     seeds removed
¾ cup / 180ml safflower oil

Canned chipotles in adobo have been popular in the United States for quite some time, and I often hear people refer to chipotle aioli, which often means store-bought mayo blended with a canned chipotle. But by definition, a true aioli includes garlic and olive oil, whereas a mayonnaise excludes the garlic and uses a neutral-flavored oil as I do here. While you can make a cheater version of this by blending store-bought mayonnaise with chipotles, making your own mayonnaise is nearly as simple, requiring only the blender and a couple of extra minutes, and it's much tastier.

Many mayonnaise recipes will tell you to use two egg yolks, but I prefer to use one whole egg, because I hate to have to waste half the egg, and mayonnaise still emulsifies when you include the white, although it may be a bit thinner, which is fine. Be sure to remove the seeds from the chipotle before blending it, since you want the finished mayonnaise to be silky. If you forget, you can also strain your finished mayonnaise.

In a food processor or a blender, pulse the egg, lime juice, salt, and chipotle until well combined. With the motor running, add the oil in a slow drizzle, processing until the mayonnaise emulsifies and turns creamy. Partway through, be sure to turn off the processor, scrape the sides, and process again so as not to waste anything. Alternatively, you can do all of this by hand, using a whisk and beating vigorously for about 8 minutes. (In the blender, it should take 4 to 5 minutes.)

This mayonnaise is best used on the day you make it, although it can be stored in a sealed container in the refrigerator for up to 2 days. For a spicier mayonnaise, leave in the chipotle seeds and then press the finished mayonnaise through a fine-mesh strainer using a silicone spatula.

MAYONESA CON LIMÓN / LIME MAYONNAISE VARIATION

Follow the main recipe but omit the chipotle chile.

QUESOS Y CREMA ÁCIDA

The commercial Mexican cheeses and other dairy products sold in the United States are problematic for me. In Mexico, we can seek out organic, additive-free queso fresco (our version of ricotta) and crema ácida (our version of sour cream). I love a good queso Chihuahua, which we use in quesadillas because it melts so well, or a dry and salty aged queso cotija, grated over a stew, or a freshly made queso fresco. Just like the cheeses from any other culture, great Mexican cheeses are best made by people who take pride in seeking the truest flavor they can get from every small batch.

In the United States, most Mexican cheeses and creams at Mexican markets are largely uninspiring, highly processed foods, shrink-wrapped in heavy plastic and with about as much flavor as you'd imagine they would have based on how they look. I don't think there is much point in seeking them out on some quest for authenticity. They simply won't taste that good, even if they have Spanish names. If you have a market where they are selling locally made or interesting-looking Mexican cheeses, then by all means try them. I am sure that cheese makers will catch up with the trend for increasingly high-end Mexican food. But if you can't find what looks like good Mexican cheese, then I recommend substituting a great-quality cheese that is not typically Mexican, and I will make suggestions for what I would use.

For instance, if you're looking for a mild cheese that melts well, then instead of Chihuahua cheese, you might swap a really good whole-milk mozzarella. For something grated and sharp, I usually opt for a ricotta salata. I don't use American sour cream. Like most Mexicans, I find its taste too sour, and I don't like its consistency. Instead, I either make crema ácida ahead of time to use in recipes, or if I need it right away, I buy crème fraîche, which is closer in flavor to Mexican crema and has a lovely richness. I like to make queso fresco, but again—if I don't have the time, I'll substitute a good ricotta. I have no problem cooking Mexican food with these non-Mexican cheeses. While it's easy to find amazing-tasting Mexican cheeses in Mexico, that's not yet the case elsewhere, and since the goal is for these dishes to taste terrific, I'm more than willing to make this concession.

QUESO FRESCO STRAINED FRESH CHEESE

2 cups / 480ml whole milk
½ cup / 120ml buttermilk
½ cup / 120ml cream
¾ tsp sea salt

This recipe involves cooking a combination of milk, buttermilk, and cream on the stove until curds form, then straining them for a period of time that will vary depending on how dense you want the resulting cheese to be. The buttermilk is the agent that curdles the cream and the milk. (Some people will use a bit of vinegar to the same end.) The result is a bright and clean-tasting cheese that works well in a lot of the recipes on this book, both savory and sweet. If you feel like experimenting, you can swap goat's milk for cow's milk, and the result will taste fabulous.

Line your colander with cheesecloth. You want the cheesecloth to drape over the lip of the colander, giving you enough excess to tie up the suspended cheese curds as they drain. Set the colander in the sink.

Combine the milk, buttermilk, cream, and salt in a Dutch oven or heavy-bottom stockpot. Place over medium-high heat and stir as the liquid heats up, using a spatula or whisk to keep the forming curds from settling at the bottom of the pot, where they could scorch. As the liquid reaches about 175°F / 80°C, the curds (which look like clumps) and whey will separate, and the curds will rise to the top.

Turn off the heat and pour the contents of the pot into the prepared colander. Use a rubber spatula to ease the curds down onto the cheesecloth. You can gently press out the moisture, but don't press hard, since you don't want to mash the curds into the cloth. Tie the four corners of the cloth and suspend the curds over a bowl (I hang the cheesecloth from my sink faucet) to let them drain for at least 30 minutes, or longer, depending on how thick you want the resulting cheese to be. It will have the texture of ricotta after 30 minutes, and if you wait 6 to 8 hours, it will have the consistency of cream cheese.

Queso fresco can be stored in a sealed container in the refrigerator for up to 1 week.

CREMA ÁCIDA MEXICAN SOUR CREAM

Plan ahead because you need a couple of days for the cream to sour. You just have to stir cream and buttermilk in a jar and let it sit for a couple of days, and it's ready to go. Be sure to use cultured buttermilk, or else nothing will happen. And, if you can find it, use pasteurized organic cream instead of ultra-pasteurized. It should still work with the more common ultra-pasteurized, but you might want to add an extra tablespoon of butter-milk. Another option is to use Greek yogurt in place of the buttermilk as a culturing agent, which leads to a slightly more sour flavor but can also result in a thicker cream. If you don't have the time to make this or haven't planned ahead, then use crème fraîche in any recipe calling for crema ácida.

MAKES 2 CUPS / 480G

2 cups / 480ml cream
¼ cup / 60ml cultured buttermilk

In a glass jar, combine the cream and buttermilk. Cover the mouth of the jar with several layers of cheesecloth or a dish towel and let it sit for 24 hours at room temperature (between 70° and 75°F / 20° and 25°C). If your home is chilly (as mine often is in San Francisco), you can set your jar on top of your refrigerator, which tends to be warmer, or in the oven with the oven light on. After 24 hours, screw on the lid of the jar, and refrigerate for 24 hours before using.

Crema ácida can be stored in the sealed jar in the refrigerator for up to 10 days.

CHILES ASADOS ROASTED PEPPERS

All kinds of Mexican recipes call for roasted peppers. We love to stuff them, fry them, and cover them in sauce, but also to slice them into strips and cook them in stews. The most common pepper for stuffing is the poblano, due to its size and sturdiness. But we roast all sorts of peppers, big and small, mild and spicy, fresh and dried. I'm giving you the template for poblanos, but feel free to use these directions no matter what kind of pepper you want to roast. One of my favorite stuffed chiles is the chile manzano, but it's seriously spicy (and can be hard to find), so don't lie about loving heat if you make that one.

Keep the size of the chiles in mind. People can typically eat one large stuffed poblano, or two if the chiles are smaller.

MAKES ABOUT 7 OZ / 200G

4 to 6 large poblano chiles,
  or as many as you want to roast

On an ungreased comal or in a cast-iron skillet over high heat, roast the chiles, turning them over every couple of minutes using tongs or your hands (carefully, so you don't get burned). You're looking for uniform blistering, but you don't want them to become too soggy in the process, especially if you intend to stuff them, since they need to hold their shape. The process will probably take 10 to 15 minutes. Once they are well blistered and before the flesh is completely charred through in any spots, place the peppers in a plastic container with a tight-fitting lid or in a bowl that you can cover with a plate (not a towel or anything porous) and set aside to "sweat" for about 10 minutes, or until they are cool enough to handle.

Remove the charred skin from the whole chiles, trying your best not to puncture them if you intend to stuff them. If you intend to use your roasted chiles for rajas, or strips, then it obviously matters less if the chile tears. If you are careful, you should be able to remove just the thin skin and none of the flesh of the chile. Begin by using the back of a chef's knife to rub away the large pieces. Then use your fingers to pick off the smaller bits. Be thorough, since the lingering bits of blackened skin taste bitter and have a reputation for causing indigestion. Once the chile is thoroughly peeled, use a sharp knife to make a slit from the stem to the tip. Reach inside and, using either your fingers or a knife, remove the veins connecting the seeds to the chile, as well as the seeds. (I don't like to rinse my chiles under water because it removes some of their great flavor.)

Store in a sealed container in the refrigerator for up to 1 week.

TORTILLAS

Tortillas play a starring role in every section of this book. They are served fresh at the table, wrapped in a cloth in a basket or in a wooden box with a lid to hold their warmth. They're a key ingredient in so many of my favorite dishes, from chilaquiles to enchiladas. And, of course, they can get folded around just about anything—to serve as the base for a taco—or fried to make a tostada. If you've ever tasted a fresh, hot corn tortilla, I don't have to tell you how much better they are than the commercially produced kind with preservatives and stabilizers to ensure that they stay "fresh" for weeks, sealed in plastic bags. So if you have the time, it's definitely worth making your own.

Corn tortillas are composed of three ingredients: corn, water, and powdered lime (calcium hydroxide, not the citrus). In Mesoamerica, corn was one of the main crops, a staple of the diet. Ancient Mesoamericans discovered that soaking dried corn in a mixture of water and lime (the mineral found in limestone) breaks down the kernels until they're soft enough to mill. It also releases amino acids that turn the corn into a complete protein and allow our bodies to digest the nutrients more easily than they would if the tortillas were made with regular cornmeal. This process, called nixtamalization, produces the raw product used to make fresh masa, a grainy, wet dough that can be yellow or white, depending on the variety of corn (although in Mexico, corn is almost always white). To make a tortilla, you roll the masa into a ball, press it flat, and cook it on a comal.

Just as a pancake tastes best when transferred directly from the pan to your plate, a tortilla tastes best when it's hot from the comal. A fresh tortilla should be soft and pliable. When folded, it shouldn't break or snap back open. As they cool, tortillas stiffen. You can reheat them, but they're never as tender and irresistible as when they're first made. If you do reheat them, warm them on an ungreased comal or in a skillet and not a microwave. Microwaves heat the water in the tortillas, causing them to quickly dry out after the water evaporates as the tortillas cool down. In general, you can reheat tortillas once and seldom more than that.

That said, like my mother, you may not want to slave at the stove flipping tortilla after tortilla while your family and friends feast. Even when you get the hang of making tortillas, it still takes time. If you want to throw together

a Mexican meal quickly, you can't make tortillas from scratch. In Mexico, we eat tortillas all day long, and most of us aren't making them before every meal. I usually keep a bag of good tortillas in the fridge and more in the freezer, and heat them up as needed.

I'm giving you some options for how to get the best tortillas you can, depending on how much time you have. I'll start with the "purest" option, teaching you how to make your own tortillas, and then I'll share some ideas for how to get decent tortillas on those occasions when you don't have the time to cook them from scratch.

Make tortillas from fresh masa

If you live in a community with a tortillería or a Mexican restaurant where they make fresh tortillas, they probably have fresh masa that they will sell to you. In San Francisco's Mission District, a tortillería called La Palma sells fresh masa, which they scoop into a plastic bag, for about a dollar per pound. I usually buy 2 to 3 pounds at a time. You want to use up fresh masa within a day of buying it, or it will begin to ferment and will make your tortillas taste sour. Some people suggest freezing fresh masa, but I don't generally advise doing that because the tortillas made from thawed masa can be heavy. However, if you have extra masa, a solution is simply to make more tortillas than you need and freeze the ones you don't eat. Stack the cool tortillas, loosely wrap them in plastic, and place in the freezer for 30 minutes. As soon as the tortillas have begun to freeze, pry them apart, restack them in a sealed container, and store in the freezer for up to 1 month. When you are ready to use them, thaw each tortilla slightly before reheating it on a comal or in a skillet. These reheated tortillas will taste remarkably close to fresh ones because the iciness they assume from being frozen helps offset the moisture that's lost as they cool down after reheating.

Make tortillas from masa harina

If you don't have access to a tortillería or any place selling fresh masa, you can still make good tortillas by hand using masa harina. Sold in bags or in bulk, masa harina looks like cornmeal but is actually dried-out masa, which you reconstitute by adding water until it has the consistency of Play-Doh. Maseca used to be the go-to brand, and it's still for sale at most conventional grocery stores. But it's a big company that doesn't use exclusively organic corn, and these days it's easy to find superior-quality, non-GMO, organic masa harina that tastes much better. (Bob's Red Mill makes one.) While tortillas made from masa harina won't be quite as tender and delectable as ones made from fresh masa, any fresh hot tortilla is going to taste amazing, especially to people who aren't used to this luxury. I encourage everyone to make their own tortillas from scratch, even if it is from masa harina.

Buy fresh tortillas from a tortillería or Mexican market
If your town has a tortillería or well-stocked Mexican market where they make fresh corn tortillas, buy bags to keep in the refrigerator (if you plan to eat them soon) or in the freezer. While these are never quite as good as homemade, they are often good nonetheless, and certainly better than the supermarket kind. If the plastic bag has an ingredient list, check to make sure that there aren't added preservatives. In San Francisco, the tortillerías make a variety of corn tortillas—some with blue corn, others flavored with nopales, or cactus. They also make thicker "artisanal" tortillas that might look tempting but won't work for a lot of the dishes in this book, including tacos and enchiladas, because they're too fat to fold and will flop back open. Buy the thinner ones if you're going to use them for recipes. Before freezing tortillas, take them out of the bag, pry them apart, then gently restack them before putting them back in the bag. If they are stuck together when they go into the freezer, they will freeze into a clump and you won't be able to thaw and use them one at a time later.

Buy organic tortillas from the grocery store
When purchasing supermarket tortillas, make sure to seek out organic corn tortillas labeled non-GMO. They might be in the freezer section, which is fine. They need to be frozen because they lack any preservatives. Fresh food is alive. I sometimes also buy organic tortillas made from a blend of 50 percent corn and 50 percent flour. While this blend isn't typical in most parts of Mexico, the wheat flour lends softness to the tortilla, making it suitably chewy and pliable—a decent ready-made vehicle for tacos.

TORTILLAS DE MAIZ CORN TORTILLAS

MAKES 12 (6-INCH / 15CM)
TORTILLAS

2 cups / 520g fresh masa
Water, as needed
or
2 cups / 260g masa harina
1 to 1¼ cups / 240 to 300ml water

If you double this recipe and freeze half, you'll be glad later. To press and cook the tortillas, you will need a tortilla press; a large resealable bag or a plastic produce bag, cut into two equal sheets a little larger than the plates of the tortilla press; and an oblong comal that fits over two burners at once or two skillets or frying pans.

_____

If using fresh masa, make sure that it has the consistency of stiff cookie batter. If it doesn't, add water, 1 tsp at a time, until it does.

If using masa harina, in a medium bowl, combine the masa harina and 1 cup / 240ml water and mix well. Continue adding water 1 Tbsp at a time until you have formed a smooth and thick dough that has the consistency of stiff cookie dough.

Form 12 golf ball–size balls and lay a moist dish towel over them so they don't dry out.

Warm an ungreased comal or two skillets over medium heat.

Lay a precut sheet of plastic on the bottom of a tortilla press and place a ball of masa on top of the plastic. Place a second sheet of plastic on top of the ball and then squeeze the press firmly so that the dough is sandwiched between the two plates. You want the tortilla to be about ⅛ inch / 3mm thick. Open the press and remove the flattened masa, which will be stuck between the two sheets of plastic. Place it on your left palm (if you're right-handed) and use your right hand to peel off the top sheet of plastic. Then flip it over and transfer it to your right hand, so that it rests in your right palm. Carefully peel off the other sheet of plastic, freeing the raw tortilla.

Gently deposit the raw tortilla onto the preheated comal or skillet. You should hear a faint sizzle as it hits the metal. Watch for the edge of the tortilla to begin turning opaque, a signal that it is cooking. When this happens (after 30 to 45 seconds), flip it to the other side and let it cook for 30 to 45 seconds, until the whole thing starts to turn opaque. Now flip it back to the first side and let it cook for a final 30 seconds. After the second flip, it should start to puff up a little, a sign that all of the water in the masa has evaporated and the tortilla is done.

Getting your technique down takes some fiddling. If the edges of your tortilla look grainy and dry, add 1 Tbsp water to your dough, massaging it in thoroughly. But don't add too much water, or the masa will stick to the plastic and to the

CONTINUED

bottom of your pan. Make sure that your tortillas aren't too thinly pressed and that the thickness is uniform, which makes it easier to flip them. You may also need to adjust the heat of your stove if you feel they're cooking too quickly or too slowly. Once you get the moisture and temperature right, each tortilla should take a total of about 2 minutes to cook through. At this point, you should be able to press and cook two tortillas at a time, one on each side of the comal (or in each hot skillet). As each tortilla is finished cooking, set it in a basket or a deep bowl and cover the growing stack with a dish towel to keep them warm as you add to it. Wrapped up well, in a basket or a box with a lid, they should stay warm for about 1 hour.

You can reheat a tortilla on a hot comal or in a skillet, flipping it a few times until it's completely heated through. It's okay if your tortilla gets a little charred. The black flecks add flavor. You can also reheat them in a stack. Begin by heating one tortilla. After you flip it, add another on top of the already hot side of the first one. After 30 seconds, flip them both together so that the cold side of the second one is now on the hot surface of the pan, and add a third tortilla to the top of the pile. Keep flipping and adding until you have as many warm tortillas as you need. There's really no limit. Once they're stacked, they will all keep each other warm.

TORTILLAS DE HARINA FLOUR TORTILLAS

MAKES 12 LARGE (10-INCH / 25CM) OR 24 SMALL (6-INCH / 15CM) TORTILLAS

4 cups / 500g all-purpose flour
2 tsp baking powder
1 tsp sea salt
½ cup / 110g lard
1½ cups / 360ml hot water

While I eat corn tortillas much more often than flour tortillas, I like the latter very much, too. Instead of pressing masa, you knead white flour with water and a bit of lard, then roll this dough out. While most of the recipes in this book call for corn tortillas, you can always substitute flour ones. Children in particular tend to love quesadillas made from flour tortillas (and it's fun to roll them out together). Flour tortillas are typically larger than corn ones—partly because you aren't limited by the size of the tortilla press. They're popular in the north of Mexico, where the people have been more nomadic and have needed to eat on the road. These big, soft but sturdy tortillas did the job as edible containers. The biggest flour tortilla is called a *sobaquera*, which comes from the word *sobaco*, or "armpit," because these were rolled around food and carried in the armpit (which was believed to add extra flavor).

_____

In a large bowl, mix the flour, baking powder, and salt.

In a small saucepan over low heat, melt the lard, then remove it from the heat.

Make a well in the center of your flour mixture and pour the melted lard into it, stirring to incorporate until the mixture has a pebbly texture. Then add the hot water, little by little, stirring and integrating it into the dough, kneading with your hands until it's smooth and stretchy.

On a floured countertop, form the dough into a long rope that you can cut into the number of tortillas you want. Depending on the desired size, you should make between 12 and 24 balls. Roll each piece into a ball, then roll them into very thin disks.

Line a basket with a dish towel and preheat the oven on the lowest setting (or turn on the oven light).

Preheat a large comal or skillet over medium-high heat. You don't need to grease it, since the lard in the dough will keep your tortillas from sticking. Add a tortilla and cook for 30 to 45 seconds, flip it with a metal spatula and cook the other side for another 30 to 45 seconds, until the whole thing starts to turn opaque. Now flip it back to the first side and let it cook for a final 30 seconds. After the second flip, the tortilla should be golden on both sides and starting to puff up a little, a sign that all of the water in the masa has evaporated and the tortilla is done.

Put each tortilla in the basket and place in the warm oven until ready to serve.

ARROZ RICE

Every morning at Tacos Cala, the taqueria adjacent to my sit-down restaurant, we make a large pot of white rice, which goes on the fresh corn tortillas as the base for every taco de guisado. We use long-grain white rice from Rue & Forsman Ranch. As is usually the case with careful and conscientious farming, their rice tastes better than most supermarket brands. If you cook it carefully, as outlined in this recipe, you'll end up with distinct grains that are soft but not at all mushy.

In Mexico, we call rice a *guarnición*, which translates to "a garnish" or "an accompaniment." Although these two words mean different things in English—a garnish adds color and a bit of flavor, and an accompaniment tends to mean the starchy base that soaks up a saucy dish—Mexican rice often does both at once, because it's typically cooked in water in which vegetables have been pureed, so it brings more color to the plate. I love red rice (which is cooked in pureed tomatoes) and green rice (which is cooked with blended poblano chiles and cilantro), but on my tacos de guisado (see page 221), I usually prefer an unflavored cooked rice blend because it doesn't compete with the flavors of the stews. We begin by frying the uncooked rice in a bit of oil, until each grain is opaque, before adding the cooking water. Then we don't touch it at all while it cooks. This leads to fluffy cooked rice, every grain distinct.

(see page 221)

Add the oil to a medium heavy-bottom saucepan. Add the garlic and rice and turn the heat to medium-high. Fry, stirring constantly, until each grain of rice is opaque.

Add the water, cilantro, and salt and bring to a boil. Decrease the heat to maintain a simmer, cover the pot with a lid, and cook for 15 minutes without stirring. Check the rice for doneness by tasting a few grains. They should be tender but not mushy, separate and distinct. If needed, cook for 3 to 5 minutes longer. Taste and add more salt if needed. Remove the garlic and cilantro before serving.

While cooked rice can be stored in a sealed container in the refrigerator for up to 3 days and reheated, I suggest making it just before you intend to eat it, because it tastes better when freshly cooked.

MAKES 4 TO 6 SERVINGS

2 Tbsp olive oil
1 garlic clove
2 cups / 400g long-grain white rice
2 cups / 480ml water
1 sprig cilantro
1 tsp sea salt, plus more as needed

ARROZ ROJO RED RICE

MAKES 4 TO 6 SERVINGS

½ cup / 120ml water, plus more
    as needed
4 Roma tomatoes, cored
½ white onion, cut into chunks
2 Tbsp olive oil
1 garlic clove
1 sprig cilantro
1 cup / 200g long-grain white rice
1 tsp sea salt
½ cup / 50g fresh or frozen
    (unthawed) peas (optional)
½ cup / 60g minced carrots
    (optional)

Red rice—rice flavored (and colored) with pureed tomatoes—is a staple dish in Mexico. For the tastiest results, choose the ripest, reddest tomatoes you can find. Typically we use peas and carrots as I call for here, but feel free to use other similar vegetables—just chop them into small, even cubes and try to keep the amounts roughly the same, preserving the vegetable to rice ratio.

————————

In a blender, combine the water, tomatoes, and onion. Blend completely. You need 2 cups / 480ml of liquid to cook the rice, so top off the tomato mixture with more water, as needed.

Add the oil to a heavy-bottom saucepan over medium heat until it's hot but not smoking. Add the garlic, cilantro, and rice and fry, stirring constantly, until each grain of rice is opaque.

Add the pureed tomato mixture and the salt to the pan. Add the peas and carrots. Bring the mixture to a boil, then decrease the heat to low, return to a simmer, and cover the pot with a lid. Let the rice simmer undisturbed for 15 minutes. Check the rice for doneness by tasting a few grains. They should be tender but not mushy, separate and distinct. If needed, cook for 3 to 5 minutes longer. Remove the garlic and cilantro before serving.

While I recommend making this rice right before serving, if you make it ahead of time, empty the cooked rice onto a baking sheet and spread it out until it has cooled; this will keep the rice on the bottom of the pot from overcooking and becoming mushy. Transfer the rice to a sealed container and refrigerate for up to 3 days. You can reheat the rice by steaming it. To do so, place a steamer basket in a pot over gently boiling water, spoon the rice into the basket, place the lid on the pan, and steam for 2 to 3 minutes.

ARROZ VERDE GREEN RICE

Colored green by a blend of poblano chile and cilantro, this is one of my favorite rice recipes. For variety, you could also toss in a handful of minced fresh spinach leaves, kale, or a spicier green pepper.

In a small saucepan over high heat, bring the water or chicken stock to a boil, then add the chile and decrease the heat. Let the chile simmer for about 10 minutes until soft. Pour the cooking liquid and the chile into a blender. For a uniformly green rice, add the cilantro and liquefy. For more flecked rice, liquefy only the chile and the liquid and wait to add the cilantro to the cooking pan. You need 2 cups / 240ml of the liquid to cook the rice, but you can top off the green liquid with more water, as needed.

Add the oil to a medium heavy-bottom saucepan and warm over medium heat until hot but not smoking. Add the garlic, onion, and rice and fry, stirring constantly, until each grain of rice is opaque.

Add the poblano liquid, salt, and the cilantro if not added earlier to the cooking liquid. Bring the mixture to a boil, then decrease the heat to low; return to a simmer and cover the pot with a lid. Let the rice simmer undisturbed for 15 minutes. Check the rice for doneness by tasting a few grains. They should be tender but not mushy, separate and distinct. If needed, cook for 3 to 5 minutes longer. Taste and add more salt if needed. Remove the garlic before serving.

While I recommend making this rice right before serving, if you make it ahead of time, empty the cooked rice onto a baking sheet and spread it out until it has cooled; this will keep the rice on the bottom of the pot from overcooking and becoming mushy. Transfer the rice to a sealed container and refrigerate for up to 3 days. You can reheat the rice by steaming it. To do so, place a steamer basket in a pot over gently boiling water, spoon the rice into the basket, place the lid on the pan, and steam for 2 to 3 minutes.

MAKES 4 TO 6 SERVINGS

2 cups / 480ml water or chicken stock, plus more as needed
1 poblano chile, cut in half lengthwise, stemmed, seeded, and veins removed (or not, depending on how spicy you want this to be)
½ cup / 10g cilantro leaves, minced
2 Tbsp olive oil
1 garlic clove
½ white onion, minced
1 cup / 200g long-grain white rice
1 tsp sea salt, plus more as needed

DRIED BEANS

Different varietals of heirloom black beans can be smaller than jelly beans or as big as the largest favas, with glossy skins that shimmer like beetle shells. But you'd never know it if your only exposure to beans has been in canned form, where the beans are cooked to a paste, and jammed into a can, and taste of tin. If this is the case, I wouldn't be surprised if beans didn't particularly excite you.

Beans excite me. At Contramar, just as in my own home, a meal isn't complete without a large bowl of soupy beans, which make the perfect side dish to just about anything else within these pages. Since all they need is to cook in water and salt, maybe with an aromatic or two, you'd think it would be hard to ruin them. But I've had enough badly cooked beans to know that this is not the case.

To start, buy the best dried beans you can. Lots of shops now carry heirloom dried beans, so look for ones that may have been grown near you. But no matter where you live, you can order phenomenal heirloom beans online, thanks to Steve Sando of Rancho Gordo, who has done so much in the United States to elevate Mexican produce by making previously hard-to-find Mexican ingredients accessible. Rancho Gordo beans come in so many enticing varieties, and when buying from a company like it, you can be sure that the beans aren't stale, like the ones in the packages on supermarket shelves that have been sitting there for who knows how long. A package of dried heirloom beans costs just a few dollars more than a bag of conventional dried beans, but a little goes a long way and they're gorgeous—a pleasure to look at as well as to eat.

My way of cooking beans is mostly characterized by what I don't do. I don't presoak dried beans because this can make the skins blister. We don't salt the cooking water because it prolongs the cooking time; it's better to add salt once the beans have cooked enough so that you can taste them, so that you don't add too much. I don't let the water boil too hard because that breaks their skins. I let them simmer gently, stirring occasionally to make sure they all get evenly cooked. I do add garlic to the cooking water, as well as a sprig of epazote, an avocado leaf, or a healthy pinch of oregano or marjoram.

Epazote has a pleasant petrol taste, while the avocado leaf lends a hint of anise. Both are available at Mexican markets and impart a nice aromatic touch to the beans as they cook.

For the first 45 minutes or so of the cooking time, you can neglect your beans. But in the last 15 to 20 minutes, you need to pay closer attention. In order to be sure the beans are completely cooked but not falling apart, you must take them off the stove at the right moment. Dried beans tend to take about an hour to cook, although it's impossible to generalize because the size and freshness of the beans affect the cooking time. The only way to know when they're getting close to ready is to start tasting them. But you should know that when you first taste a hot bean that has just come out of the pot, it will be deceptively soft. They firm up quite a bit as they cool down. You want your cooked beans to taste custardy, not to resist your teeth in the slightest. If you feel any kind of a crunch, let the beans cook for another 5 minutes and then test again. Once you're satisfied with their doneness, add the salt, ½ tsp at a time, tasting between additions, and then let the beans cool in their cooking water (which makes a tasty broth in its own right).

FRIJOLES AGUADOS SOUPY BEANS

MAKES 4 TO 6 SERVINGS

2 cups / 360g dried beans
1 garlic clove
1 sprig epazote, 1 avocado leaf,
    or 1 Tbsp dried oregano or
    marjoram
Sea salt

In Mexico, black beans are pretty ubiquitous. But we also love to eat red and pinto beans, and all of the recipes I am giving you for beans can be made with other colored beans. There is no standard cooking time for dried beans. It varies based on their size and freshness. (The older the bean, the longer it will take to cook.) You need to pay attention and use your senses to guide you when you're cooking dried beans, because the secret to making really good beans is finding that elusive sweet spot between over- and under-cooking them. A few minutes too long and their skins will split, and they will fall apart. But if you take them off the stove prematurely, they will taste chalky and bland. I'm against the current trend of undercooking beans. The better a bean is cooked, the more complex the flavor. When testing a cooked bean for doneness, bite it and make sure there is no resistance. Once they're custardy, turn off the heat and let them cool in their broth.

A top-quality bean produces a rich and savory broth. We call it *caldo de frijoles* (soup of beans), and it's often on our lunch menu at Tacos Cala. It's delicate but nourishing. Don't let it go to waste! You can also use this broth to poach eggs.

Rinse the beans thoroughly, removing any debris, then place them in a medium pot and cover with about 4 inches / 10cm of water. In Mexico, we traditionally use a tall clay pot, but any pot will do as long as there's room for the beans to expand as they absorb the cooking water. Add the garlic and the epazote, avocado leaf, oregano, or marjoram.

Bring the water to a boil, then immediately decrease the heat to maintain a low simmer and cover the pot with a lid. After 30 minutes, stir the beans, because the ones at the bottom of the pot will cook faster and you want them all done at the same time. Add more water if needed to maintain 2 to 3 inches / 5 to 7.5cm over the top of the beans. Cover and let simmer for another 15 minutes, then taste a bean for doneness. The beans probably will not be finished yet, but at this point, you should start checking them every 10 minutes, stirring gently each time and adding more water if needed. Let the beans cook until they are just a bit softer than you think they should be but still whole, with their skins intact. When you're satisfied that they're well cooked, season with salt.

I bring these beans to the table warm, in a bowl of their broth, for people to serve themselves. The beans can be stored in a sealed container in the refrigerator for up to 1 week and gently reheated over low heat, as needed. They can also be frozen for up to 6 months, thawed, and reheated over low heat.

FRIJOLES REFRITOS REFRIED BEANS

At my restaurants in Mexico City and San Francisco, I refry beans in vegetable oil because I want the menu to have as many vegetarian options as possible, especially in the basic dishes. To enhance the flavor of these beans, I fry minced onion in oil; olive oil and safflower oil work equally well.

Some purists argue that olive oil doesn't belong in Mexican food, since olives aren't native to central America. Well, neither are the pigs from which we get lard. It's true that olive oil isn't the most commonly used oil in Mexico, but my Italian maternal grandmother, Nonna, lived with us for part of every year, and she always cooked with it as matter of course, so I grew used to the taste of a mildly fruity olive oil in my Mexican food. When deep-frying, I use safflower oil, or another oil with a high smoke point. But there are dishes in which I enjoy the additional flavor imparted by olive oil, so that's what I suggest when it's what I would personally use.

_____

In a bowl, mash the beans to a coarse paste with a potato masher or fork, gradually adding a few tablespoons of the reserved bean cooking liquid periodically as you mash, until you achieve the consistency you want. You don't want any beans left whole, but it's okay if some texture remains. If you prefer very smooth refried beans, you could use a blender or an immersion blender, but I like mine a bit chunky, so I mash by hand.

Warm the oil in a skillet over medium heat until it's hot but not smoking. Add the onion and cook, stirring until translucent but not browned, about 5 minutes. Add the mashed beans and the salt and then stir constantly for about 5 minutes. Drizzle in more of the remaining bean cooking liquid if needed to maintain the desired consistency. The beans should form a thick but creamy paste. Taste and add more salt if needed.

The beans can be stored in a sealed container in the refrigerator for up to 5 days. They can also be frozen for up to 6 months, thawed, and reheated in a skillet over low heat.

MAKES 4 TO 6 SERVINGS

2 cups / 120g drained Frijoles Aguados (facing page)
1 cup / 240ml reserved bean cooking liquid (facing page)
¼ cup / 60ml safflower or olive oil
½ white onion, minced
½ tsp salt

FRIJOLES REFRITOS EN MANTECA BEANS REFRIED IN LARD

MAKES 4 TO 6 SERVINGS

2 cups / 120g drained Frijoles
    Aguados (page 84)
1 cup / 240ml reserved bean
    cooking liquid (page 84)
¼ cup / 50g lard
½ tsp sea salt

As you flip through this cookbook, you'll notice that I use lard as an ingredient in some dishes. Is this "modern"? Maybe. While I've used it in my cooking forever, lard seems to be making a comeback. Like other animal fats, it doesn't deserve the bad reputation it got during the days of the fat-free craze. We now know that lard is lower in saturated fat than butter, and since it's less likely to burn at high heat, you need less of it to cook with. Also, just as you can buy organic meat that is pasture-raised and antibiotic-free, you can buy lard from these same animals. Lard does not result in "heavier beans." On the contrary, beans cooked in lard are more unctuous and silkier than their oil-cooked counterparts. As is so often the case, there's a reason a tradition lasts: because the food tastes better.

At home, I refry beans in lard if I have any, or in reserved bacon fat, which is basically the same thing, except it's smoked. I hate to waste, and I enjoy the smoky taste this imparts upon the beans.

Again, feel free to use any color of bean. I've made excellent refried beans with everything from black to pinto to cannellini beans. The method and ratios remain the same.

———————

In a bowl, mash the beans to a coarse paste with a potato masher or fork, gradually adding a few tablespoons of the reserved bean cooking liquid periodically as you mash, until you achieve the consistency you want. You don't want any beans left whole, but it's okay if some texture remains. If you prefer very smooth refried beans, you could use a blender or an immersion blender, but I like mine a bit chunky, so I mash mine by hand.

Warm the lard in a skillet over medium heat, until it's melted. When you put the tip of a wooden spoon in the hot lard, the wood should sizzle. Add the mashed beans and the salt and then cook, stirring constantly for about 5 minutes. Drizzle in more of the remaining bean cooking liquid if needed to maintain the desired consistency. They should form a thick but creamy paste.

The beans can be stored in a sealed container in the refrigerator for up to 5 days. They can also be frozen for up to 6 months, thawed, and reheated in a skillet over low heat.

CALDO DE POLLO CHICKEN STOCK

MAKES ABOUT 1 QT / 960ML

1 white onion, thinly sliced

2 garlic cloves

1 fennel bulb, cut in half, or
    2 stalks celery

2 carrots

2 bay leaves (preferably fresh)

2 lb / 910g bone-in, skin-on
    chicken breasts

About 5 cups / 1.2L water

1 tsp sea salt

I am giving you a two-for-one recipe here, for poaching chicken breasts in what becomes a light chicken stock to be used in any number of recipes. I like the dark meat of chicken, too, but it doesn't shred as well as the breast, so when recipes call for poached and shredded chicken, I usually prepare it this way, using just the breast and reserving the broth. I encourage you to play with what you put in the pot with your chicken. I am very free about what I put in mine. It's a great way to use up tired vegetables and any aromatic herbs. If I have parsley, I will throw some in, as well as a few sprigs of cilantro. I don't add much salt to this stock, since I use it in recipes that will have more salt in them. If you have the carcass of a whole chicken left over, you should definitely use that to make a stock. (But you won't end up with poached chicken to use in other recipes.)

In a large stockpot combine the onion, garlic, fennel, carrots, bay leaves, chicken, water, and salt to a boil over high heat. Decrease the heat and simmer for 20 minutes. Remove the chicken and let it cool. Once you can handle it, tear the meat off the bones and reserve it to use in another dish. Return the bones to the pot and let the stock simmer for an additional 40 minutes.

Line a colander with several layers of cheesecloth and set the colander over a bowl. Strain the stock through the colander. Chill the stock if you don't need to use it immediately. Chicken stock will last in a sealed container in the refrigerator for about 5 days, but I use what I need immediately and freeze the rest in containers so that I always have some available.

CALDO DE PESCADO FISH STOCK

Because my cuisine is so seafood focused, a good fish or shrimp stock is one of my staples. I use it as the base for a lot of other dishes, since it adds a complexity of flavor that water does not as it reduces and combines with other ingredients. As is the case with a chicken stock, it's a great way to get a second use from the fish or seafood that you were already planning to cook and eat. You only need a bit to make your stock. The collar, bones, and head of a fish all work well—or the heads and shells of shrimp—as well as a few vegetables cut into smaller pieces than you would use in a chicken stock, since seafood stock isn't cooked for as long and the smaller pieces release their flavor faster. I don't salt my seafood stocks because I want to be able to salt the dish that it goes into later.

It's nice to make a shrimp stock if you're going to be using it for a shrimp dish and a fish stock for a fish dish, although that's not strictly necessary. You probably wouldn't be able to taste the difference. However, it can also be a practical and economical way to use up the whole animal. If you're going to make a shrimp stock, buy shrimp with their heads and shells on and then use those for your stock. If you're cooking fish, you could ask at the market for the head and bones (which they will often give you very inexpensively, if not for free) to use for your stock.

Collars of 2 fish, or the head, bones, and fins of one large fish, or the heads and shells of 1 lb / 455g shrimp
3 carrots, cut into small (about 1-inch / 2.5cm) chunks
4 stalks celery, cut into chunks
½ white onion, cut into chunks
1 Roma tomato, cored
2 garlic cloves
4 bay leaves (preferably fresh)
10 black peppercorns
2 allspice berries
1 chile piquín
5 cups / 1.2L water

In a large stockpot over high heat, bring the fish bones or shrimp shells, carrots, celery, onion, tomato, garlic, bay leaves, peppercorns, allspice, chile, and water to a boil. Then, decrease the heat and simmer for 45 minutes.

Line a colander with several layers of cheesecloth and set the colander over a bowl. Strain the stock through the colander. Chill the stock if you don't need to use it immediately. A seafood stock will last in a sealed container in the refrigerator for about 2 days, but I use what I need immediately and freeze the rest in a container so that I always have some available.

2 DESAYUNO

BREAKFAST

People in Mexico enjoy a substantial breakfast. In Mexico City, it's common to find bankers and art dealers tucking into plates of chilaquiles or huevos con chorizo at 10:00 AM.

The notion of brunch isn't particularly popular, maybe because our regular breakfast foods tend to be considered brunch foods in the United States. We mostly eat savory foods in the morning; our morning sweet comes in the form of pan dulce (sweet rolls). Mexican breakfasts almost always feature eggs, cooked every conceivable way.

I never tire of eggs. An accessible and affordable protein, eggs have so much versatility, from how they're cooked to what you eat them with and which salsas you pour over them. They give you tons of energy to get through the busiest days. And if you've overindulged the night before, they're the perfect hangover cure. Also, the chile that's often cooked with eggs (and prominent in salsas) gives an instant boost of vitamin C—always a good thing in the morning.

If you haven't cooked a lot of Mexican food before, breakfast is a great entry point to the cuisine. Not only is it such an important meal in Mexican culture but these dishes are also hard to mess up and often more impressive than the sum of their parts, given how easy they are to put together.

I've given recipes to serve four to six people for almost all of my breakfast dishes so that you can make a quantity to serve friends or family. But everything can be scaled down to serve one or two very easily, and most of these dishes are simple enough that they're worth cooking even if you don't have company. I often throw together a pan of huevos a la Mexicana on a weekday morning. It's one of my son Lucas's favorite breakfasts.

While I'll suggest certain salsas that are typically served with particular breakfast dishes, always feel free to substitute any of the staple salsas that you may already have in your fridge. There really isn't a salsa that doesn't taste good on eggs. You'll notice a lot of the same ingredients repeat in breakfast dishes: onions, garlic, cilantro, chile, tomatoes. You can mix and match any of these dishes, and they will taste fantastic.

Breakfast food is comfort food, no matter the culture. And it's an even greater comfort to enjoy these foods with family and friends first thing in the day before any distractions set in.

PATAS DE ANÍS ANISE ROLLS

MAKES 20 ROLLS

2¼ tsp (1 package) active dry yeast
½ cup / 120ml warm water
1 tsp granulated sugar, plus ½ cup / 100g and more for sprinkling
4¼ cups / 530g all-purpose flour, plus more for sprinkling
1 tsp sea salt
4 eggs
3 egg yolks
1½ cups / 330g unsalted butter, softened
1 tsp aniseeds
½ cup / 120ml warm milk

Bread is actually a significant part of the Mexican diet, dating back to the arrival of the European colonizers. Their appetite for baked goods caught on, as you can tell by counting the bakeries in any neighborhood in Mexico City. When I opened Contramar, I wanted fresh-baked bread on every table alongside fresh-made tortillas, so next door, I also run a bake shop where I sell our bread as well as the kinds of pastries people typically eat with coffee or hot chocolate, like these patas. *Patas* translates to "hooves" (as in, the feet of a pig). This recipe comes from my paternal grandmother, Doña Concha, who was from Campeche, in southeast Mexico. The rolls are flavored with anise, and they are shaped by rolling flattened dough around the handle of a spoon that you slide out gently, letting the rolls rise in that baguette shape before baking them.

In the bowl of your stand mixer fitted with the dough hook, combine the yeast, water, and 1 tsp sugar. Stir to dissolve the yeast, then let it rest for about 10 minutes, until bubbles form and it looks a bit frothy.

With the mixer running on medium speed, add the remaining ½ cup / 100g sugar, the flour, salt, eggs, 2 of the egg yolks, ¾ cup / 160g of the butter, and the aniseeds and mix for about 5 minutes, or until a soft and sticky dough forms. Add the milk and knead on medium speed for about 5 minutes more, until the dough pulls away from the sides of the bowl.

Lightly flour your work surface. Portion the dough into 20 balls. Using a rolling pin, flatten a few balls into very thin disks (about ¼ inch / 6mm). Spread about 1¾ tsp butter on top of each dough disk and sprinkle with flour.

Preheat the oven to 350°F / 180°C. Butter two baking sheets.

Gently roll each flattened disk around the handle of your biggest wooden spoon, forming a long, baguettelike shape with the handle at the center of the cylinder. Ease the handle of the spoon out and place the roll on a prepared baking sheet. Continue with the rest of the dough balls, placing the shaped rolls approximately 2 inches / 5cm apart so they don't stick together as they rise. Cover the pans with a dish towel and set aside to rise in a warm spot for about 40 minutes, or until they double in size.

Whisk the remaining egg yolk. Using a pastry brush, gently brush the tops of the rolls with the egg and sprinkle with sugar.

Bake for 12 to 15 minutes, until golden brown. Serve warm or at room temperature the day they are baked.

CONCHAS DE PINOLE PINOLE SWEET BUNS

MAKES 12 BUNS

Concha Dough Buns
2 ¼ tsp (1 package) active dry yeast
½ cup / 120ml warm water
½ cup / 120ml warm milk
1 tsp granulated sugar plus
      ½ cup / 100g
½ cup / 110g unsalted butter,
      softened
1 tsp sea salt
2 eggs, at room temperature
4 cups / 500g all-purpose flour
1 tsp vegetable oil

Pinole Topping
⅓ cup / 40g powdered sugar
¼ cup / 30g all-purpose flour
¼ cup / 30g pinole flour
¼ cup / 55g cold butter, cut into
      small cubes
Pinch of sea salt

Conchas (pictured on page 308) are one of the best-known pan dulce, or sweet roll, often found heaped in the windows of panaderías, or bakeries. The base of the concha is a briochelike bread, shaped into a round bun. On top is a cap of butter cookie dough that gets baked right onto the bread dough, so it forms a sweet, crumbly crust on the soft roll. The conventional concha topping is flavored with vanilla or chocolate, but you can add whatever you want to it. I like to use ingredients native to Mexico, like pinole or mesquite (see variation). Pinole is toasted corn, ground very finely, sweetened and seasoned with a hint of cinnamon or cocoa powder. You can purchase pinole at Mexican markets and online.

Like all pastries, conchas are the most delicious on the day they're baked. But conchas can also get a second life, toasted, as a sandwich bun. Salty refried beans, spread on a sweet and buttery pinole concha, taste especially good. (An Asian friend of mine remarked that this is reminiscent of the salty beans sometimes found in Asian sweet breads.) I also love to toast half a split bun and use it as the base for an open-face dessert "sandwich" of arroz con leche.

———————

To make the dough: In the bowl of your stand mixer fitted with the dough hook, dissolve the yeast in the water and milk. Add the 1 tsp of the granulated sugar and wait for the liquid to bubble and become slightly frothy—5 to 10 minutes. Add the remaining ½ cup / 100g granulated sugar, the butter, salt, eggs, and all-purpose flour. Mix on medium speed for about 10 minutes, until the dough forms a smooth and elastic ball that pulls away from the sides of the bowl. Oil the dough with the oil and then return it to the mixing bowl. Cover the bowl with a dish towel and set aside to rise in a warm spot for about 2 hours, until doubled in size.

Butter a baking sheet.

When the dough has risen, divide it into 12 balls. They should weigh about 2.5 oz / 75g each. Place the rolls on the baking sheet, positioning them approximately 2 inches / 5cm apart so they don't stick together as they rise.

To make the topping: In a clean bowl for your mixer, fitted with the paddle attachment, combine the powdered sugar, all-purpose flour, pinole flour, butter, and salt and mix until it achieves a cookie dough consistency.

Lay a large sheet of parchment paper on your work surface. Gather up the dough and place it on the parchment. Top with another large sheet of parchment and, using a rolling pin, roll out the dough as you would roll out butter cookie dough to ⅛ inch / 3mm thick. Remove the top piece of parchment and, using a 2-inch / 5cm biscuit cutter (to match the diameter of the rolls), punch out twelve circles. Carefully lay a circle on each roll. For a simpler method, you can use moistened fingertips to gently pat about 1 Tbsp of the topping onto each bun, spreading it (without pressing it into the dough) so that it covers most of the surface area.

Cover the baking sheet with a dish towel and set aside in a warm place to rise for 30 minutes, or until they're about doubled again.

Preheat the oven to 375°F / 190°C.

Bake the conchas for about 20 minutes, until the topping is nicely browned. Let cool just until cool enough to handle and then serve. The fresh rolls are best eaten the same day. Store leftover rolls in a sealed container to be split and used for sandwiches the next day.

CONCHAS DE MESQUITE / MESQUITE SWEET BUN VARIATION

To make these rolls with mesquite flour, which comes from the mesquite plant and tastes subtly piney, substitute ¼ cup / 40g for the pinole flour. It's available in bulk at most health foods stores.

HUEVOS POCHADOS EN SOPA DE FRIJOLES
EGGS POACHED IN BEAN SOUP

MAKES 4 TO 6 SERVINGS

1 recipe Frijoles Aguados (page 84)
4 to 6 eggs
Maldon sea salt or another
    finishing salt
Salsa of your choice for serving

Eggs poached in a blended black bean soup make a simple and satisfying meal at any time of day. You can make a single serving by poaching just one or two eggs in a cup of soup. But if you are practiced at poaching eggs, go ahead and poach more at the same time to feed a group. When your spoon breaks into the egg, the runny yolk blends with and enriches the broth, creating a satisfying meal from humble components.

———————

In a saucepan, using an immersion blender, blend the beans and enough bean broth so that you end up with the consistency of a creamy soup, not refried beans.

Bring the pureed beans to a boil over medium heat, then decrease the heat to low and bring to a simmer.

When the beans are simmering, crack an egg into a small measuring cup, ideally one with a long handle. Gently lower the measuring cup into the simmering bean soup, submerging the bottom of the measuring cup in the soup and then easing the egg out. Repeat with the remaining eggs, distributing them evenly in the saucepan.

The cooking time will depend on how you like your poached eggs. Cook for 4 minutes for eggs with well-set whites around a still-runny yolk. If you poach more than 6 eggs at once, you will need to increase the cooking time by about 30 seconds per egg, since each one absorbs heat and lowers the temperature of the soup.

When you think your eggs are cooked, ladle each one with the bean soup in which it was poached into individual serving bowls. Top with a sprinkle of salt and a spoonful of salsa, and serve immediately.

HUEVOS CON MIGAS
SCRAMBLED EGGS WITH FRIED TORTILLA BITS

When a tortilla is a few days old, it becomes too stiff to fold into a taco without cracking in half and starts to turn a bit glassy at the edges. That's when you should cut the tortillas into little squares and let them dry out completely. Then you can store them in an airtight container and have them ready when you want to make these eggs. *Migas* means "crumbs or bits," and refers to the dried-out pieces of tortilla. When you fry them, first they soak up the oil and become soft and then they turn crispy. Scrambled with eggs, they're absolutely delicious, making another breakfast dish that somehow manages to be much more than the sum of its parts. Stale tortillas? Who knew they could taste this good. But nothing goes to waste in my kitchen, which is one reason I love to make these eggs.

_____

In a bowl, whisk the eggs, crema or crème fraîche, and salt until well combined.

Warm the oil in a pan over high heat until it's hot but not smoking. It may seem like a lot, but you'll see that the tortillas are very absorbent. Drop a piece of tortilla into the oil and listen for a sizzle. When you hear it, add the rest of the tortillas and stir them with a wooden spoon while they cook. They will soften as they soak up the oil, and then they'll turn crispy. Right after this happens, carefully discard the excess oil and turn the heat to low.

Add the egg–crème fraîche mixture to the pan and scramble together with the fried tortillas. Taste and add more salt if needed. Serve immediately, topped with a spoonful of salsa and the sliced avocado.

MAKES 4 TO 6 SERVINGS

8 to 12 eggs
2 Tbsp Crema Ácida (page 65) or crème fraîche
½ tsp sea salt, plus more as needed
⅓ cup / 80ml safflower oil
4 or 5 stale corn tortillas, cut into ⅜-inch / 1 cm squares and dried out
Salsa of your choice for serving
1 avocado, cut in half, pitted, peeled, and cut into ½-inch / 12mm-thick slices

HUEVOS A LA MEXICANA MEXICAN-STYLE EGGS

This is a slightly fancier version of a very common and basic Mexican break-fast, although it still comes together in minutes if you have the salsa already made. (When you make this salsa, be sure to core the tomatoes well—completely removing the seeds and their surrounding juices—if you don't remove them, they'll make your eggs watery.) Custardy, soft-scrambled eggs complement the creamy texture of the chèvre cheese and get a nice hit of acid from the tomatoes and chile in the salsa. If tomatoes aren't at their prime or you want a simpler variation, you may omit the tomatoes; these eggs will still be delicious when cooked with just the fried onion and serranos.

_____

Warm the salsa in a large skillet over medium heat.

Meanwhile, in a bowl, whisk the eggs and salt. Add the chèvre and keep whisking until it's fairly well incorporated, although it's fine if some clumps remain since they will melt during cooking.

In a large skillet over low heat, melt the butter. Add the egg-cheese mixture and cook, stirring constantly so the eggs stay moist and creamy. Continuously agitate the eggs while they cook, never letting them stick to the bottom of the pan. When the scrambled eggs are a creamy yellow and just beginning to set, remove the pan from the heat and top with the hot salsa. Garnish with the cilantro. Serve immediately with the tortillas, beans, and avocado.

MAKES 4 TO 6 SERVINGS

1 recipe Salsa Mexicana (page 49)
8 to 12 eggs
½ tsp sea salt, plus more as needed
3 oz / 80g soft chèvre, cut into ½-inch / 12mm rounds
1 Tbsp butter
Cilantro, chopped
8 to 12 Tortillas de Maiz (page 72)
1 recipe Frijoles Aguados (page 84; optional), warmed
1 or 2 avocados, cut in half, pitted, peeled, and cut into ½-inch / 12mm-thick slices (optional)

HUEVOS RANCHEROS FRIED TORTILLAS, FRIED EGGS, AND SALSA

MAKES 4 TO 6 SERVINGS

1 recipe Salsa Mexicana (page 49)
    and/or another salsa of
    your choice
About ½ cup / 120ml vegetable oil,
    plus more if needed
8 to 12 fresh Tortillas de Maiz
    (page 84)
8 to 12 eggs
Sea salt
¼ white onion, finely minced
1 avocado, cut in half, pitted,
    peeled, and cut into ½-inch /
    12mm-thick slices

For huevos rancheros, fried eggs are laid on top of fried corn tortillas, and then hot salsa is ladled on top. You can use any salsa you want. This is another great vehicle for Salsa Mexicana, but it's equally good with Salsa Verde (page 50) or Salsa de Chile Morita (page 55). The trick, especially when making huevos rancheros for a group, is to time the frying of the tortillas and the eggs so that both are hot when you're ready to serve them. I recommend prefrying a stack of tortillas and keeping them warm in a covered container so that you can focus on the slightly more sensitive task of frying eggs, which must be served immediately upon cooking. It's too hard to fry both eggs and tortillas at the same time. You don't need much oil for tortilla frying. In fact, less oil is better; too much can result in a soggy mess.

_____

Heat the salsa in a saucepan over low heat. Let it simmer while you fry the tortillas and then the eggs.

Start by frying as many tortillas as you're going to need, so that you'll have two per person. You need a container with a lid to keep them warm after you fry them. I have a basket that I like, but a stainless-steel pot with a lid works, too. Line the bottom of the container with a brown paper bag to absorb the oil and place next to you when you start frying the tortillas.

Warm 1 Tbsp of the oil in a skillet over medium heat. (You'll know it's hot enough when the edge of a tortilla sizzles slightly when dipped in the oil.) Drop in one tortilla at a time and let it fry for no more than 30 seconds per side, flipping it with tongs. Remove the tortilla from the pan, letting the excess oil drain off into the pan, and then place the tortilla on the paper bag at the bottom of the pot and cover with the lid. Continue in this way, stacking each fried tortilla on top of the one you just fried, adding more oil to the pan when needed. Once the tortillas are done and staying warm in a container with the lid on, it's time to fry the eggs.

CONTINUED

Pour ¼ cup / 60ml of the oil in the same pan in which you fried your tortillas and bring it back up to that sizzling temperature. In my family, we always fry eggs in a fair bit of oil, because it results in lacy, crisp-edged eggs every time, and you don't need a nonstick pan. Once the oil is hot, gently crack 2 eggs into the pan at once. The oil may splatter a bit, so be on guard. Using a spoon, baste the whites with the hot oil while they're frying, making sure they cook completely and get crispy on the edges. Fry until the whites are totally set but the yolks are still a little runny. The eggs should cook in about 1 minute.

Place 2 fried tortillas on a serving plate. Using a slotted spoon, remove the eggs one at a time, shaking off the excess oil and depositing them on the fried tortillas. Ladle the warm salsa in a ring around the egg whites, leaving just the yolks exposed. Season the yolks with a pinch of salt, sprinkle with onion, and lay a few slices of avocado on top and serve. Repeat with the remaining tortillas and eggs.

HUEVOS DIVORCIADOS / FRIED EGGS WITH RED AND GREEN SALSAS VARIATION

If you ladle green salsa on one half of the plate, over one fried egg, and red salsa on the other half, over a second fried egg, this dish becomes *huevos divorciados* (divorced eggs), for obvious reasons. Use any green- and red-colored salsas that you like. You can apply the same principle to other dishes, too, like chilaquiles (see page 118) to make chilaquiles divorciados, for example.

HUEVOS EN CAMISA "EGG IN A SHIRT"

MAKES 1 SERVING

1 ball freshly made Tortillas de Maiz
    dough (see page 72)
1 egg
Sea salt
Salsa of your choice for serving

There's a saying in Mexico that when a girl's tortillas puff up, it's a sign that she is ready to get married. In that case, I would've been in trouble, because I became my family's tortilla maker at age seven, studying what Victoria—the woman who helped at our house—did and practicing dutifully until I got my tortillas to puff up like hers. Once I could make tortillas, I learned how to cook huevos en camisa, which was one of my favorite childhood snacks and is now one of my son Lucas's favorite things to munch on whenever we're making tortillas together.

Huevo en camisa translates to "egg in a shirt." In this case, the tortilla is the shirt that the egg is wearing. This is the way it works: right after the second flip, when the masa is puffed with air, you make a quick slit in the tortilla, break an egg right into it, and put the whole thing back on the comal or skillet so that the egg cooks inside the tortilla. It's incredibly simple—and delicious.

If you can cook huevos en camisa, it means you've mastered the technique of making fresh tortillas, and this dish lets you show off your skills.

Warm an ungreased comal or skillet over medium-high heat.

Following the instructions on page 72, form a tortilla and drop it onto the comal or into a skillet over medium-high heat. After the second flip, when the tortilla puffs up, transfer it to a cutting board and quickly use a paring knife to make a slit in the puffed edge. Crack an egg directly into the slit. Return the tortilla, now encasing the raw egg, to the comal or skillet. Fry the tortilla for about 1 minute on each side, until the egg is fried inside its tortilla "shirt."

Season with the salt and serve with salsa. Eat immediately.

HUEVOS LIBANESES LEBANESE-STYLE EGGS

MAKES 4 TO 6 SERVINGS

Labneh
2 cups / 490g full-fat yogurt
¼ tsp sea salt
Squeeze of lemon
Up to 1 Tbsp finely minced fresh
    herbs, such as chives, mint,
    tarragon, or basil (optional)

¼ cup / 60ml olive oil
1 white onion, finely minced
3 serrano chiles, stemmed,
    seeded, veins removed (or
    not, depending on how spicy
    you want this to be), and
    finely minced
1 tsp sea salt, plus more as needed
8 to 12 eggs
4 to 6 rounds pita bread, wrapped
    in aluminum foil
2 Tbsp za'atar

Mexico is a melting pot of cultures and culinary influences. The Lebanese are one of the more recent groups to have settled there, and at markets in places such as Oaxaca, Puebla, and Veracruz, pan árabe (freshly baked pita) and labneh (strained yogurt cheese) are sold alongside tortillas and chiles. Labneh is a key ingredient in huevos Libaneses and is easy to make from scratch if your market doesn't sell it. In my version, eggs are baked in ramekins on top of sautéed minced onion and serrano chiles that keep the cooked egg from sticking. Right when they come out of the oven, you slide a dollop of tangy labneh under each one so that it melts, blending together with the hot yolk after the egg is pierced. Sprinkle with za'atar—a blend of sumac, thyme, oregano, sesame seeds, and salt—and serve with warm pitas instead of tortillas.

While you can find labneh for sale at some markets, it's very easy to make at home. The process is similar to making fresh ricotta, only you strain yogurt instead of cooked milk. You can make it interesting by adding minced fresh herbs or experimenting with different kinds of yogurt. Goat's milk yogurt, for instance, will make labneh that tastes more like chèvre. After an hour or two, it will resemble ricotta. After 8 hours, it will have the texture of cream cheese.

———————

To make the labneh: Line a colander with several layers of cheesecloth and set the colander over a bowl. In a second bowl, combine the yogurt, salt, lemon juice, and herbs. Pour the mixture into the colander and set aside to drain, or gather the edges of the cheesecloth and suspend it over the sink, hanging it from the faucet. The liquid (whey) will drain out, leaving just the solids behind. After a few hours (8 hours at most), open the cheesecloth and scrape the labneh into a container with a lid. It will keep in the sealed container in the refrigerator for up to 1 week.

When you're ready to make the eggs, preheat the oven to 400°F / 200°C.

In a large skillet over medium-high heat, warm the oil until hot but not smoking. Drop in the onion and chiles at the same time (the onion keeps the chiles from burning). Sauté, stirring constantly, until the onion is translucent but has not browned. Add the salt.

CONTINUED

Divide the sautéed onion-chile mixture evenly among four to six 8 oz / 240ml ramekins or other oven-safe dishes. Immediately crack 2 eggs into each ramekin, place on a baking sheet, and bake for about 8 minutes, until the whites have set. (You want the yolks to stay a little runny.) After 5 minutes, add the foil-wrapped package of pitas to the oven to warm while the eggs cook.

Remove the ramekins and pitas from the oven, tuck a spoonful of labneh beneath each egg, and sprinkle with the za'atar. Cut the warm pitas into wedges, wrap them in a dish towel, and place in a basket.

Serve the ramekins with the pitas for people to sop up the tangy, creamy juices.

HUEVOS LIBANESES SKILLET VARIATION

If you want less fuss, you can also gently crack all of your eggs right on top of the sautéed onion and chiles into the skillet and place the whole thing in the oven. Then, when the eggs are baked, sprinkle them with za'atar and spoon each egg, together with some of the hot onion-chile relish, on top of a spoonful of labneh that you've placed on each person's plate. It's slightly less elegant but just as delicious.

HUEVOS TIRADOS EGGS SCRAMBLED WITH REFRIED BEANS

This is not the most photogenic of breakfasts—it's basically "a plateful of brown," as my son says—but don't judge a breakfast by its color!) Refried black beans get mixed right into the eggs as they scramble. Then the whole thing is shaped into a mound and served alongside fried plantains and topped with a spoonful of salsa. You can't go wrong with cooked or raw salsa verde. The tomatillos impart a nice note of acidity to this rich and savory dish. (They also add a splash of color to that plateful of brown.) When the eggs and beans are cooked together, the eggs lend their fluffi-ness to the beans. The combination seems strangely light, even though it's definitely another hearty breakfast to keep you going until midafternoon.

Begin by making the fried plantains and leave them in the oven at low heat to stay warm while you make the huevos tirados.

Warm the oil or lard in a large skillet over medium heat until it's hot and/or melted but not sizzling. Decrease the heat to low and crack the eggs into the skillet. Immediately puncture their yolks, sprinkle with the salt, and add the beans. Using a big wooden spoon or spatula, scramble the eggs and beans together in the pan, stirring the mixture continuously to integrate the eggs and beans while they cook.

Spoon the egg-bean mixture into a log on each plate. Place a small handful of fried plantains on the side and garnish with the avocado. Top with a spoonful of salsa and serve.

MAKES 4 TO 6 SERVINGS

1 Tbsp safflower oil or lard
8 to 12 eggs
½ tsp sea salt
1 cup / 240g Frijoles Refritos (page 85)
1 recipe Fried Plantains (page 123)
1 avocado, cut in half, pitted, peeled, and thinly sliced
Salsa Verde (page 50) or another salsa of your choice for serving

EVERYTHING CAN BE A TACO

From the moment I decided to write this cookbook, I knew it would not have a taco chapter. There are already so many taco cookbooks published in the United States, with precise recipes dictating exactly which toppings to use with which fillings and which salsas. The truth is, I find these notions somewhat silly. They miss the whole point of what makes tacos great, which is that you don't need a recipe to make one—not the way Mexicans make and eat them, and not the way I've been making and eating them for as long as I can remember.

When I was young, as soon as my brother and I got home from school, we'd head straight for the fridge, digging around to see what we could throw together. And whatever looked good inevitably made its way into a rolled tortilla. Leftover pipian mole from our neighbors' party? Perfect. Carnitas, sautéed vegetables, cheese, sliced avocado—everything tasted better in taco form. Anchovies and butter—the weirdest combination—was a personal favorite. Because our mom is Italian, we ate our share of pasta, and my brother and I loved to slap together spaghetti tacos. (Don't knock them until you've tried them.) Like all children in Mexico, we also loved to melt an obscene amount of butter on a hot tortilla, sprinkle it just as liberally with sugar, and call that a taco. No one disputed our claim. Another classic in our household was a manchego cheese and quince paste taco. I now make a sweet tamal for dessert at Cala, inspired by that winning combo.

In Mexico, there are no rules about what constitutes this food—which can be a snack, a complete meal, or a quick breakfast—other than that it be wrapped in a tortilla and eaten with your hands. Once you hold a taco, you must never let go of it until you finish it. That's actually the only legitimate taco rule. And the tortilla has to be soft; otherwise, it's a tostada.

At Tacos Cala, we don't serve spaghetti tacos or butter-sugar ones. But the tacos on our menu are different from any of the others I've sampled in California. My inspiration comes from many taquerias, like Tacos Hola, which is across from my apartment in the Condesa district in Mexico City,

and their tacos de guisado, or "tacos filled with stew." Tacos Hola is just one little room at street level, with a modest awning and a single table on the sidewalk in front. At 8:30 every morning, they crank up a metal grate and start serving tacos made from the stews bubbling on the stove. Most people eat standing up. It's very informal. They wrap a plastic bag around each plate—to rip off and throw out when you hand it back—so that they can slip another plastic bag around the plate for the next customer and don't have to do any dishes. I didn't copy the plastic-bagged plates at Tacos Cala. But the stews, yes—if not the exact recipes, then the idea that a great taco is made from something delicious that has bubbled for a while in a pot and then ladled onto a bed of rice and beans lining a fresh, hot tortilla. These tacos don't need extra add-ons, except for maybe a little sprinkling of minced cilantro or a spoonful or two of salsa. The guisados beg to be tasted, not covered up.

In my guisados, I make use of whatever is fresh and exciting at the farmers' market, or I find a new vehicle to transform leftover ingredients from dinner into lunch. On any given day, the menu at Tacos Cala might include a mole; a picadillo, or sauté of ground beef; rajas, or strips of poblano chile cooked in a cream sauce with potatoes; a greens or mushroom sauté; or braised tongue in salsa verde. It could be as refined as an octopus stew or as elemental as a soft-boiled egg. No shredded cheese or sour cream. Freshly made red and green salsas are the only condiments available—always both, so people have a choice of color as well as taste.

Although there aren't many components to these tacos, a lot of care goes into every part. Each tortilla is served hot off the comal, freshly made within the hour, strong enough to hold a stew yet tender and soft as you bite into it. The rice glistens a little from being lightly fried before it's boiled. The black beans are whole and intact yet creamy on the inside. Each of these things may seem plain and basic—and in a way they are—but it takes attention to get them right and that comes across in the taste, even if people don't realize why they taste so good. It's also about the ratios. No part should dominate, and the taco should be generous but not overstuffed. No matter how tempted you may be, don't heap fillings onto your tortilla. This is finger food. You must be able to eat it without things falling out.

While the guisados vary from day to day, a soft-boiled egg is the one constant on the taco menu, and the only taco for which I will provide a recipe. I want to give you my template, so that you see the ratios and can make tacos at home like the ones I love. While I've shared my recipes for rice and beans in the basics chapter, you don't have to use both (or either one), and you could certainly substitute another color of bean or rice. Whatever you make, cook it carefully, and the results will be delicious.

Just as a sandwich is something you make with what's at hand, throwing in whatever looks good, the same applies to tacos. Just about anything in this book can have a second life when wrapped in a tortilla. So when you like a recipe—especially if it's one that requires a bit of extra work, such as a mole—make more than you need. The next day, when you're digging through the fridge for a quick bite, you'll be glad you did. Just make sure to have good corn tortillas in the freezer, ready to be heated on a comal.

Everything can be a taco!

TACOS DE HUEVO SOFT-BOILED EGG TACOS

At Tacos Cala, we make a big batch of soft-boiled eggs right before lunch. We peel them and keep them in the same pot of hot water they boiled in, so that they're still warm, for up to 2 hours, for serving on tacos. You can do the same if you're making these tacos for a brunch. Also, it's likely that people will want a second taco, so this will keep their second egg from getting cold while they're eating the first. What follows is the most basic recipe for the plainest taco on my menu. Even though I've had it a million times, it's still one that I'm drawn to regularly. The soft-boiled yolk merges so well with the salsa, combining to form a rich and tangy sauce that seeps down into the rice and beans. Plain or not, it competes with any guisado. I recommend using two salsas, each one a different color.

You need hot tortillas, rice, beans, and eggs. Each of these parts must be warm when you're ready to assemble and serve the tacos. Ideally, you'll have made the salsas and beans a day ahead; warm them over medium-low heat while you prepare the rest. Cook the rice and then put a pot of water on to soft-boil the eggs while the rice is steaming. Then you can either make or reheat your tortillas, so they're hot and fresh when you and your family or friends are ready to put together the tacos.

MAKES 4 TO 6 SERVINGS

8 to 12 eggs, at room temperature
Arroz (page 77)
8 to 12 Tortillas de Maiz (page 72)
1 recipe Frijoles Aguados (page 84)
Maldon sea salt or another
    finishing salt
1 or 2 of your favorite salsas

Bring a pot of water to a boil and then add the eggs, one at a time, gently lowering them into the water with a spoon. (To be sure your eggs don't crack, use Jacques Pépin's trick of poking a tiny hole with a needle in the rounder end of each shell.) Set a timer and let the eggs boil for 1 minute. Then put a lid on the pot, turn off the stove, and let them sit in the hot water for 7 minutes more. Meanwhile, prepare a big bowl of ice water. Remove the eggs from the hot water with a slotted spoon, reserving the hot water in its pot, and transfer the eggs to the ice water for 1 minute. This keeps the shells from sticking. Peel the eggs and place them back in the hot water until ready to serve, or for as long as 2 hours.

Spread a generous 1 Tbsp of rice across a tortilla, patting it down and leaving a border of ⅜ inch / 1cm at the edge. Top with 1 Tbsp of beans, strained from their cooking broth. Slice a soft-boiled egg in half lengthwise and place both halves cut-side up over the beans. Finish with a pinch of salt and fold the tortilla to close. Repeat to fill the remaining tortillas. Pass the salsa at the table for people to spoon into their own tacos. Minimalism at its most delicious.

CHILAQUILES FRIED TORTILLAS SIMMERED IN SALSA

MAKES 4 TO 6 SERVINGS

1 Tbsp plus 1 cup / 240ml safflower
    oil, plus more as needed
1 qt / 960ml Salsa Verde (page 50)
    or another cooked salsa of your
    choice
12 Tortillas de Maiz (page 72), each
    cut into 6 to 8 wedges
¼ cup / 60g Crema Ácida (page 65)
    or crème fraîche
8 to 12 eggs
½ cup / 60g finely minced
    white onion
½ cup / 10g cilantro leaves, minced
½ cup / 75g (⅜-inch / 1cm) cubed
    feta cheese
1 or 2 avocados, cut in half, pitted,
    peeled, and cut into about
    8 slices

Chilaquiles are a kind of deconstructed enchilada. Stale tortillas get fried until they're crispy, then softened in a hot salsa and served with toppings. You can also make an even easier version by using tortilla chips. Just buy really good ones (thick and crispy, ideally from a taqueria) so they'll hold their shape rather than turning to mush in the pot. (Though to be honest, I've had a surprisingly tasty plate of chilaquiles made from Doritos, not that I'm advising such a thing.) You can serve chilaquiles at an elegant brunch, but they're also something you can fix for yourself quickly if you've got the components. I always put a fried egg on mine, but they're also good with shredded chicken or crumbled chorizo. Although it's not a traditional Mexican cheese, I love crumbled feta on chilaquiles, because its tanginess goes well with the tomatillo salsa.

———————

Warm the 1 Tbsp oil in a skillet over medium heat. Pour the salsa into the pan and let it cook at a low simmer for 10 to 15 minutes, thickening slightly.

In a large saucepan over medium-high heat, warm the remaining 1 cup / 240ml oil, which should be 2 inches / 5cm deep so you can submerge the tortilla wedges. Line a plate with a brown paper bag. Working in about three batches, drop the tortilla wedges into the saucepan and use a slotted spoon or tongs to turn them over as they fry for 2 to 3 minutes, until golden brown. Transfer the chips to the prepared plate and continue frying the rest. The chips should be very crispy after they cool. Transfer any remaining oil to the frying pan in which you will cook your eggs; you should have about ¼ cup / 60ml oil.

Turn off the burner under the skillet and wait for the salsa to stop simmering. Add the crema ácida or crème fraîche to the salsa and stir until it's well integrated. Drop all of your chips into the pan. Stir them once or twice to coat with the sauce, being gentle and trying to break as few as possible. As soon as they have absorbed most of the sauce, stop stirring.

Warm the oil in the frying pan over medium-high heat until it is sizzling. Once the oil is hot, gently crack 2 eggs into the pan at once. The oil may splatter a bit, so be on guard. Using a spoon, baste the whites with hot oil while they're frying, making sure they cook completely and get crispy on the edges. Fry until the whites are totally set but the yolks are still a little runny. The eggs should cook in about 1 minute. Using a slotted spoon, transfer the eggs to a plate and repeat for the remaining eggs.

Spread a cup of the saucy chips on each plate. Top each with 2 fried eggs and garnish with a sprinkling of the onion, cilantro, feta, and avocado before serving.

TORTAS

Does it seem strange to you to make a sandwich out of salsa-drenched chilaquiles piled onto a roll? If so, then you need to think outside the box—or inside the bread. While the taco is probably the best-known Mexican dish outside of Mexico, tortas are just as popular and delicious. And, as anything can be a taco, as long as it's eaten in a warm tortilla, nearly everything can go on a roll and become a torta. In Mexico we use bolillos or teleras (soft sandwich rolls), but you can cut a baguette into quarters and it'll serve the same purpose. If you get a great baguette, it'll likely taste better than some bolillos, which can be mediocre when mass-produced. You could also use a ciabatta, and though it wouldn't be as crusty as the typical telera, it would still taste great as the foundation for a Mexican sandwich. As to what you put inside? The first torta that blew my mind as a child had a chile relleno inside it. My mouth still waters just thinking of it. Often people will spread a thin layer of refried beans on one side of the torta, to serve the same purpose that mayonnaise would on a sandwich, keeping produce or wet fillings from soaking the bread immediately. Toppings are up to you, but I will never object to pickled red onions and sliced avocado. In the chapters to come, you'll see a few more torta recipes, when I can't resist sharing a particular favorite. But don't hesitate to make a torta out of any of the other dishes in here that strike your fancy, especially if it's lunchtime and you have a nice baguette and some good leftovers sitting around.

TORTAS DE CHILAQUILES Y MILANESA
SANDWICHES WITH CHILAQUILES AND BREADED CUTLETS

MAKES 4 TO 6 SERVINGS

1 lb / 455g chicken or veal, cut into
    4 to 6 round pieces no more
    than ½ inch / 12mm thick
1 tsp sea salt
1 cup / 240ml whole milk
1 recipe Chilaquiles (page 118),
    sauce and tortillas only
3 Tbsp / 45ml safflower oil
4 to 6 bolillos (Mexican sandwich
    rolls) or 1 large ciabatta or
    baguette, cut into 4 to
    6 sandwich-size pieces
2 eggs, whisked
1 cup / 40g fine dried bread
    crumbs
4 to 6 Tbsp / 60 to 90g Crema
    Ácida (page 65) or crème fraîche

This sandwich, served at a breakfast place near my apartment in the Roma district in Mexico City, is a must-have for many of my regular visitors. It's a filling breakfast to say the least and will keep anyone going for hours of sightseeing. While you could certainly make chilaquiles to eat on a torta, the sandwich is a great vehicle for such leftovers. Here chilaquiles get a second (arguably better) life, heaped on a freshly fried veal cutlet and tucked into a toasty roll.

When you are ready to make the sandwiches, begin by making the chilaquiles, then set them aside in a pot with a lid to keep them warm while you fry the steak cutlets.

———————

Pound the meat until it's as thin as possible. Season the meat on both sides with the salt and soak it in the milk for at least 1 hour or overnight in the refrigerator to further tenderize it.

Warm the oil in a heavy-bottom skillet over medium-high heat until it's hot but not smoking.

While the oil is heating, preheat the oven to 350°F / 180°C. Wrap the bread in aluminum foil and place it in the oven to warm up while you fry the cutlets.

Place the eggs in a shallow bowl and the bread crumbs in another shallow bowl. Line a plate with a brown paper bag. Dip each tenderized cutlet in the whisked eggs, then dredge it in the bread crumbs. Fry as many cutlets as you can fit in the pan without crowding them, flipping each cutlet after it cooks for 2 to 3 minutes on each side, becoming crispy and brown. Transfer the cutlets to the prepared plate to drain.

Split the bread lengthwise. Place a cutlet on one side and top with the chilaquiles. Garnish with a spoonful of crema or crème fraîche, close the sandwich, and serve hot.

Tortas de Chilaquiles LA ESQUINA DEL CHILAQUIL, Alfonso Reyes 139, Hipódromo Condesa

HUEVOS MOTULEÑOS CON PLÁTANOS FRITOS
FRIED EGGS WITH TOMATO SAUCE AND FRIED PLANTAINS

Each fried egg is served sunny-side up on a fried tortilla, per the instructions for Huevos Rancheros, generously covered in a cooked tomato salsa infused with the taste of ham, and brightened with fresh green peas when they're available. Frozen peas also work fine, and garbanzo beans make a hearty variation. The fried slices of plantain, which is native to the Yucatán Peninsula, where this dish originated, provide a sweet complement to the salty, smoky sauce.

————————

To make the sauce: Warm the olive oil in a heavy-bottom skillet over medium heat until it's hot but not smoking. Add the onion and chile and cook until the onion is translucent but not browned. Add the garlic and cook for 1 minute more, just until you can smell its fragrance. Add the tomatoes to the skillet along with the tomato paste, salt, and pepper and simmer over low heat. Measure out the peas and ham and set aside to add after you fry your plantains (if you add them at this point, they will overcook).

Preheat the oven to its lowest temperature. Line a platter with a brown paper bag and place in the oven to warm.

To make the fried plantains: Warm the vegetable oil in a heavy-bottom stockpot over low to medium heat. (Plantains have a lot of sugar in them, so they will burn easily if the oil is too hot.) Drop in one slice of plantain and make sure it sizzles slightly before dropping in as many as you can fit in a single layer without crowding. Let them cook for about 2 minutes per side, using a spatula to flip them. They should look appetizingly golden when done. Remove them with a slotted spoon and place them on the prepared platter in the oven to stay warm while you fry the rest.

Once the plantains are fried and keeping warm in the oven, add the peas or garbanzo beans and ham to your simmering tomato sauce. Taste and add more salt if needed. If your ham is cured, the sauce may already be salty enough without adding more salt.

Cook the tortillas and eggs as directed on page 105, frying the tortillas and setting them aside to stay warm while you fry 2 eggs at a time.

When you're ready to serve, slide a fried egg onto a fried tortilla on each plate and ladle the sauce over them. Serve with the fried plantains on the side, slices of avocado on top, and a bowl of black beans at the table for people to help themselves.

Motuleño Sauce
2 Tbsp olive oil
1 white onion, coarsely chopped
1 habanero chile, stemmed, seeded, veins removed (or not, depending on how spicy you want this to be), and chopped
1 garlic clove, chopped
4 Roma tomatoes, cored and chopped, or 4 canned whole tomatoes
1 Tbsp tomato paste (optional; use only if the tomatoes are at all pink)
½ tsp sea salt, plus more as needed
Pinch of freshly ground white pepper
½ cup / 50g shucked sugar snap peas, frozen peas, or fresh garbanzo beans
½ cup / 75g minced cooked ham

Fried Plantains
¼ cup / 60ml vegetable oil
2 or 3 very ripe (black) plantains, peeled and cut into ¼-inch / 6mm-wide disks on the diagonal
Sea salt

4 to 6 tortillas
8 to 12 eggs
1 avocado, cut in half, pitted, peeled, and sliced (optional)
1 recipe Frijoles Aguados (page 84)

CARNITAS SLOW-COOKED PORK

MAKES 2 ½ LB / 1.2KG

¼ cup / 50g lard or reserved
    bacon fat
3 lb / 1.4kg boneless pork
    shoulder or butt, cut into
    1½-inch / 4cm chunks
1 orange, quartered
4 bay leaves (preferably fresh)
¼ white onion
3 garlic cloves
1 Tbsp sea salt, plus more as
    needed
5 black peppercorns

Carnitas—slowly cooked and crisped pork—can be eaten at different times of the day in Mexico, but they are most commonly a breakfast food, and they star in one of my favorite breakfasts, Tortas Ahogadas (page 126).

Carnitas start as chunks of pork, braised until the meat starts falling apart and then fried until they turn brown and crispy. There are as many ways to make carnitas as there are recipes for Thanksgiving stuffing. Actually, like Thanksgiving stuffing, most people in Mexico know how they like their carnitas and don't need a recipe at all. I've seen people throw everything into the braise, from Coca-Cola to Fanta to sweetened condensed milk. I prefer to let the taste of the meat shine, which is why I start by picking the best pork I can buy. I look for a fatty cut that's evenly marbled, which means the pig was well fed but also had a chance to exercise. It should have a light and healthy pink color. I also ask to smell the meat before buying it. Raw, it should have virtually no smell. Cooked is another story, since the savory aroma of roasting pork will fill your whole house.

This process takes a few hours, but you don't have to do much except keep an eye on the pot until the end, when stirring is required to keep the carnitas from sticking to the pan. I usually make carnitas when I need to feed a crowd. I serve them with fresh tortillas, guacamole, and lime wedges, plus rice and beans to eat on the side, and I have people assemble their own tacos at the table. I always set some aside, too, to enjoy the next day all by myself.

———————

Melt the lard or bacon fat over medium heat in your largest heavy-bottom stockpot or Dutch oven. (A heavy base will help to keep the pork from burning while it cooks down.) Decrease the heat to low and place the pork in the pot, fatty-side down. Squeeze the orange over the pork and add the juiced rinds, bay leaves, onion, garlic, salt, and peppercorns. Simmer over the lowest heat possible, uncovered, for about 1½ hours, stirring occasionally to make sure that all of the pieces are cooking evenly.

Remove and discard the orange peel and bay leaves. Now increase the heat to medium-high and continue cooking for another 1½ hours, stirring more regularly as the fat renders out and the pork begins to look more shredded and browned. Once you're sure that the meat is cooked through, add more salt to taste. (Salting the meat in stages serves two purposes: salting it raw brings out the maximum flavor from the meat while it cooks. But holding back ensures that you don't oversalt, since you have to wait until the pork is fully cooked before you can taste it and add more salt only if needed.)

In the last 10 minutes of cooking, start removing the chunks that look done, transferring them to a colander set over a bowl to drain the excess oil. There should be a range of textures to the carnitas—some pieces will be crispy, some stringy, some chewy. You want that mixture. Serve hot.

Carnitas can be stored in a sealed container in the refrigerator for up to 3 days. Reheat on an ungreased comal or in a skillet over medium heat or on a baking sheet in a 350°F / 180°C oven for about 10 minutes.

TORTAS AHOGADAS SALSA-DROWNED CARNITAS SANDWICHES

Salsa Ahogada
2 Tbsp olive oil
1 white onion, coarsely chopped
1 serrano chile, stemmed,
    seeded, veins removed (or not,
    depending on how spicy you
    want this to be), and coarsely
    chopped
1 garlic clove
4 Roma tomatoes, cored and
    chopped
1 Tbsp tomato paste (optional;
    use only if the tomatoes are
    at all pink)
2 cups / 480ml water
2 tsp sea salt, plus more as needed
5 black peppercorns, or a pinch of
    freshly ground black pepper
3 whole cloves, or a pinch of
    ground cloves
4 allspice berries, or a pinch of
    ground allspice
1 Tbsp ground cumin
1 Tbsp dried oregano
3 dried chiles de árbol
2 bay leaves (preferably fresh)
¾ cup / 180ml white vinegar

1 lb / 455g Carnitas (page 124)
4 to 6 bolillos (Mexican sandwich
    rolls) or 1 large ciabatta or
    baguette, cut into 4 to
    6 sandwich-size pieces
1 cup / 240g Frijoles Refritos
    (page 85)
½ cup / 60g Cebollas Rojas
    Encurtidas (page 39)
1 avocado, cut in half, pitted,
    peeled, and thinly sliced

These "drowned" sandwiches are a specialty of the state of Jalisco, famously eaten in Guadalajara on the streets of popular neighborhoods as a filling breakfast with the power to relieve a hangover. You eat them standing, in spite of the fact that the entire sandwich gets doused in a spicy, vinegary red sauce that doesn't exactly make for tidy consumption. You can order them media ahogada (half-drowned, for which just the cut part of the sandwich gets dipped) or bien ahogada (completely submerged).

Don't get out your white tablecloth when serving these for brunch. If you and your guests are not afraid of getting your hands messy (or averse to eating a sandwich with a knife, fork, *and* spoon), these sandwiches are worth the fanaticism that they inspire. When featured at brunch at Cala, I serve them bien ahogada, with each sandwich sitting in its own bowl of sauce and lots more ladled over the top. If you have access to good Mexican birote (the hard-crusted bolillo from Jalisco), use that or substitute the best sandwich rolls or baguettes with a good crust.

This is one recipe that has its own salsa (rather than a staple salsa) because as good as this salsa is, it's really only eaten on this sandwich.

Whole spices have much more flavor (and fragrance) than ones that have been ground, especially if those ground spices aren't very fresh. But if you use whole cloves and peppercorns, make sure you have a blender strong enough to pulverize them completely. Alternatively, you can grind your whole spices in a spice grinder before adding them to the blender. It's worth the extra couple of minutes.

———————

To make the salsa: Warm the oil in a medium heavy-bottom skillet over medium heat until it's hot but not smoking. Add the onion, serrano chile, and garlic and fry, stirring constantly, until the onion is transparent but not browned and the garlic is golden and aromatic. Add the tomatoes and the tomato paste, 1 cup / 240ml of the water, and the salt. Simmer for 10 minutes.

While the mixture is simmering, warm an ungreased comal or skillet over medium heat. Stirring constantly, toast the peppercorns, cloves, allspice, cumin, oregano, chiles de árbol, and bay leaves together for 1 to 2 minutes, until you can smell them but before the chiles blister or turn brown. Remove the comal or skillet from the heat and transfer the contents to a blender jar, provided you have a powerful blender. If not, use a spice grinder to pulverize the spices before placing them in the blender jar. Add the tomato mixture, vinegar, and remaining 1 cup / 240ml water to the blender and liquefy. Pour the mixture into a medium saucepan and simmer over medium heat for 20 minutes, or until the salsa has thickened and reduced by at least one-third. Taste and add more salt if needed. Keep the salsa hot until you are ready to serve it under (and over) your tortas.

If you're reheating cold carnitas, preheat the oven to 350°F / 180°C or warm an ungreased comal or skillet over medium-high heat on the stove top. Heat the carnitas in the oven or on the comal or in the skillet for about 10 minutes, flattening them with a spatula, until a nice crispy outer layer develops while the interior stays soft and a bit creamy.

Preheat the broiler. Split the bread lengthwise and broil for 3 minutes, until the slices are hot and toasty.

Spread about 2 Tbsp of the beans on one side of each roll. On the other side of each roll, distribute about ½ cup / 135g carnitas. Distribute a couple of slices of pickled onions and a couple of slices of avocado on each half and close each sandwich. Cut each sandwich in half on the diagonal.

For each serving, pour 1 cup / 240ml of the hot salsa ahogada into a deep plate or shallow bowl. Place both halves of a sandwich, cut-side down, in the sauce. Now ladle more sauce over the top of the sandwich and garnish with more pickled onions.

Serve with a knife, fork, spoon, and lots of napkins!

CONTINUED

TORTAS AHOGADAS CON CARNITAS DE PESCADO / SALSA-DROWNED SANDWICHES WITH FLAKED FRIED FISH VARIATION

This variation on Tortas Ahogada, using fried fish instead of pork, is something we invented at Contramar to use up tuna scraps from the tuna tostada that has become our signature dish. We use line-caught albacore or yellowfin, but this would work with any fish that is fatty enough to hold up in the deep fryer. The fried pieces should develop a crispy outer edge but still stay moist (though thoroughly cooked) on the inside—just like pork carnitas. Make the fried fish for the tortas ahogada: Buy 1 lb / 455g albacore, yellowfin, halibut, or any other firm-fleshed, fatty fish. Line a plate with a brown paper bag. Pour 2 cups / 480ml vegetable oil into a saucepan big enough so that all of your pieces of fish will be completely submerged. Warm the oil over medium-high heat until it is hot enough that a piece of fish sizzles when dropped in. Drop in the rest of the fish, making sure not to crowd the pan, cooking the fish in two batches if necessary. Don't stir the fish pieces around as they fry; just let them cook until they're a golden honey color. Using a slotted spoon, transfer the fish to the plate to drain. Season with sea salt and serve warm. Store in a sealed container in the refrigerator for up to 2 days.

CHORIZO ROJO RED CHORIZO

12 guajillo chiles, stemmed
and seeded

3 morita chiles, stemmed
and seeded

2 cups / 480ml white vinegar

7 garlic cloves

Leaves of 3 sprigs thyme

2 tsp dried oregano

15 black peppercorns, or 1 tsp
freshly ground black pepper

5 cloves, or a healthy pinch of
ground cloves

7 allspice berries, or a healthy
pinch of ground allspice

2 bay leaves (preferably fresh)

¼ cup / 65g sea salt

2¼ lb / 1kg ground pork

Ambitious home cooks love to make all kinds of staples from scratch these days, and the internet is full of recipes for homemade chorizo. But mostly these recipes offer a kind of chorizo for dummies, telling cooks to season ground pork with wimpy amounts of ground chile, plus a few measly tablespoons of vinegar, and then cook it immediately. No!

Chorizo is a spicy pickled meat. Like any pickle, it needs to be fully saturated in a brine of vinegar and salt. To give chorizo the zesty complexity that makes it, well, a chorizo, you have to soak whole dried chiles (a lot of them) in the vinegar, blend it all up with the other herbs and spices, and then massage it into the meat. Finally, and this is very important, the flavored meat must sit for a few days, pickling, soaking up those flavors, and drying out, before you cook it.

Traditionally, this is done by stuffing the seasoned meat into casings and hanging the sausages for several days to dry out. Now, I realize that this is impractical for most of us, especially in smaller kitchens. It's the one step that I skip, since I don't believe that my practical solution sacrifices flavor or texture. What I do instead is to completely clear out one refrigerator shelf and place my seasoned ground pork there, on a baking sheet that I cover with a dish towel so the meat can breathe as it dries out. I recommend letting chorizo pickle for three days before cooking. Double the recipe if you want to freeze some for later. Chorizo is amazing as a taco filling, scrambled with eggs, crumbled over chilaquiles, or fried with potatoes.

Get the best organic ground pork that you can, with the highest percentage of fat available, not a lean one. If possible, ask a butcher to coarsely grind a particularly fatty cut of raw pork for you. Keep in mind that many people actually buy extra fat to grind into their sausages. Most will render out during cooking, but the extra fat keeps the finished chorizo from sticking to your pan.

On a comal or in an ungreased skillet over medium heat, toast all the chiles for 1 to 2 minutes, flipping them with tongs to heat each side. Make sure they don't brown or blister, or they will turn bitter. When you can smell them, place them in a saucepan. Cover them with water and bring to a simmer, then turn off the stove and let them soak for 20 minutes, until they are soft. Drain the chiles and discard the soaking water.

Combine the chiles, vinegar, garlic, thyme, oregano, peppercorns, cloves, allspice, bay leaves, and salt in a blender and blend. (If your blender isn't very powerful, you could use a spice grinder before adding them to the blender, or use ground versions of the spices, but don't skip any. Flavor is what chorizo is all about.)

Place the pork in a large bowl and add the pungent marinade. Wearing plastic gloves, massage the marinade into the pork until it's totally incorporated into the meat, which will turn the deep red color that's characteristic of chorizo.

Line a baking sheet (one that will fit on your cleared refrigerator shelf) with parchment paper and spread the seasoned meat over it from edge to edge. Punch holes in the surface of the meat with your fingertips so it can aerate. Lay a dish towel (or another sheet of parchment paper) on top of the meat and set it in the fridge to cure for 3 days. Every day, take it out and punch new holes in the surface of the meat. After 3 days, you can fry the amount you want to cook and transfer the rest to a sealed container for use later.

This chorizo will keep in the fridge for about 1 week or in the freezer for up to 2 months. Thaw in the refrigerator before using.

CHORIZO VERDE GREEN CHORIZO

MAKES 5 CUPS / 1.4G

3 oz / 85g fresh spinach

5 serrano chiles, stemmed, seeded,
    and veins removed (or not,
    depending on how spicy you
    want this to be)

3 poblano chiles, stemmed,
    seeded, and veins removed
    (or not, depending on how
    spicy you want this to be)

½ cup / 60g raw pumpkin seeds

1 cup / 240ml white vinegar

4 garlic cloves

1 tsp freshly ground white pepper

2 bay leaves (preferably fresh)

5 cloves or ½ tsp ground cloves

2 tsp dried oregano

3 Tbsp / 45g sea salt

1½ lb / 650g ground pork, fattiest
    and coarsest grind available

1 lb / 455g 75% lean ground beef

The method of making this green chorizo is very similar to the red one on page 130, but it has a very different flavor thanks to the use of serranos, poblanos, and spinach, instead of the dried red chiles, and a tasty combination of beef and pork. It still has a lot of heat and offers a fresh alternative to people who may have tried only red chorizo.

———————

Fill a large saucepan halfway with water and bring to a boil over high heat. In the sink, place a bowl and fill it with water and ice cubes. Once the water is boiling, drop in the spinach, and cook for 30 seconds, until it turns bright green. Using a slotted spoon, transfer it into the bowl of ice water and let it soak for 1 minute. Drain it into a colander and use your hands or a wooden spoon to squeeze out as much liquid as possible.

In a blender, combine the blanched spinach, serranos, poblanos, pumpkin seeds, vinegar, garlic, pepper, bay leaves, cloves, oregano, and salt. Blend until everything is liquefied.

Place the pork and the beef in a large bowl. Add the green mixture and, wearing plastic gloves, massage it into the meat until it's totally incorporated.

Line a baking sheet (one that will fit on your cleared refrigerator shelf—see recipe introduction on page 130) with parchment paper and spread the seasoned meat over it, from edge to edge. Punch holes in the surface of the meat with your fingertips so it can aerate. Lay a dish towel (or another sheet of parchment paper) on top of the meat and set it in the fridge to cure for 3 days. Every day, take it out and punch new holes in the surface of the meat. After 3 days, you can fry the amount you want to cook with and transfer the rest to a sealed container for use later.

This chorizo will keep in the fridge for about 1 week or in the freezer for up to 2 months. Thaw in the refrigerator before using.

MOLLETES CON CHORIZO
BROILED OPEN-FACED SANDWICHES WITH REFRIED BEANS, CHEESE, AND CHORIZO

This is a typical college breakfast or easy snack or dinner. Buttered crusty bread (a baguette works great) gets spread with refried beans, covered in cheese and crumbled chorizo, then broiled, open-faced, and served with pico de gallo for a little freshness.

———————

Preheat the broiler. Split the bread lengthwise. Spread one side of the bread with about 1 tsp of the butter. On the other side, spread 2 Tbsp of the beans. Place the rolls on a baking sheet. Top the beans with the cheese and chorizo.

Broil for 3 to 5 minutes, until the cheese is melted and bubbling. Serve with the pico de gallo on the side.

MAKES 4 TO 6 SERVINGS

4 to 6 bolillos (Mexican sandwich rolls) or 1 large ciabatta or baguette, cut into 4 to 6 sandwich-size pieces
2 Tbsp unsalted butter, softened
1 cup / 240g Frijoles Refritos (page 85)
1 cup / 80g grated sharp Cheddar or Chihuahua cheese or another sharp cheese you like
1 cup / 350g crumbled Chorizo Rojo (page 130) or Chorizo Verde (page 132), cooked in a skillet and drained
1 cup / 240ml Pico de Gallo (page 44)

BOMBAS CON FRIJOLES
BEAN AND CHEESE–FILLED SWEET BUNS

This is a great way to use day-old conchas, sweet rolls with a buttery cookielike topping that are shaped like the shells for which they are named. Toasting under the broiler revives them beautifully, and the sweet buns form an unexpectedly delicious base for the savory beans and sharp melted cheese.

_____

Preheat the broiler.

Cut your conchas in half. Spread each side with about 2 Tbsp of the refried beans. Place the rolls on a baking sheet. Divide the cheese evenly among them.

Broil for 3 to 5 minutes, until the cheese is melted and bubbling. Close the sandwiches and serve immediately.

MAKES 4 TO 6 SERVINGS

4 to 6 Conchas de Pinole
   (page 96)
1 cup / 240g Frijoles Refritos
   (page 85)
1 cup / 80g shredded toma cheese,
   queso Oaxaca, or sharp
   Cheddar cheese

3 ANTOJITOS
Y PRIMEROS

FINGER FOOD AND FIRST COURSES

Mexico is a country full of people who love to eat and who seize every opportunity to taste as many things as possible. A Mexican meal almost always starts with an antojito or a primero, both of which correspond loosely to the American appetizer course.

Antojito means "little craving" and applies to a lot of common street food as well as to bar snacks, or the nibbles you might be served after arriving at someone's house before a meal. These are Mexican canapés, rich but tiny. The goal is not to fill up on antojitos (tempting though it may be) but to savor something small and delicious while chatting with friends. In fact, on menus, antojitos are often listed under a section called *para compartir*, or "to share."

Another way that Mexican antojitos may be listed on menus is *para picar*, or "to pinch on." This definitely applies to dishes like sopes (thick, fried masa disks that hold various toppings) as well as to tostadas, something that I've always served at my restaurants; these dishes can be confusing to guests from some European cultures who may wonder whether this type of food qualifies as refined dining if eaten out of hand. (In Paris, they eat burgers with a knife and fork and often seem perplexed by the way we eat tacos.) This is not something that troubles me. I love finger foods and see no contradiction between white tablecloths and tostadas, although I was one of the first to serve street food like this at a white-tablecloth establishment.

These days, family-style dining is in fashion, so I guess everyone has caught on. Food always tastes best when it's shared with people whose company you enjoy as much as the food itself. And with shared plates, the more friends you get together for a meal, the more things you get to try!

Compared to antojitos, primeros are more like the traditional first course served at a dinner party or formal restaurant and include the salads and soups we love to begin meals with in Mexico. I'm not sure why soup is so popular in a country where it never gets particularly cold, but we eat it every which way—brothy, creamy, hot, and chilled, at home and at restaurants—and never tire of it. While the soups in this section are filed under primeros, there's absolutely no reason you couldn't make a meal out of any one of them, paired with a basket of warm tortillas or a loaf of bread. The chapters in this book are meant to introduce you to the way we compartmentalize food in Mexico, but of course you are welcome to deviate to your heart's desire.

You might notice that there are not a lot of salads in this chapter. Mexicans don't automatically launch a meal with salad. For whatever reason, the European tradition of including a salad with every meal didn't take root. What did take root is the European tradition of thinking of a rice or pasta dish as a primero rather than as a fuerte, or main course. This isn't intuitive to people from the United States, even those who are vegetarian, who view heavy starches as mains. But in Italy, pasta is a primi, just as the Mexican fideo (a hearty casserole of fried noodles) is considered a primero, unless it's made more substantial by the inclusion of seafood. In general, dishes that include meat are considered fuertes, while vegetarian ones tend to be primeros, except for ceviches and aguachiles, which are lighter and feature raw seafood and therefore stay in the appetizer category.

I just want to give you some understanding of why I've organized my recipes the way I have, based on the Mexican way of eating. But it doesn't matter what you call a dish, how you classify it, or when you choose to eat it. All that matters is that you enjoy it.

PEPITAS PREPARADAS ROASTED PUMPKIN SEEDS WITH CHILE AND LIME

MAKES 2 CUPS / 280G

4 chiles de árbol, stemmed
    and seeded
2 cups / 240g pumpkin seeds
1 lime, cut in half
1 tsp sea salt

Every culture has its version of bar nuts, and this is ours. Pumpkin seeds get toasted with chiles, doused with lime juice, and sprinkled with salt, which of course just makes you want to drink more. This is the easiest thing in the world to make, but also one of the best. Make sure to get unroasted and unsalted pumpkin seeds without their shells, which is not the way that they come when you scoop them straight out of a pumpkin. They should be green, a little shiny, and relatively flat. Mexican markets sell them as pepitas.

———————

Preheat the oven to 350°F / 180°C.

Warm a medium skillet over low heat. Place the chiles in the skillet and let them toast for 1 to 2 minutes while agitating them. As soon as you can smell the chiles, add the pumpkin seeds to the skillet and move them around constantly as they toast for another 3 to 4 minutes. Pumpkin seeds burn easily, so you want to monitor them closely and keep them from sticking to the pan. Once you can smell a nice toasted aroma (*not* the smell of burnt seeds), remove the pan from the heat and empty the pumpkin seeds and chiles into a bowl. Remove and discard the chiles. Squeeze the lime juice over the seeds, toss, sprinkle with the salt, and toss again.

Coat a baking sheet with oil or use a sheet of parchment paper to keep the seeds from sticking. Spread the seeds evenly on the prepared baking sheet and bake for 10 to 15 minutes, using a spatula to turn them over after the first 5 minutes. You are looking for the seeds to dry out, but they shouldn't turn much darker.

Serve the seeds while they're still warm. Theoretically, these seeds can be stored in a sealed container for up to 1 week—*if* you have any left.

ENSALADA DE CALABACITAS Y ESPÁRRAGOS
SUMMER SQUASH AND ASPARAGUS SALAD

5 or 6 young zucchini or yellow
squash or a mix, sliced into
ribbons ⅛ inch / 3mm thick
1 bunch of asparagus, fibrous base
of each stalk trimmed off and
discarded, sliced crosswise into
⅛-inch / 3mm-wide pieces
1 tsp sea salt, plus more as needed
3 Tbsp / 45ml extra-virgin olive oil
¼ cup / 60ml freshly squeezed
lime juice

This is a super-simple salad, made to show off the season's first and freshest
asparagus and either zucchini or yellow squash (or both) that are young
and tender enough to be enjoyed raw. I like the combination of green zucchini and yellow squash on the plate, but it's not essential to use the two.
What is important is that you buy the smallest and most delicate zucchini
or squash that you can find. When buying asparagus, test to make sure that
a stalk snaps neatly. When the disks of asparagus get tossed with ribbons
of fresh zucchini or squash, and dressed in a light lime vinaigrette, they look
like springtime on a plate.

———————

Place the zucchini and/or squash and asparagus in a colander, toss with the salt,
and leave it in the sink to drain for 5 to 10 minutes. Don't leave it for much longer
or the squash will get too limp.

In a bowl, whisk together the oil and lime juice. Add the squash and asparagus
slices and toss gently to coat. Taste and add more salt if needed.

Serve on individual salad plates or in shallow bowls.

ENSALADA VERDE CON ADEREZO DE PEPITAS GREEN SALAD WITH PUMPKIN SEED DRESSING

MAKES 4 TO 6 SERVINGS

1 serrano chile, stemmed, seeded, and veins removed (or not, depending on how spicy you want this to be)

1 small garlic clove, toasted lightly in a dry skillet over low heat

½ cup / 60g raw pumpkin seeds

1 Tbsp flat-leaf parsley leaves

2 Tbsp freshly squeezed lime juice

½ cup / 120ml extra-virgin olive oil

½ tsp sea salt, plus more as needed

4 to 6 cups / 80 to 120g of the best, freshest lettuce you can find

This salad showcases the best lettuce at its peak freshness. Depending on the season, I might include chicory, radicchio, purslane, Little Gem, or whatever looks beautiful and delicious. Where lettuce is concerned, you should definitely use your eyes to guide your selection. Don't buy a head of lettuce that looks at all wilted. The leaves should be springy, never brown-tinged at the edges. Try to buy whole heads and avoid those fatigued mesclun mixes sold in plastic. Aside from the freshest possible lettuce, the ground pumpkin seed dressing also sets this otherwise simple salad apart, adding a creamy robustness to the vinaigrette.

———————

In a food processor, blend the chile, garlic, pumpkin seeds, parsley, lime juice, oil, and salt. Set aside.

Wash and dry the lettuce well, being careful not to crush or bruise the leaves. Toss with the dressing in a large bowl, taste, and add more salt if needed. Serve immediately.

Any leftover dressing can be stored in a sealed container in the refrigerator for up to 1 week.

ENSALADA DE NOPALES, AGUACATES, TOMATES Y CALABACITAS
CACTUS, AVOCADO, TOMATO, AND SUMMER SQUASH SALAD

The dressing for this summer salad is the liquid strained from pico de gallo, which gives the piquancy of a fresh salsa without its visible ingredients. It's where all the flavor comes from in this light dish.

Make sure that you either buy cactus paddles that have been dethorned or remove them yourself. When you serve the paddles raw, as in this recipe, you must first coat them in salt for 1 hour, which brings out their natural slime, which you then rinse off.

When serving squash raw, I always choose baby squash, ideally from a farmers' market or a garden, because they taste sweeter. I like to use yellow and green squash together in this salad, and I slice it with a mandoline, sometimes cutting on the vertical and sometimes on the horizontal, creating a variety of interesting shapes on the plate. To make a heartier meal, spoon cooked beans (cannellini are nice) into each bowl as a base for the salad and to soak up the dressing, and top the salad with crumbled queso fresco, goat cheese, or feta.

Place the cactus paddle in a bowl, sprinkle both sides with 1 tsp salt, and set aside for 1 hour. Transfer the cactus to a colander and rinse them thoroughly until they no longer feel slimy. Cut the cacti into ¼-inch / 6mm-wide strips and transfer to a large salad bowl.

Place the squash in a colander, add 1 tsp salt, and leave it in the sink to drain for about 10 minutes while you assemble the rest of the salad. Don't leave it for much longer or the squash will get too limp.

Meanwhile, in a food processor, combine the tomatoes, onion, chiles, and the remaining 1 tsp salt and pulse until minced but still chunky. You don't want to liquefy these ingredients, because you will be straining the pico de gallo to use only the juices, and the liquid that strains out should be clear, not pink, which it will become if you blend it too thoroughly. Suspend a fine-mesh strainer over a bowl and pour the contents of the food processor into the strainer, catching the juices in the bowl. Remember that you are keeping the juices that strain out, not discarding them.

MAKES 4 TO 6 SERVINGS

1 cactus paddle, dethorned

3 tsp sea salt, plus more as needed

5 or 6 baby squash, preferably yellow and green and differently shaped, sliced about ⅛ inch / 3mm thick

4 Roma tomatoes, cored and cut in half

½ white onion

2 or 3 serrano chiles, stemmed, seeded, and veins removed (or not, depending on how spicy you want this to be)

¼ cup / 60ml extra-virgin olive oil

¼ cup / 60ml freshly squeezed lime juice

1 avocado, cut in half, pitted, peeled, and thinly sliced

¼ cup / 5g cilantro leaves, minced, or cilantro flowers if available

4 radishes, thinly sliced on a mandoline and placed in a bowl of ice water to curl

CONTINUED

ENSALADA DE NOPALES, AGUACATES, TOMATES Y CALABACITAS, continued

Being careful not to crush or break the sliced squash, gently press out the excess moisture and transfer the squash to the large bowl with the cactus. Don't rinse the squash, since the leftover salt will season the salad. Add 3 Tbsp / 45ml of the oil and the lime juice and toss gently to coat. Taste and add more salt if needed.

Serve on individual salad plates or in shallow bowls. Divide the vegetables evenly. Top each portion of squash and cactus with a few slices of avocado. Ladle with the pico de gallo broth and drizzle with the remaining 1 Tbsp oil. Garnish with the cilantro or cilantro flowers and a few slices of radish before serving.

ENSALADA DE NOPALES Y VERDOLAGAS CON RICOTTA SALATA

CACTUS AND WATERCRESS SALAD WITH RICOTTA SALATA

This is a wonderful salad that really puts cactus center stage, showing how this vegetable can be enjoyed raw as well as cooked. Make sure that you either buy cactus paddles that have been dethorned or remove the thorns yourself. Because you need to salt and rinse the paddles whenever you serve them raw (see page 147), I don't add a lot of salt to this vinaigrette. While a more traditional cheese for this salad might be a dry queso fresco, good ones are hard to come by outside of Mexico, so I typically reach for ricotta salata.

————————

Place the cactus paddles in a bowl, sprinkle with the sea salt, and let rest for 1 hour. Transfer the paddles to a colander and rinse them thoroughly until they no longer feel slimy. Cut them into ½-inch / 12mm-wide slices and transfer to a medium serving bowl.

Add the radishes, onion, watercress, and cilantro to the bowl. In a jar or a small bowl, combine the oil, lime juice, and finishing salt and shake or stir to mix. Dress the salad and toss to coat.

Serve within 1 hour of dressing the salad, topping each portion with 1 Tbsp ricotta salata right before you serve it.

MAKES 4 TO 6 SERVINGS

1 lb / 455g cactus paddles, dethorned
½ cup / 130g sea salt
3½ oz / 100g radishes, sliced on a mandoline
½ red onion, slivered
6 cups / 120g watercress, rinsed, dried, and torn into manageable bites
2 Tbsp chopped cilantro leaves
½ cup / 120ml extra-virgin olive oil
½ cup / 120ml freshly squeezed lime juice
1 tsp Maldon sea salt or another finishing salt
4 to 6 Tbsp / 20 to 30g grated ricotta salata

AGUACATE RELLENO DE CAMARONES
AVOCADO STUFFED WITH SHRIMP

This is a kind of Mexican-style shrimp Louie. A chopped salad, heavy on the bay shrimp, is tossed with chipotle mayonnaise and a squeeze of lemon and then served in halved avocados and sprinkled with toasted pumpkin seeds for crunch. Part of what makes this so good is the study in textural contrasts: the creamy avocado beneath the crisp chopped salad and the meaty bay shrimp contrasted with the raw vegetables. It's a super-simple recipe that will nonetheless steal the stage at a luncheon or make a lovely starter at an elegant dinner. The chipotle mayonnaise—one of my favorite tricks—whips together in a snap in a blender but lends the dish an illusion of complexity. For the most elegant presentation, do your best to dice your fennel, radishes, onion, and tomato into cubes of the same small size and shape; that uniformity elevates the look of this dish.

———————

Use a large spoon to carefully scoop the flesh of each halved avocado out of its shell, setting the intact avocado halves on a serving platter or, if you intend to serve them individually, on salad plates.

In a medium bowl, combine the cabbage or lettuce with the fennel, radishes, onion, and tomato. Add the shrimp, mayonnaise, lemon juice, and salt and toss. Taste and add more salt or lemon juice as needed.

Serve a generous scoop of shrimp salad in each avocado half. It's fine if it spills over—no one will complain! Garnish each serving with a sprinkle of pumpkin seeds and fresh oregano or thyme leaves. Eat within 30 minutes, before the avocado begins to turn brown.

MAKES 4 TO 6 SERVINGS

2 or 3 avocados, cut in half and pitted

¼ head napa cabbage or 2 heads Little Gem lettuce (you want something crunchy), finely chopped

1 fennel bulb, cut into ¼-inch / 6mm dice

2 radishes, cut into ¼-inch / 6mm dice

¼ white onion, cut into ¼-inch / 6mm dice

5 oz / 140g cherry tomatoes, diced

1 lb 6 oz / 630g cooked bay shrimp, well drained

3 Tbsp / 45g Mayonesa con Limón (page 62)

Juice of 1 lemon, plus more as needed

1 tsp sea salt, plus more as needed

Leaves of 2 or 3 sprigs cilantro, minced

ENSALADA DE PULPO OCTOPUS SALAD

MAKES 4 TO 6 SERVINGS

4 Yukon gold potatoes
2 Tbsp sea salt
1 cooked octopus (see page 247),
    chopped into ½-inch / 12mm
    pieces
1 large fennel bulb, diced
½ cup / 10g parsley leaves,
    chopped
⅔ cup / 160ml extra-virgin olive oil
Juice of 2 lemons
Maldon sea salt or another
    finishing salt

This was one of my favorite things that my beloved nonna made, a dish we always prepared when we stayed at the beach in Zihuatanejo, where it was easy to get octopus. It exemplifies everything I love about Italian home cooking: simple food showcasing the freshest ingredients, prepared with love. Octopus is easy to cook if you have a pressure cooker and it's so naturally delicious that it needs little adornment besides this bright lemony dressing flecked with lots of parsley.

————————

In a medium saucepan, cover the potatoes with water, leaving their skins on to preserve the starch. Add the salt and bring to a boil. Decrease the heat and let them simmer for 15 to 20 minutes. Test the potatoes with a fork for doneness; they should be soft but not falling apart. Transfer to a colander to drain. Remove their skins (they should slip right off) and let the potatoes cool until you can handle them. Cut the potatoes into ½-inch / 12mm cubes.

Place the potatoes in a serving bowl and add the octopus, fennel, and parsley. Dress with the oil and lemon juice. Taste and add the finishing salt if more salt is needed. Since the potatoes and octopus were both cooked in salted water, you may not need additional salt.

Store the salad in the fridge until you're ready to serve; use the same day it is made.

ESQUITES ROASTED CORN IN ITS OWN BROTH

MAKES 4 TO 6 SERVINGS

6 ears white corn, shucked
1 Tbsp sea salt, plus more
  as needed
¼ cup / 5g coarsely chopped
  epazote or cilantro
3 chiles piquín
1 recipe freshly made Mayonesa
  con Chipotle (page 62) or
  Mayonesa con Limón (page 62)
Grated queso Cotija or
  ricotta salata for serving
2 limes, cut into quarters
Ground chile piquín for serving

Are esquites a salad? A soup? Neither and both. Esquites are a favorite Mexican street snack, always eaten in the fall when corn is fresh and plentiful. Kernels of corn get cut off the cob, boiled, and then served in a bit of the cooking liquid, mixed with toppings such as mayonnaise, grated queso Cotija (I substitute ricotta salata when I don't have access to good Cotija), lime, and ground chile piquín. It's usually served in a Styrofoam cup and eaten with a spoon while standing up. In Mexico, no one will invite you to their house to eat an esquite. It's a to-go food. But it's also something I crave when I'm not in Mexico, so I like to re-create it at home. I make mine a bit more refined than the street version. Instead of merely boiling the corn, I like to roast the ears first and then slice off the kernels, which imparts a nice toasty flavor. I throw fresh epazote in the broth, along with some chile piquín. It's important to use white corn for esquites. The best variety is cacahuazintle, which has big kernels, but any sweet white corn will do.

I recommend placing the toppings in the center of the table for people to choose what they'd like to add. Mayonnaise and cheese are delicious and make the broth turn creamy, but I prefer just lime and ground chile. Esquites can be enjoyed hot, at room temperature, or cold. At parties, the pot is often left on the stove for hours, so people can come back for more.

Place a comal or skillet over high heat and oil it lightly so that the corn doesn't stick. Place the ears of corn on the comal or skillet and rotate every 30 seconds or so, until they are lightly charred on all sides, 4 to 5 minutes total. Let the corn cool to the touch, then slice off the kernels.

Place the kernels in a medium saucepan over medium-high heat and add water to barely cover, then add the salt, epazote, and chiles. Bring to a boil, then decrease the heat and let simmer for 5 minutes. You have to make sure that the corn is cooked through but not overcooked to the point of being mushy. It should be soft enough to chew easily while still retaining a slight crunch. Remove the chiles. Divide the kernels and liquid evenly among serving bowls and serve warm, passing the mayonnaise, cheese, limes, and ground chile for people to add if they wish.

Esquites can be stored in a sealed container, covered, in the refrigerator for 2 to 3 days. Reheat in a saucepan over low heat.

SOPA DE AGUACATE FRÍA COLD AVOCADO SOUP

This chilled avocado soup was a real 1970s thing in Mexico. It was the signature dish of a family friend, the wife of an art historian, and it always seemed so fancy to me, especially when served at her luncheons by waiters in white gloves. I couldn't believe it when I found out that the recipe involved blending avocados with cream cheese and a Knorr seasoning cube. Instead of cream cheese, I use fresh goat cheese, and I crumble ricotta salata on top. And I skip the Knorr. Blending the avocados, goat cheese, and chicken stock gives this soup a super-creamy texture. It's lighter and silkier than guacamole but has the same effect—you keep wanting more. Make this soup within an hour of when you intend to serve it because it will separate and turn watery if you make it further ahead than that.

——————

In the jar of a blender, liquefy the avocados, goat cheese, stock, cilantro, chile, salt, and pepper. Chill for 20 minutes before serving.

Ladle the soup into bowls. Crumble the ricotta salata over the top of the bowls and serve.

If you have soup left over, add a squeeze of lime to prevent it from turning brown. It can be stored in a sealed container in the refrigerator for 1 to 2 days. Rewhip it in the blender before serving.

MAKES 4 TO 6 SERVINGS

3 avocados, cut in half, pitted, and peeled
6 oz / 170g soft goat cheese
2 cups / 480ml Caldo de Pollo (page 88)
½ cup / 10g cilantro leaves
1 serrano chile, stemmed, seeded, veins removed (or not, depending on how spicy you want this to be), and minced
1 tsp sea salt
Healthy pinch of freshly ground black pepper
Ricotta salata for serving

SOPA DE FLOR DE CALABAZA SQUASH BLOSSOM SOUP

MAKES 4 TO 6 SERVINGS

2 Tbsp butter

1 leek, white parts only, thoroughly washed and sliced into fine rings

2 qt / 2L water

2 Tbsp sea salt

3 sprigs epazote or oregano

1 garlic clove

Kernels from 2 ears of white corn

2 small zucchini, finely chopped or sliced on a mandoline

1 big bunch of squash blossoms, stems and sepals removed, coarsely chopped

Zucchini burst into flower in the late summer. Their saffron yellow flowers have a short season, so I like to eat as many as I can, in every possible way. I love them sautéed with onion and garlic, in quesadillas with epazote, and stuffed with ricotta and anchovies. But my favorite form in which to enjoy these delicate beauties might be in this soup, made with the corn that is harvested at the same time as the squash is flowering. They make a perfect pairing. It's a great starter course that comes together very quickly. You don't need a stock to form the base of this soup because the fried leeks, garlic, and epazote do the trick while they're simmering in the water.

———————

In a medium to large Dutch oven or heavy-bottom stockpot melt the butter over medium-high heat until shimmering but not smoking. Add the leek and fry for 3 to 4 minutes, until light gold, stirring to keep it from sticking and browning too much. Add the water and the salt, 2 sprigs of the epazote or oregano, and the garlic. Bring to a boil, then decrease the heat to low and simmer for 15 minutes to reduce. Add the corn and cook for 2 minutes, then add the zucchini and cook for an additional 2 to 3 minutes. Remove and discard the garlic. Toss in the squash blossoms and immediately turn off the stove.

Mince the remaining sprig of epazote or the leaves of the remaining sprig of oregano.

Ladle the soup into serving bowls and sprinkle with the herbs to add a nice perfume to the soup. Serve the soup immediately, since the flowers look and taste best right after they're cooked.

SOPA DE PAPAS Y PORO POTATO-LEEK SOUP

Potatoes and leeks go hand in hand. Many cultures make soup from this duo. In France, they have their vichyssoise and, in Mexico, we have our sopa de poro y papas. We use a tomato-y chicken stock and no cream, and we leave the potatoes and leeks chunky. This is a very homey soup that's also found in a lot of fondas, which are restaurants that serve a prix fixe meal of three courses, usually a soup, a guiso (main), and a dessert (including an agua fresca). I don't recommend freezing this soup, because potato-based soups tend to turn grainy after they're defrosted.

In the jar of a blender, combine the garlic, tomatoes, stock, and salt and blend to liquefy.

In a large Dutch oven or heavy-bottom stockpot, warm the oil over medium-high heat until it's shimmering. Add the leeks and fry until translucent, 3 to 4 minutes. Add the contents of the blender and the potatoes and bring to a boil. Decrease the heat and simmer for about 10 minutes, or until the potatoes are soft. Taste and add more salt if needed. Garnish with the oregano or thyme and serve.

This soup can be stored in a sealed container in the refrigerator for up to 1 week.

MAKES 4 TO 6 SERVINGS

1 garlic clove
4 Roma tomatoes, cored and quartered
5 cups / 1.2L Caldo de Pollo (page 88) or vegetable stock (if making a vegetarian version)
1 Tbsp sea salt, plus more as needed
1 Tbsp olive oil
2 large leeks, cut in half lengthwise, thoroughly washed, and white parts only cut into 1⁄8-inch / 3mm-thick slices
2 potatoes, peeled and diced or cut into thin sticks
Leaves of a few sprigs oregano or thyme

SOPA DE HONGOS MUSHROOM SOUP

MAKES 4 TO 6 SERVINGS

¼ cup / 60ml olive oil

1 cup / 200g finely sliced green
    onions, white parts only

1 chile de árbol

1 tsp sea salt, plus more as needed

2 garlic cloves, minced

8½ oz / 240g mushrooms, diced

Chiffonade of 8 to 10 epazote
    leaves

1 qt / 960ml Caldo de Pollo
    (page 88) or vegetable stock
    (if making a vegetarian version)

Chiffonade of 4 or 5 squash
    blossoms (optional)

Unlike the cream of mushroom soup traditionally served in the United States, there is no dairy in this soup, nor are the chopped mushrooms blended into the broth, so you can really see and taste them. People in Mexico commonly prepare this soup during the rainy season in August, when there are all sorts of mushrooms available in the markets. I like to use a combination of different types of mushrooms and have made delicious versions using a blend of trumpet, king, maitake, and shiitake. If you don't have access to this variety of mushrooms, cremini or common white button mushrooms are perfectly tasty. I would avoid only porcinis, which deserve to stand on their own, and portobellos, which would make your soup too brown.

One other thing that sets this mushroom soup apart is that I fry a chile de árbol in the oil before I sauté the green onion. You don't need to stem or seed the chile because you are simply frying it to flavor the oil (and soup) and then will discard it. The soup isn't spicy, but I love how the smokiness of the dried chile combines with the earthiness of the sautéed mushrooms. I also like to throw in a handful of chopped fresh squash blossoms just before serving to add a burst of yellow.

In a medium to large Dutch oven or heavy-bottom stockpot, warm the oil over medium-high heat until shimmering but not smoking. Drop in the chile and fry for 30 seconds. Add the green onions and ½ tsp of the salt and cook until the onion is translucent but not browned. Add the garlic and sauté for 1 to 2 minutes more, just until you can smell it. Add the mushrooms, epazote, and remaining ½ tsp salt. Salting in stages like this allows the different flavors to come out, and salting the mushrooms separately encourages them to release their tasty juices.

Let the mushrooms cook down for about 5 minutes, until they are translucent. Then add the stock and bring to a boil. Immediately decrease the heat and let simmer gently for 10 minutes. Taste and add more salt if needed.

Remove the chile and stir in the squash blossoms. Some people prefer to serve a whole squash blossom on top of each bowl of soup, which is pretty but is more for looks than taste.

This soup can be stored in a sealed container in the refrigerator for up to 4 days.

CHILPACHOLE DE JAIBA SPICY CRAB SOUP

This bright-red crab soup is a common party dish in coastal parts of Mexico, typically made with a fierce quantity of different spicy chiles. People sometimes serve it in shot glasses, throwing it back before they lose their nerve. For a less-macho version, you can decrease the number of chiles de árbol. But a chilpachole is, by definition, spicy. If you mild it down, it won't really earn its name. For fun, you can leave pieces of whole crab, still in the shell, in the soup when you serve it. Or pick out all of the meat ahead of time for a more refined presentation. In San Francisco, where Dungeness crab are plentiful, that's what I use for this soup, but you can use any meaty crab or even an equal amount of lobster and it will be just as delicious!

_____

Start by making sure that your crab is well cleaned, so that all of the innards have been removed. Place the crabs in a large heavy-bottom stockpot and cover them with water. Add the bay leaves, cinnamon, and ¼ cup / 65g salt. You may notice that this is a lot of salt; when you boil crab, you want the water to be as salty as the ocean. The salt will permeate the meat and give it good flavor. Bring to a boil over high heat, then decrease to low and simmer. Cover the pot and let the crabs cook for 15 minutes, until the shells turn bright red. Using tongs, remove the crabs from the pot, place in a colander, and rinse immediately under cold water. If you skip this step, the crabs will continue to cook after leaving the pot and could become tough.

Warm an ungreased comal or skillet over medium heat. Begin by toasting only the chiles de árbol, since they have thinner skin than the guajillos and will be finished more quickly. As they toast, stir constantly or rotate with tongs for 1 to 2 minutes and remove them from the heat as soon as they start to smell nutty, before they brown or blister. Set them aside while you toast the guajillo chiles, onion, garlic, and peppercorns, agitating them as you did the chiles de árbol, for 2 to 3 minutes. Remove the guajillos from the heat once they look lightly browned and you can smell their toasted fragrance but before they smell burnt. Remove the stems of the chiles.

In the jar of a blender, combine the toasted chiles de árbol and guajillo chiles mixture, tomatoes, remaining 2 tsp salt, ground black pepper, oregano, cinnamon, and ½ cup / 120ml water and liquefy.

MAKES 4 TO 6 SERVINGS

6 lb / 3kg fresh Dungeness or
    other crab, cut in half and well
    cleaned
4 bay leaves (preferably fresh)
1 cinnamon stick
¼ cup / 65g sea salt, plus 2 tsp
2 chiles de árbol, stemmed
    and seeded
2 guajillo chiles, stemmed
    and seeded
¼ white onion
1 garlic clove
12 black peppercorns, or ½ tsp
    freshly ground black pepper
4 Roma tomatoes, cored
1 tsp dried oregano
1 tsp ground cinnamon
4½ cups / 1L plus 65ml water
2 Tbsp olive oil
2 sprigs epazote
1 lime, cut into quarters
1 avocado, cut in half, pitted,
    peeled, and sliced
¼ cup / 5g cilantro leaves, minced
Tortilla chips for serving

CONTINUED

Over medium heat, in a 4- to 6-qt / 960ml to 1.4L Dutch oven or large heavy-bottom stockpot, warm the oil. When the oil is shimmering, pour in the contents of the blender and fry this sauce for 1 to 2 minutes, until the red color deepens. Add the remaining 4 cups / 960ml water and the epazote, bring to a boil over high heat, then decrease to low and simmer while you remove your crabmeat from the shells. Add all of the meat back to the pot and cook for 1 minute more—just long enough to heat the crab through. Remove the epazote and discard.

Divide the chilpachole into soup bowls to serve. Bring the lime, avocado, and cilantro to the table for people to help themselves. A bowl of fresh tortilla chips also makes a nice accompaniment, to scoop up the large chunks of crabmeat from the bottom of your bowl.

CALDO RISCALILLO SHRIMP BROTH

MAKES 4 TO 6 SERVINGS

2 guajillo chiles, stemmed
and seeded

2 ancho chiles, stemmed
and seeded

2 cascabel chiles, stemmed
and seeded

1 Roma tomato, cored

1 garlic clove

1 cup / 240ml water

2 qt / 2L Caldo de Pescado
(page 89)

1¾ oz / 50g dried shrimp

2 sprigs epazote

2 tsp sea salt, plus more as needed

12 to 18 raw medium shrimp,
peeled, deveined, cleaned,
and cut in half or into
bite-size pieces

½ white onion, minced

½ cup / 10g cilantro leaves,
chopped

2 serrano chiles, stemmed,
seeded, veins removed
(or not, depending on how
spicy you want this to be),
and finely minced

2 limes, quartered

1 avocado, cut in half, pitted,
peeled, and thinly sliced

This light and zesty shrimp soup has always been on the menu at Contramar. It's one of the early dishes that we named after the bay where my partners and I first came up with the concept for the restaurant. At the beach restaurants, there's always a soup like this one on the menu. To make the broth, we blend our adobo sauce with a seafood stock intensified by dried shrimp that gives a punch of concentrated flavor. You can buy dried shrimp at Mexican or Asian markets, although the Asian shrimp tend to be smaller, so make sure the weight is comparable. At Contramar, we serve a very simple version of this, without adding the fresh shrimp. I'm including them here to make the dish more substantial, but you can leave them out if you prefer. Serve this soup with chopped onion, cilantro, serrano chiles, and sliced avocado for your guests to garnish their bowls as they please.

On an ungreased comal or in a skillet over medium-high heat, lightly toast the guajillo, ancho, and cascabel chiles, stirring them constantly or turning them with tongs, until they have released their scent but are not dark or blistered. Add them to a blender jar together with the tomato, garlic, and water and liquefy. Empty the contents of the blender into a medium to large Dutch oven or heavy-bottom stockpot and turn the heat to low.

In the jar of the blender, combine the stock and dried shrimp and liquefy. Pour this mixture into the pot with the blended chiles. Add the epazote and salt and bring to a boil. Decrease the heat to low and simmer for about 10 minutes, until reduced and thickened. Taste and add more salt if needed. Add the raw shrimp and cook for 3 to 4 minutes, just until they turn pink.

Ladle the soup into bowls and serve immediately, passing the onion, cilantro, serranos, limes, and avocado at the table for guests to help themselves.

This soup can be stored in a sealed container in the refrigerator for 2 to 3 days.

SOPA VERDE CON ALBÓNDIGAS DE PESCADO GREEN SOUP WITH FISH MEATBALLS

MAKES 4 TO 6 SERVINGS

1 recipe Caldo de Pescado (page 89), made using 2 lb / 910g cod or another white-fleshed fish
1 bunch of cilantro, rinsed well
1 bunch of parsley, finely chopped
4 garlic cloves
2 serrano chiles, stemmed, seeded, and veins removed (or not, depending on how spicy you want this to be)
2 tsp sea salt, plus more as needed
2 new potatoes, cut into ½-inch / 1cm cubes
4 eggs
1 cup natural puffed rice cereal
Pinch of freshly ground black pepper
1 cup / 140g all-purpose flour
Lime wedges for serving

Albondigas, or meatballs, are a favorite Mexican comfort food. In this soup, I substitute fish for the meat and thicken the fish balls with puffed rice cereal, a trick I discovered when I had a bag from the health food store. It's the perfect binding agent in the meatballs because it helps them to stick together while allowing the flavors of the fish and the cilantro and parsley in the broth to shine through.

When you buy your fish to make this soup, ask for the collar. The cartilage near the fish head makes for a tasty and gelatinous broth, and the meat that comes off the collar will add fat to help the fish balls hold together. Remember that you can be somewhat loose with this stock recipe, adding whichever vegetables and herbs you want to use up from your refrigerator.

_____

In a large Dutch oven or heavy-bottom stockpot over high heat, bring the stock to a boil. As soon as the stock comes to a boil, decrease the heat to low and simmer for about 30 minutes. Carefully strain out the fish and vegetables; discard the vegetables and set the fish aside to cool until you can handle it.

Place the strained stock in the jar of a blender. You will have about 2 qt / 2L. Add all of the cilantro, half of the parsley, the garlic, chiles, and 1 tsp of the salt and liquefy.

Pour the contents of the blender into the pot and add the potatoes, which will thicken the soup. Place the pot over low heat and, as the soup simmers, make your fish balls.

Break 3 of the eggs into a bowl and whisk. Once the fish is completely cool, pick out any small bones and flake the fish into the eggs. Add the remaining parsley, cereal, remaining 1 tsp salt, and pepper and mix well. With your hands, pat the mixture into golf ball–sized rounds. Break the remaining egg into a separate small bowl and beat well. Spread the flour on a plate. Roll each fish ball first through the beaten egg and then through the flour.

Drop the fish balls into the simmering broth and let them cook for 8 to 10 minutes, until firm and cooked through. Taste the soup and add more salt if needed. Serve immediately, with a squeeze of lime.

This soup can be stored in a sealed container in the refrigerator for 2 to 3 days. To reheat, bring to a simmer in a saucepan over low heat.

SOPA DE LIMA YUCATECAN LIME SOUP

Sopa de lima is like a cousin of the better-known tortilla soup. Originally from the Yucatán, the real thing is made with lima agria, a special species of lime that's nearly impossible to find outside of Mexico. To approximate the simultaneously tart and sweet flavor, I use a bit of orange juice as well as lime and lime zest. This is a great soup when you're battling a cold, since the vitamin C boosts your system even as the hot chicken broth comforts you. And everything's better topped with fried tortilla strips.

In a Dutch oven or heavy-bottom stockpot over medium heat, warm the olive oil until it's shimmering but not smoking. Add the onion and garlic and cook until the onion is translucent but not browned. Add the tomatoes and bring to a boil. Pour the stock into the pot and add the epazote or hoja santa and salt. Return to a boil and add the chicken breasts, then decrease the heat and simmer for 15 to 20 minutes until the chicken is completely cooked.

While the chicken is poaching in the broth, line a plate with a brown paper bag.

Warm the safflower oil in a skillet over high heat until it's approximately 350°F / 180°C. When you drop a tortilla strip into the oil, you should hear it sizzle and see little bubbles surrounding it. When the oil is hot enough, drop all of the tortilla strips in at once and fry for 1 to 2 minutes before flipping them over to continue to fry for another 1 to 2 minutes on the other side. They should turn a darker shade of gold and curl. Using a slotted spoon, remove them from the oil and place them on the prepared plate to drain.

Once the chicken is poached, remove it from the stock and set it aside until it's cool enough to handle. Remove and discard the epazote or hoja santa. Add the orange juice, lime zest, and lime juice to the soup. Taste and add more salt if needed, depending on how salty your broth was.

Ladle the broth into serving bowls. Shred the chicken and divide it among the bowls. Top with the fried tortilla strips and serve hot.

This soup can be stored in a sealed container in the refrigerator for 2 to 3 days. To reheat, bring to a simmer in a saucepan over low heat.

MAKES 4 TO 6 SERVINGS

½ cup / 120ml olive oil
1 cup / 140g diced white onion
1 garlic clove, minced
3 or 4 Roma tomatoes, diced
2 qt / 2L Caldo de Pollo
    (page 88)
1 sprig epazote or hoja santa leaf
1 tsp sea salt, plus more as needed
2 large chicken breasts
½ cup / 120ml safflower oil
6 Tortillas de Maiz (page 72),
    cut into skinny strips
Juice of ½ orange
Zest and juice of 1 lime

TIRITAS DE ZIHUATANEJO ZIHUATANEJO-STYLE CEVICHE

Tiritas translates to "strips" and refers to the skinny slices of raw fish in this ceviche, which is popular in the coastal town of Zihuatanejo. This is a delicious starter on its own, but it's also one of my favorite taco fillings. I like the contrast of red onions with a white-fleshed fish. If you want to make a milder version, be sure to scrape out and discard both the veins and the seeds of the chiles.

––––––––––

In a medium bowl, combine the fish, onion, chiles, lime juice, and salt. Stir to coat and then set in the refrigerator to chill for 10 to 15 minutes before serving. (Less time and it will still be raw, but more time and it will start to become tough.) Before serving, taste to check that you like the texture and to see if it needs any more salt.

You can store ceviche overnight in the refrigerator, but the lime will thoroughly "cook" the raw fish, and ceviche starts oxidizing after a day. Ceviche is tastiest the day it is made, so don't make more than you intend to serve and eat.

MAKES 4 TO 6 SERVINGS

1 lb / 455g very fresh firm-fleshed fish, such as halibut or mahi-mahi, filleted and cut into thin (about ½-inch / 12mm) slices

1 small red onion, slivered

2 serrano chiles, stemmed, seeded, veins removed (or not, depending on how spicy you want this to be), and cut into slivers

1 cup / 240ml freshly squeezed lime juice

2 tsp sea salt, plus more as needed

CEVICHE CONTRAMAR CONTRAMAR'S CEVICHE

MAKES 4 TO 6 SERVINGS

½ red onion, thinly sliced
   lengthwise
1 tsp sea salt, plus 1 Tbsp
1½ lb / 650g sashimi-grade
   firm-fleshed white fish, such as
   halibut or mahi-mahi, filleted and
   cut into ½-inch / 12mm cubes
50g / ½ cup minced celery
2 serrano chiles, stemmed,
   seeded, veins removed (or not,
   depending on how spicy you
   want this to be), and sliced
   lengthwise into very thin strips
1 manzano chile, stemmed,
   seeded, veins removed (or not,
   depending on how spicy you
   want this to be), and sliced into
   thin rings
1 cup / 240ml freshly squeezed
   lime juice
½ cup / 10g cilantro leaves,
   coarsely chopped
Drizzle of fresh cold-pressed
   olive oil
Pinch of Maldon sea salt or
   another finishing salt
Tortilla chips for serving

This ceviche has a little bit more going on than the standard ceviche, with the addition of minced celery, manzano chile, and cilantro. Instead of cutting the fish into strips, you cut it into cubes. You don't want the cubes to be too tiny but just the right size to put in your mouth without having to cut them, since this is a dish often served in a large bowl for people to scoop up with tortilla chips.

——————

Place the onion in a bowl of cold water with the 1 tsp salt and let soak for 5 minutes, then drain.

In a bowl large enough to hold all of your ingredients, sprinkle the remaining 1 Tbsp salt over the fish and stir. Add the celery, serranos, and manzano and mix. Drain the onion and add to the bowl. Pour the lime juice over everything, sprinkle with the cilantro, and drizzle with the oil. Right before serving, add the finishing salt. Serve immediately with the tortilla chips to scoop up the fish.

Ceviche is at its prime the day it is made, so don't make more than you intend to serve and eat.

CEVICHE DE DORADO CON CHILE ANCHO Y JAMAICA MAHI-MAHI CEVICHE WITH ANCHO CHILE AND HIBISCUS

MAKES 4 TO 6 SERVINGS

1½ lb / 650g mahi-mahi, diced into
    bite-size pieces
1 tsp sea salt
2 Tbsp vegetable oil
1 ancho chile, stemmed, seeded,
    and cut into rings
1 oz / 30g whole organic dried
    hibiscus flowers
1 cup / 240ml freshly squeezed
    lime juice
¼ cup / 60ml olive oil
1 Tbsp diced chives
1 avocado, cut in half, pitted,
    peeled, and diced
1 tsp Maldon sea salt or another
    finishing salt

I made up this bright and slightly messy-looking ceviche in the early days of Contramar, and it has been a favorite on the menu ever since. A ceviche is typically sour from the lime juice that "cooks" the raw fish. This one is also, but part of its tartness comes from the inclusion of hibiscus flowers, the same kind that get steeped to make one of the most popular aguas frescas. The hibiscus adds a subtle note of floral sweetness. And all of the acid is balanced by the diced avocado, its richness rounding out the dish. When slicing your ancho chile, use a pair of kitchen scissors instead of a knife to quickly snip them into tidy rings.

———————

Place the mahi-mahi in a medium bowl and sprinkle with the sea salt. Line a plate with a brown paper bag.

In a small skillet over medium-high heat, warm the vegetable oil until it's hot but not sizzling. Add the ancho and fry for about 1 minute. Transfer the chile to the prepared plate to drain. Using the same pan and hot oil, fry the hibiscus flowers until crisp, then place them on the plate to drain. When the chile and hibiscus are cool enough to handle, place them on a cutting board and chop them together until you have a deep red crumble of little bits and set aside.

To the bowl with the mahi-mahi, add the lime juice, olive oil, chives, and chile-hibiscus mixture and toss to combine. Add the avocado and finishing salt. Serve immediately.

Ceviche is at its prime the day it is made, so don't make more than you intend to serve and eat.

AGUACHILE DE CAMARÓN
SALTED RAW SHRIMP BATHED IN LIME, CHILE, AND CILANTRO

An aguachile, like a ceviche, is made by drenching raw seafood in lime juice. But unlike ceviche, where you leave the raw seafood to "cook" for fifteen minutes in this marinade while the proteins break down, aguachile is served immediately while the seafood (most often shrimp) is still raw. An aguachile tends to be spicier than a ceviche, thanks to the inclusion of chile tepín, a really spicy chile from the north. If you can't get it, chile piquín makes a good substitute. With the parsley and cilantro blended into this aguachile, the raw shrimp get bathed in a bright green sauce that looks as vibrant as it tastes.

_____

Arrange the shrimp on a serving platter or individual plates (not a bowl). Sprinkle 1 tsp of the salt over the shrimp.

In a small bowl, sprinkle ½ tsp of the sea salt over the onion. (This will leach some of the moisture from the onion so that it's less crunchy.)

In another small bowl, sprinkle the remaining ½ tsp sea salt over the cucumber and add about 1 Tbsp of the lime juice.

In the jar of a blender, combine the parsley, cilantro, water, and remaining lime juice and liquefy. If it's frothy (which it probably will be), let it sit for about 5 minutes to settle.

Pour the contents of the blender over the shrimp and then scatter the onion and cucumber over the top. Drizzle with the oil and sprinkle with the finishing salt. Serve immediately.

Aguachile is at its prime the day it is made, so don't make more than you intend to serve and eat.

MAKES 4 TO 6 SERVINGS

1¼ lb / 575g raw medium-size shrimp, peeled, deveined, and butterflied
2 tsp sea salt, plus more as needed
½ red onion, thinly sliced lengthwise
1 cucumber, peeled, cut in half, and thinly sliced
1 cup / 240ml freshly squeezed lime juice
½ cup / 10g parsley leaves
Packed ½ cup / 10g cilantro leaves
¼ cup / 60ml water
1 tsp chile tepín or chile piquín
2 Tbsp fresh cold-pressed olive oil
Maldon sea salt or another finishing salt

COCTEL DE CAMARÓN SHRIMP COCKTAIL

MAKES 4 TO 6 SERVINGS

1 cup / 240ml tomato juice
1 Tbsp fish sauce
1 Tbsp Valentina Salsa Picante
1 Tbsp Búfalo Salsa Clásica
    (typical Mexico hot sauce
    from the 1960s)
½ cup / 115g ketchup
½ cup / 120ml freshly squeezed
    orange juice
3 Tbsp / 45ml freshly squeezed
    lime juice
1 lb / 455g cooked bay shrimp
¾ cup / 100g chopped
    white onion
¾ cup / 120g diced tomatoes
    (use whatever is lovely: cherry
    tomatoes, heirloom, Roma)
½ cup / 10g cilantro leaves,
    chopped
Sea salt
1 avocado, cut in half, pitted,
    peeled, and cubed

Shrimp cocktail, a beloved beach snack, has definitely infiltrated Mexico City. Traditionally, people who make shrimp cocktail will often have a jar of seasoned vinegar on hand that contains a lot of the salt and spices that give this dish an almost pickled flavor. But it takes a few weeks for the vinegar to season properly, so it isn't practical when you have an urgent craving for this dish. I've approximated that flavor with two different bottled hot sauces that are supermarket staples in Mexico (and available at most Mexican markets I've visited in the States)—the bright red Valentina Salsa Picante, Cholula, or Guacamaya Salsa Picante, and the darker Bufalo Salsa Clásica, which contains smoky chipotle peppers—as well as two different fresh citrus juices and some fish sauce for a hint of umami. While this is the recipe for a standard shrimp cocktail, feel free to use cooked prawns, clams, oysters, crab, and/or scallops, all of which taste great bathed in this sauce. A mixed seafood cocktail is called a campechano.

If you happen to have a collection of canning jars, this dish looks adorable served in them.

In a medium bowl, combine the tomato juice, fish sauce, Valentina and Búfalo hot sauces, ketchup, orange juice, and lime juice. Add the shrimp, onion, tomatoes, and cilantro and stir so that everything is well coated in the sauce. Taste and add sea salt as needed.

Chill until you're ready to serve. Right before serving, add the avocado. This is best the day it's made, although it will keep in a sealed container in the refrigerator for 1 day.

Coctel de Camarones at EL JAROCHO DE LAS LOMAS, Jose de Iturrigaray 105, Lomas-Virreyes

TUNA TOSTADA

The raw tuna tostada remains one of our most popular menu items at Contramar, twenty years after we opened. This seems fitting, given that it was the ceviche and the tostadas on the beach at Zihuatanejo that inspired my friends and me to open a seafood restaurant in Mexico City.

Back in the 1990s, Nobu had a huge influence worldwide. Those very refined bright flavors of good "fusion food" were exploding everywhere. In Mexico, people of my generation loved the combination of Japanese and Mexican flavors: raw fish, ponzu, and chile. Sushito was the first chain to make sushi accessible in Mexico City, with chipotle mayonnaise and chiles serranos toreados, and people went nuts for it. That was the context and inspiration for our raw tuna tostada.

Even though Japanese fusion cuisine was influential when we opened Contramar, no other Mexican restaurants were serving raw tuna back then. It's hard to believe, given that the tuna tostada has now been copied in restaurants around the world and is sometimes even listed as "Contramar's Tuna Tostada" on other menus! I'm not complaining. In restaurants, imitation is flattering; I'm glad people like our tostadas enough to want to make their own.

Our recipe doesn't include a lot of ingredients, and that's why every detail matters so much. Take those fried leeks. I always choose the biggest ones that I can find, because I only use the whites at the center of the leek, and I want them to hold their ring shape in the fryer. If they're too small, they brown too fast and crumble. Since they keep cooking after they're removed from the oil, it's crucial to take them out when they're barely golden. This may seem like nitpicking, but if you let them get too brown, they will taste unpleasantly bitter and throw the whole thing off. It's not hard to get it right, but you have to pay attention. Similarly, I make sure to strain the chile seeds from my chipotle mayonnaise so that it's really silky, and I coat the fish lightly with olive oil before marinating it with fresh ponzu, so the acid from the citrus doesn't "cook" the flesh. Not only does this enhance the taste, it also keeps the fish looking pink and pretty, which matters when you're serving raw fish.

The tuna tostada at Contramar is a classic now. While I never grow tired of the original, there are infinite possibilities for the tostada, and I love exploring them all. It's the same for tacos as it is for tostadas. Everything can be a tostada. Like a big chip, the crispy fried tortilla is the perfect base to support whatever ingredients you want to showcase. It's like an architectural process for me. On top of the fried shell, I usually begin by putting down a layer of something creamy—the foundation—to support the featured ingredient, which is then capped by something ornamental that adds a final burst of flavor and texture to the whole.

I'm going to break down the steps that I use for making the tuna tostada, which can serve as a template for any other kind of tostada that you might like to make. I will also give you a few of my other current favorite tostada recipes, but please make substitutions based on whatever appealing ingredients are locally available to you.

For imitation-worthy results, be attentive to the steps but unafraid of being creative.

TOSTADAS DE ATÚN O TRUCHA
TUNA OR TROUT TOSTADAS

MAKES 8 (6-INCH / 15CM)
TOSTADAS

1 thick leek, white part only,
    thoroughly washed and sliced
    into ⅛-inch / 3mm-thick rounds
2 cups / 480ml rice bran oil,
    safflower oil, or any vegetable
    oil with a high smoke point
8 stale corn tortillas
12 oz / 340g sashimi-grade tuna,
    trout, or other fatty fish, thinly
    sliced against the grain
1 Tbsp olive oil
¼ cup / 60ml soy sauce
¼ cup / 60ml freshly squeezed
    orange juice
2 Tbsp plus 2 tsp Mayonesa con
    Chipotle (page 62)
1 avocado, cut in half, pitted, peeled,
    and cut into 8 to 16 slices
Maldon sea salt or another
    finishing salt
Lime wedges

My tuna tostada is composed of layers: a smoky chipotle mayonnaise spread over the shell, topped with slices of silky tuna, briefly marinated in ponzu, capped with a scattering of crispy fried leeks and a single perfect slice of avocado. The success of this dish depends on choosing top-quality fish, of course. At Contramar, we only serve it when sustainable tuna is available, so it's not always on the menu. In San Francisco, I've substituted a locally farmed trout, although the rest of the recipe is unchanged. You can also make these with hamachi, kampachi, or albacore. But in my opinion, raw tuna and trout are especially beautiful for their deep pink color. Whatever fish you use, make sure that it's sashimi-grade and slice it as thinly as possible against the grain.

For the fried tostada shell, it's ideal to have stale corn tortillas because fresh tortillas curl up in the fryer. In Mexico, you always see people drying out their old tortillas, either to feed to the pigs and chickens or to use in chilaquiles and tostadas. If you know you are going to want to make these tostadas for a party, then plan ahead and leave your tortillas out for a day or two first. Place them in a single layer on a baking sheet with another baking sheet on top of it to keep them flat as they dry out. If you go the extra step of first making tortillas from scratch solely for the purpose of making tostadas, be sure that they're quite thin: no more than ⅛ inch / 3mm thick. A thicker tortilla will be difficult to get crisp in the fryer.

This is finger food, so I like my tostadas to be fairly small. To make smaller (than 6-inch / 15cm) ones, simply, cut your tortillas in half and then fry them.

First, place the leeks in a bowl of cold water and separate the rings. Remove any green rings and reserve these for making stock. Transfer the white rings to a dish towel to dry out for at least 15 minutes so that they're completely dry before frying.

Meanwhile, warm the rice bran or safflower oil in a large heavy-bottom saucepan or deep skillet over medium-high heat (you want the oil to be at least 2 inches / 5cm deep) to 350°F / 180°C. You can test the temperature with an instant-read thermometer or by submerging a wooden spoon in the oil, which will be immediately surrounded by little bubbles if the oil is at the right temperature.

CONTINUED

Line a plate with a brown paper bag. Fry the tortillas one at a time, for about 2 minutes each. While the tortilla is frying, use a pair of chopsticks or two forks to hold down the two edges so that the tortilla doesn't curl up. Once the tortilla is golden, remove it from the oil and let it drain on the plate. Repeat with the rest of the tortillas and let them all cool for at least 15 minutes while you prepare the rest of the ingredients. You want the tortillas fully cool or else the mayonnaise will melt.

Using the same oil in which you fried your tortillas, fry the leeks: Decrease the oil temperature slightly to 300°F / 150°C. Check the temperature with an instant-read thermometer before adding the leeks; if the oil is too hot, the leeks will turn dark and become bitter. Drop in the leeks and constantly move them around while they fry so they cook and color evenly. The *instant* you see the leeks turning golden, remove them with a slotted spoon and set them on the plate to cool completely.

While the tostadas and leeks are cooling, marinate the fish: Place the fish in a bowl and drizzle it with the olive oil so that the citrus and soy sauce don't bite into the fish and give it a gray cast. After lightly coating the fish with olive oil, immediately add the soy sauce and orange juice, toss, and let sit for 5 minutes.

Once the tortillas are cool, spread 1 tsp of the mayonnaise on each one. That may seem like very little, but you don't want it to be thick and ooze out from under the rest of the toppings. On top of the mayonnaise, distribute the sliced fish in one layer. Scatter with the fried leeks and top with the avocado. Just before serving, add a pinch of the finishing salt.

I like to serve these tostadas 4 per plate, to be passed around, with lime wedges on the side.

TOSTADAS DE CANGREJO CRAB TOSTADAS

Unlike the tuna tostada, this crab tostada doesn't have a layer of mayonnaise on the bottom because the mayonnaise is already incorporated into the crab salad so the topping sticks to the shell just fine. Celeriac or napa cabbage pairs well with the crab. I like how celeriac's texture mimics that of the crab, but I also love the distinct crunch that the cabbage provides. If you want your crab salad to have a bite, mince 1 to 2 Tbsp Salsa Brava (page 45) and add it to the mix.

—————————

In a bowl, stir the crabmeat, celeriac or cabbage, mayonnaise, chiles, and salt. Taste and add more salt if needed (depending on how salty your crab cooking water was). Divide the crab salad among the tostadas, spreading it in an even layer to cover the shell. Top each tostada with the avocado and sprouts and serve with the lime wedges.

MAKES 8 (6-INCH / 15CM) TOSTADAS

1 cup / 200g cooked crabmeat (see Chilpachole de Jaiba, page 161)

1 cup / 100g shredded celeriac or minced napa cabbage

½ cup / 120g Mayonesa con Limón (page 62)

2 habanero chiles, stemmed, seeded, veins removed (or not, depending on how spicy you want this to be), and minced

½ tsp sea salt, plus more as needed

8 tostada shells (see Tostadas de Atún o Trucha, page 182)

1 avocado, cut in half, pitted, peeled, and cut into 8 to 16 slices for garnish (optional)

Microsprouts for garnish

Lime wedges for serving

TOSTADAS DE QUELITES TOSTADAS WITH WILD GREENS

MAKES 8 (6-INCH / 15CM)
TOSTADAS

¼ cup / 60g Frijoles Refritos
    (page 85), warmed
8 tostada shells (see Tostadas de
    Atún o Trucha, page 182)
1 cup / 240g whole-milk Queso
    Fresco, strained (see page 64)
Zest and juice of 1 lemon
1 tsp sea salt
Pinch of freshly ground white
    pepper
2 cups / 40g wild greens, such
    as amaranth, purslane, or
    lamb's-quarter
3 Tbsp / 45ml extra-virgin olive oil
3 Tbsp / 45ml freshly squeezed
    lime juice
Maldon sea salt or another
    finishing salt

I am crazy about quelites, the native Mexican greens sold by farmers in Mexican markets that taste herbaceous and rugged and wild. Even in Mexico City, you can't usually find quelites at regular supermarkets, and they're not for sale at conventional US supermarkets, but I've been able to find them at farmers' markets and Central American produce shops. I believe demand for them is growing and they will become more widely available. Amaranth, one of the most common wild greens found in Mexico, is now definitely available in the United States, when it's in season in late summer. A cousin to quinoa, it's highly nutritious, with leaves that taste like spinach but nuttier. Purslane, called *verdolagas* in Spanish, is another wild green so common in California that it's considered an invasive weed. If you have some growing in your garden, you should definitely pick and eat it! Not only does it have a pleasing lemony taste, it's also extremely high in omega-3 fatty acids, which may be why it's a popular ingredient not only in Mexican cooking but also in Arabic and Chinese cuisine.

I love to braise quelites and use them as a taco filling, but they're also delicious tossed with a vinaigrette and served as a salad. That's how I serve them on these tostadas. The bitter greens and tangy lime dressing form the perfect counterpart to the less assertive queso fresco and black beans coating the tostada shell, for a starter that manages to be at once light and substantial, fresh and filling.

Technically, wild mint qualifies as a wild green, and if you'd like, you could use a very tiny bit of it, but not too much, since it will overwhelm the other flavors if used with a heavy hand.

———————

Begin by spreading a thin layer of beans on each tostada. This is the glue that the other ingredients will stick to.

In a small bowl, combine the queso fresco with the lemon zest and juice, ½ tsp of the sea salt, and the pepper, and stir to combine well. Dollop 1 Tbsp of the lemony queso fresco on top of the bean layer.

In another bowl, toss the greens with the oil, lime juice, and the remaining ½ tsp of the sea salt. Scatter the dressed quelite salad over the queso fresco and sprinkle with the finishing salt. Serve immediately while the greens are ultrafresh.

TOSTADAS DE HONGOS Y ERIZO DE MAR
MUSHROOM AND SEA URCHIN TOSTADAS

MAKES 8 (6-INCH / 15CM) TOSTADAS

8 trumpet mushrooms, well rinsed and dried

1 Tbsp olive oil

1 tsp sea salt

Zest of 1 lemon and 1 tsp freshly squeezed lemon juice

8 tsp Mayonesa con Limón (page 62)

8 tostada shells (see Tostadas de Atún o Trucha, page 182)

1 habanero chile, stemmed, seeded, veins removed (or not, depending on how spicy you want this to be), and minced or 3 Tbsp / 1g bonito flakes (optional)

8 prime-quality full tongues of sea urchin

Briny, creamy, and custardlike, sea urchin is one of my all-time favorite foods, a real luxury to savor. Here it's dolloped on top of seared and briefly marinated trumpet mushrooms. Although raw trumpet mushrooms have very little taste, this treatment gives them the approximate texture and flavor of abalone, so they pair beautifully with the raw urchin, which some people say tastes like the essence of the ocean itself. You can take this theme even further by garnishing each tostada with a few sea beans or some fresh seaweed if you have access to it. If you've never bought sea urchin before, begin by finding the best fish market in your area. Sea urchin is sold by the *hakata*, which is the Japanese term for the wooden box it comes packaged in. You want to buy ones that are whole (not broken up) and that look orangey brown, with a distinctly textured surface that resembles the taste buds on your tongue. If they look mushy, they're not fresh. Sea urchin requires no preparation work (other than the work of sourcing the freshest ones). You simply lay them on top of the tostada and enjoy their briny ocean taste and custardy texture.

Preheat the oven to 350°F / 180°C.

In a medium bowl, toss the mushrooms with the oil and ½ tsp of the salt. Place an ungreased comal or skillet over high heat and sear the mushrooms briefly for 1 to 2 minutes. Place the mushrooms on a baking sheet and bake for 8 minutes, then transfer to a plate and chill in the refrigerator for 10 minutes.

Slice the mushrooms into ⅛-inch / 3mm rounds and add the remaining ½ tsp salt and the lemon zest and juice. Set aside to marinate for 20 minutes.

Spread a heaping 1 tsp of the mayonnaise on each tostada and then sprinkle with the chile to give the tostadas some heat or with a few bonito flakes for some smoke. Distribute the marinated mushrooms evenly among the tostadas and finish by topping each one with a tongue of sea urchin.

TOSTADAS DE CAMARÓN SHRIMP TOSTADAS

A shrimp salad made with chipotle mayonnaise creates a smoky and creamy topping for these addictive tostadas. A thin layer of refried beans provides a nice counterpart, adhering the shrimp salad to the shell.

_____

In a medium bowl, mix the shrimp with the onion, tomatoes, cilantro, mayonnaise, oil, lime juice, oregano, and salt. Taste and add more salt if needed.

Spread a thin layer of beans on each tostada. This is the glue that the other ingredients will stick to. Add a spoonful of the shrimp mixture and top with some lettuce. Garnish each with the avocado and serve with the lime wedges on the side.

MAKES 8 (6-INCH / 15CM) TOSTADAS

1 lb / 455g cooked bay shrimp, minced
¾ cup / 100g chopped onion
¾ cup / 120g diced Roma tomatoes
¾ cup / 15g cilantro leaves, chopped
¾ cup / 180g Mayonesa con Chipotle (page 62)
1 Tbsp extra-virgin olive oil
1 Tbsp freshly squeezed lime juice
1 tsp dried oregano
1 tsp sea salt, plus more as needed
¼ cup / 60g Frijoles Refritos (page 85), warmed
8 tostada shells (see Tostadas de Atún o Trucha, page 180)
½ head iceberg lettuce, thinly sliced
1 avocado, cut in half, pitted, peeled, and thinly sliced
Lime wedges for serving

MASA IN MANY FORMS

Masa is to Mexican food what pasta is to Italian food. When it comes to all the things you can do with this magical stuff, tortillas are just the tip of the masa iceberg. As soon as people figured out they could get maximum nutrition from corn by nixtamalizing it, they also discovered there were endless ways to use this versatile, inexpensive, and delicious dough.

One of my favorite masa products is the sope. A sope is round like a tortilla. In fact, you start making a sope in the same way that you start making a tortilla, by rolling masa into a ball and squishing it in a tortilla press, but you press more gently, stopping when it's about ¼ inch / 6mm thick (approximately twice the thickness of a good tortilla). First, you grill this disk on an ungreased comal or in a skillet, but you only cook it partially on one side. Then you let it cool slightly before using your thumb and index finger to pinch a rim around the edge, creating a lip around a shallow depression that's made for holding whatever delicious tidbits you want to place on it. Next, you either fry the sope or place it back on the comal or skillet to finish cooking. The sope is not crispy like the fried tortilla that makes a tostada, but it is firm enough to hold toppings and be eaten without any plate needed. Sopes can be the size of a tortilla or bite-size, but they're always round in shape. I prefer to make mine on the small side, so that I can eat a few while still saving some appetite for the next antojito I want to try.

If you type the word *huaraches* into your search engine, the main image that comes up is the rustic sandals with the woven leather tops that tourists like to buy in Mexico. That's because these masa vehicles are named for the sandals with a similar oblong shape. Huaraches are a popular Mexican street food, often made on large comals stationed along bustling city sidewalks. They can hold all sorts of toppings but are typically spread with beans, crema ácida, and shredded lettuce. There really isn't a difference between the taste of sopes and huaraches, but they're common enough that you should know which name to use when you're ordering (or cooking).

When you order a quesadilla in the United States, it usually takes the form of melted cheese between two tortillas—most often flour ones—cooked in a pan or on a griddle. In Mexico, there's a lot more range to the dish. My favorite quesadillas are quesadillas doradas, or fried quesadillas. These are made not with tortillas but with fresh masa. Once again, you start as if you were going to make a tortilla, pressing a ball of masa in your tortilla press between two sheets of plastic wrap and squishing it as flat as you would a tortilla. But instead of dropping it onto a hot comal, you take off just the top layer of plastic wrap and place a spoonful of cheese (and/or other fillings) at the center of the circle of masa, then you fold the circle in half, enclosing the filling and pressing the edges to seal it. Finally, using a wide spatula, you transfer the quesadilla to a pan of oil heated to 350°F / 180°C and fry the whole thing until it's golden and crispy.

A tlacoyo is similar to the fried quesadilla I've just described, in that it's made from fresh masa and not tortillas. But other things besides cheese get pressed into the fresh masa. Tlacoyos are torpedo shaped—ovals with pointy ends. They get cooked on a hot comal or in a skillet instead of deep-fried. Tlacoyos tend to be filled with things in paste form: refried beans, mashed garbanzo or fava beans, or chicharrón (a paste made from fried pork skin). They are commonly served with salsa.

Itacates are triangles of masa blended with lard and seasoned with salt and then cooked on a comal. They don't have fillings per se, although it's common for them to be cut in half and treated like the bread for a sandwich to hold whatever you feel like placing inside. To make itacates, combine 2 cups / 520g fresh masa, 2/3 cup / 130g lard, and 1 tsp sea salt. Use a stand mixer or your hands to blend it thoroughly, then form it into triangles that could fit in the palm of your hand. Cook them on a hot comal or in a skillet for a few minutes per side. They should sizzle on the comal because of all that fat and develop a nice crust. When I was little, these were one of my absolute favorite foods, and they remain so to this day.

Quesadillas at MEDELLIN MARKET, Campeche 101, Roma Sur

SOPES PLAYEROS
FRIED MASA ROUNDS WITH BLACK BEANS, ROMAINE, AND RICOTTA SALATA

2 cups / 480g Frijoles Refritos
(page 85), warmed
2 cups / 520g fresh masa or 2 cups /
260g masa harina mixed with
1 to 1¼ cups / 240 to 300ml
water (as directed on page 72)
2 cups / 480ml rice bran oil,
safflower oil, or any vegetable
oil with a high smoke point
1 or 2 heads Little Gem lettuce,
finely chopped
¼ cup / 60g Crema Ácida
(page 65) or crème fraîche
¼ cup / 20g grated ricotta salata
1 recipe Salsa Verde (page 50)

The sope playero is a very Guerrero-style dish, commonly eaten at the beach in that region. For this one (pictured, left, on page 197), the sope is always deep-fried and often served with a cooked green sauce. I cover mine with a thin layer of refried black beans, a scattering of chopped Little Gem or romaine lettuce, a dollop of crema ácida or crème fraîche, and shaved ricotta salata (in place of the dry queso fresco used in Mexico). Because they are fried, they have enough rigidity to keep them from collapsing when you're holding them, making them a perfect passed appetizer. To make a sope, you need the same masa dough that you would use to make a tortilla, so either buy fresh masa if you have access to it or make the dough from masa harina mixed with water.

These can also be a vegetarian main dish if you make them a bit larger. You could also top them with chorizo or shredded chicken.

———————

Place your beans in a small saucepan over very low heat to reduce while you make your sopes. By the end, you want the beans to be very thick, reduced by about 50 percent.

Whether you are using fresh masa or mixing masa harina with water, make sure that your dough has the consistency of stiff cookie batter. Make a Ping-Pong–size ball and press gently, until it's about ¼ inch / 6mm thick. It should be about twice as thick as a tortilla would be. With your thumb on the inside of the sope and your index finger on the outside, pinch the edge, moving around the entire disk, to create a rim that will hold your toppings. Repeat to form 12 sopes in total.

Line a plate with a brown paper bag. In a heavy-bottom skillet over medium-high heat, bring the oil to about 350°F / 180°C. If you don't have an instant-read thermometer, test the oil by placing a wooden spoon in it. Tiny bubbles should form rapidly around the spoon once it's hot enough for frying. Carefully place 3 sopes at a time in the hot oil. Fry for about 2 minutes, until the sopes are golden but not brown. Use a slotted spoon to transfer them from the oil to the plate. They will become a bit crispier after they're removed from the oil. Repeat until all the sopes are cooked.

Taste your reduced beans to make sure they are properly salted and add salt if necessary. You want them salty because the sopes aren't, and you're going to be adding crema, so the beans are the only salty part of the dish.

Before the sopes get too cold, add a spoonful of beans to each one; the beans should spread out across the surface of the warm sope. Make sure the beans don't spill over. Scatter the lettuce over the top. Add a dollop of crema or crème fraîche and top with the ricotta salata.

Serve warm with a spoonful of the salsa.

SOPES CON PESCADO ADOBADO
FRIED MASA ROUNDS WITH FISH IN RED CHILE RUB

MAKES 12 (3-INCH / 7.5CM)
SOPES

½ cup / 120ml safflower oil
1 tsp sea salt
1 lb / 455g boneless red snapper,
    opah, or another firm-fleshed
    fish that will hold up to
    heavy cooking, cut into
    1-inch / 2.5cm cubes
2 cups / 480ml Adobo de Chiles
    Rojos (page 58)
12 cooked sopes (see Sopes
    Playeros, page 194)
½ cup / 10g purslane leaves or
    other greens, cut into ribbons
    for garnish
Ricotta salata for garnish

The adobo sauce in this recipe (pictured on the right side) is heavy on flavor, combining the smoky heat of the dried chiles with the bright hit of citrus from freshly squeezed orange and lime juices and ample garlic and other spices, making for a complex and addictive blend. The fried fish soaks it all up.

───────────

Pour the oil into a heavy-bottom saucepan over medium-high heat.

Lightly salt the fish on all sides.

To test if the oil is hot enough for frying, place one piece of the fish into the oil. If it sizzles, the oil is hot enough. Fry all of the fish at once until the pieces are cooked through, agitating the pan while the fish fries. The fish will lose water content while frying and begin to look opaque.

Now add the adobo sauce. Turn the heat to low and keep cooking, stirring gently and constantly, until the fish absorbs much of the liquid. As it cooks, the fish will break into pieces, which is fine.

Spread the fish and sauce evenly on top of the sopes. Garnish with the purslane and ricotta salata and serve hot.

QUESADILLAS DORADAS GOLDEN QUESADILLAS

MAKES 4 TO 6 QUESADILLAS

1 cup / 260g fresh masa or 1 cup / 130g masa harina mixed with ½ cup to ½ cup plus 2 Tbsp / 120 to 150ml water (as directed on page 72)

½ to ¾ cup / 40 to 60g shredded toma, whole-milk mozzarella, or another good melting cheese

1 qt / 960ml grapeseed or safflower oil

1 recipe Salsa Verde (page 50)

1 recipe Mayonesa con Limón (page 62)

You think you know quesadillas. Two tortillas with some cheese melted in the middle, right? But the quesadilla dorada, a fried quesadilla, takes this humble snack to the next level. Unlike the quesadillas you are probably familiar with, you don't sandwich cheese between two cooked tortillas, since this would fall apart in the frying. Instead, you place a generous spoonful of cheese, as well as any additional filling that you'd like, at the center of a freshly pressed circle of raw masa, folding it over and sealing the edges closed before frying the whole thing. Yum!

In Mexico, we use queso Oaxaca or queso Chihuahua; both stringy low-moisture cheeses that melt well. In the United States, my favorites are toma or whole-milk mozzarella (not fresh), although I also like ricotta. For best results, avoid anything that comes preshredded in a plastic bag. You should be able to shred a good mozzarella as if it were a poached chicken breast—with your fingers, no grater needed.

Quesadillas doradas are a kind of blank slate to which you can add all sorts of things. I love to sauté chopped chanterelles or another mushroom in a few tablespoons of butter and add that to the cheese at the center of my fried quesadilla. Braised greens taste fabulous with the melted cheese, as do squash blossoms, minced epazote, huitlacoche, shredded chicharrón (pork rind), and chorizo. If you have any leftover Tinga de Pollo (page 268), use that to make a few of these into a complete meal. As always, feel free to experiment!

Make a golf ball–size ball of masa the same way you would when making a fresh tortilla and proceed as directed for pressing tortillas (see page 72). Once the dough is flattened between the two sheets of plastic wrap, remove the top sheet of plastic from the tortilla but leave the bottom sheet. Place 2 Tbsp shredded cheese in the center of the tortilla. (If you are adding an optional filling, add 1 tsp at this point.) Lifting the bottom edge, using the bottom piece of plastic wrap as a sling, fold the circle of masa in half, enclosing the filling and pinching the edges together to seal them, as if you were making an empanada or ravioli. Repeat to form 3 to 5 more quesadillas.

Line a plate with a brown paper bag. In a large heavy-bottom skillet or wok, heat the oil to 350°F / 180°C. Gently place the quesadilla in the oil and fry until golden, 8 to 10 minutes. You could cook a few at a time but make sure they are not crowded in the pan and do not touch, since the fresh masa on the outside of one will stick to the fresh masa of another.

Using tongs, transfer the cooked quesadillas to the plate to drain and cool slightly. Repeat to cook the remaining quesadillas.

Serve the quesadillas with the mayonnaise. Like all fried foods, quesadillas doradas are best eaten warm and not reheated.

PESCADILLAS "FISH-A-DILLAS"

MAKES 4 TO 6 QUESADILLAS

3 Tbsp / 45ml vegetable oil
1 cup / 140g chopped onion
3 garlic cloves, chopped
2 Roma tomatoes, cored and diced
1 lb / 455g thinly sliced wahoo
    (ono) or mackerel
3 oz / 85g epazote or cilantro
1 tsp salt
Pinch of freshly ground black
    pepper
1 cup / 260g fresh masa or 1 cup /
    130g masa harina mixed with
    ½ cup to ½ cup plus 2 Tbsp /
    120 to 150ml water (as directed
    on page 72)
1 qt / 960ml grapeseed or
    safflower oil
1 recipe Guacamole (page 60)
½ lime

This is a dish commonly served at beachside palapas—a twist on fried quesadillas, using fish, which have become another Contramar classic. The "pesca" part refers to the fish, sautéed with a salsa Mexicana, that gets pressed into the center of the masa circle instead of cheese, or in addition to the cheese if you want a kind of Mexican tuna-melt flavor.

Heat the oil in a large heavy-bottom skillet over medium-high heat until it's shimmering but not smoking. Add the onion and cook until it is translucent but not browned, 3 to 4 minutes. Add the garlic and cook for 1 to 2 minutes, just until you can smell its fragrance. Add the tomatoes and bring all of these sauce ingredients to a boil, then decrease the heat to low and simmer for about 5 minutes. Add the fish, epazote, salt, and pepper. Continue to simmer until the fish is cooked through and the majority of the moisture from the tomatoes and onion has evaporated, about 15 minutes. Remove the pan from the heat and let it cool down while you prepare your masa.

Make a golf ball–size ball of masa the same way you would when making a fresh tortilla and proceed as directed for pressing tortillas (see page 72). Once the dough is flattened between the two sheets of plastic wrap, remove the top sheet of plastic from the tortilla but leave the bottom sheet.

Before you go to place your cooked fish at the center of your quesadillas, make sure that the stewed fish filling is not too wet, since this will keep the masa from sealing and frying properly. You may need to pour off excess liquid. Place a spoonful of the cooked fish at the center of each flattened masa disk. Lifting the bottom edge, using the bottom sheet of plastic wrap as a sling, fold the circle of masa in half, enclosing the filling and pinching the edge together to seal them, as if you were making an empanada or ravioli. Repeat to make 3 to 5 more pescadillas.

Line a plate with a brown paper bag. In a large heavy-bottom skillet or wok, heat the oil to 350°F / 180°C. Gently place the pescadilla in the oil and fry until golden, 8 to 10 minutes. You could cook a few at a time but make sure they are not crowded in the pan and do not touch, since the fresh masa on the outside of one will stick to the fresh masa of another.

Using tongs, transfer the cooked pescadillas to the plate to drain and cool slightly. Repeat to cook the remaining pescadillas.

Serve the pescadillas with spoonfuls of guacamole and a squeeze of lime. Like all fried food, pescadillas are best eaten warm and not reheated.

TORTITAS DE PLÁTANO MACHO CON FRIJOLES PLANTAIN AND BEAN FRITTERS

MAKES 4 TO 6 SERVINGS

4 half-yellow, half-black (but not
    soft) plantains, pointy tips cut off
1 Tbsp sea salt, plus more as
    needed
2 Tbsp all-purpose flour
½ cup / 40g grated queso Cotija
    or ricotta salata
½ cup / 120g Frijoles Refritos
    (page 85)
1 cup / 240ml vegetable oil
1 recipe Salsa Verde (page 50) or
    another salsa of your choosing

I inherited my love for this southeastern dish from my family in Campeche and Tabasco, where plantains grow. The mashed plantains have a subtle sweetness that's offset by the salty cheese and refried beans at the center of these fried patties. These fritters are a delicious side served with Cochinita Pibil (page 291).

——————

Place the plantains in a saucepan large enough to fit them. Add water to cover and the salt and bring to a boil over medium-high heat. Decrease heat to low and simmer for 10 minutes. Remove the boiled plantains from the water. Once they're cool enough to handle, peel them and remove their seeds, which should slip right out. Place the plantains in a medium bowl and mash them. Taste to make sure they're salty enough and add salt if needed. (No additional salt will be added after this point, but the cheese is salty so take that into consideration.) Add the flour and cheese and incorporate completely.

At this point, I like to oil my hands slightly so that I can make the patties without having the sticky plantain paste stick to them. Form the plantain paste into round or oval patties with slightly raised edges (like the rim of a sope). I like them on the smaller side, so that each one fits comfortably in my palm. Put 1 Tbsp of refried beans at the center of each patty and then push the edges closed to seal it in, so that all of the beans are contained at the center of the mashed plantains.

Line a plate with a brown paper bag. In a large heavy-bottom skillet or wok, heat the oil to about 275°F / 135°C. Because plantains have so much sugar in them, they burn easily, so you want your frying oil at a slightly lower temperature than you'd normally use. Gently lower in as many of the plantain fritters as you can fit without crowding them. Fry them for 4 to 5 minutes per side, until they're golden brown. Using tongs, transfer the fritters to the plate to drain.

Serve the fritters hot, with spoonfuls of the salsa.

TACOS DORADOS FLUTE-SHAPED FRIED TACOS

To make my son, Lucas, very happy, I only have to make tacos dorados for dinner. Lucas is an adventuresome eater. He's not picky. I either trained him well or got lucky to have a son who enjoys trying new foods. (Most likely, it's both.) But I don't know a kid on Earth who wouldn't love these fried tacos. They are often called taquitos or flautas. They're a good vehicle for using up leftover chicken: grilled, poached, even rotisserie. The secret to a good taco dorado is to make sure it stays rolled up while you fry it so that the chicken stays tucked inside. I use one or two toothpicks to keep each taco shut, threading the toothpick like a needle through both layers of tortilla to hold the tube shape. Just make sure to take the toothpicks out before serving them—especially to kids!

_____

It's always a good idea to warm the tortillas on an ungreased comal or in a skillet first so they're soft and don't spring open or fall apart when you roll them up. Once the tortillas are soft and ready to be rolled, place about 2 Tbsp of the chicken at the center of a tortilla, roll it tightly into a cigar shape, and then thread it with a toothpick to keep it closed. Repeat for the remaining tortillas and filling.

Line a plate with a brown paper bag. In a 10-inch / 25cm heavy-bottom skillet, heat the oil to 350°F / 180°C. When the oil is hot, using tongs, place as many of the rolls into the oil as you can fit comfortably into the pan without crowding. This means you will do batches of two or three at a time. Turn and fry them to a uniform golden color—4 to 5 minutes total. Using a slotted spoon, transfer the rolls to the plate to drain and cool slightly. Sprinkle with the salt.

To serve, place a dollop of crema or crème fraîche on top of each one, then scatter over the chopped lettuce and ricotta salata. Pass the salsa at the table.

MAKES 4 TO 6 SERVINGS

4 to 6 Tortillas de Maiz (page 72)
4 to 6 oz / 115 to 170g shredded
    cooked chicken (page 88)
1 cup / 240ml grapeseed or
    safflower oil
Sea salt
3 to 4 Tbsp / 45 to 60g Crema
    Ácida (page 65) or crème fraîche
1 head Little Gem lettuce, coarsely
    chopped
3 to 4 Tbsp / 15 to 20g grated
    ricotta salata
1 recipe Salsa Verde Cruda
    (page 43)

TORTILLA ESPAÑOLA CON CHILE SERRANO
SPANISH EGG TORTILLA WITH SERRANO CHILE

1 cup / 240ml olive oil

1½ lb / 650g Yukon gold potatoes, peeled

1 tsp sea salt

1 garlic clove

½ white onion, minced

1 serrano chile, stemmed, seeded, veins removed (or not, depending on how spicy you want this to be), and minced

6 large eggs, whisked

1 recipe Mayonesa con Limón (page 62), Salsa Verde (page 50), or Salsa de Chile Manzano (page 46)

Tortilla Española—a frittata of egg and fried potato—is one of the most basic and comforting Spanish foods. It is still an absolute classic, and we cannot think of Spanish food without it. It's usually cut into wedges, sometimes dolloped with aioli, and accompanied by wine or coffee. It's so easy to make that everyone has their own system for doing so. This recipe is from my son's paternal grandmother, Meche, who is a Mexican of Spanish descent and cannot live without chiles serranos. I love the addition of minced serranos fried with the onion that makes her version a tiny bit spicy. The only laborious part of this recipe is that you must fry the potatoes first so that they become crispy before cooking them together with the eggs. Some people cheat and use potato chips—a classic student hack, and if the chips are kettle-fried, it's not half bad. But unless you're stuck in a dorm kitchen, it's worth taking the time to fry chunks of real potatoes, making this a great entrée for a brunch, a snack to munch on with friends, or even a full meal accompanied by a salad.

———————

Line a plate with a brown paper bag. In an 8- to 10-inch / 20 to 25cm nonstick heavy-bottom skillet, warm the oil over medium-high heat for about 3 minutes, until hot enough that a chunk of potato sizzles when dropped in. Rather than cutting my potatoes into perfect cubes, I like to use a paring knife to cut each potato into ½-inch / 12mm chunks, letting them fall directly into the hot oil. I find that the uneven ridges produce more surfaces to get crispy when fried. However, feel free to cut your potatoes into perfect cubes of the same size if you prefer. They'll taste great no matter what you do. Let the potatoes fry for about 10 minutes or until uniformly golden but not a deep brown, occasionally stirring them. You don't need their insides to cook fully, since they will continue cooking with the eggs. Once they are golden on all sides, use a slotted spoon to transfer them to the plate to drain. Sprinkle them with ½ tsp of the salt immediately after removing them from the oil, so that the salt sticks.

Pour all but about 3 Tbsp / 45ml of the hot oil into a jar (reserve it for reuse later) and return the skillet to the stove. Place the garlic in the hot oil and leave it for just 1 to 2 minutes, until it begins to turn golden and you can smell its aroma. Then remove and discard it. (You want the scent of the garlic and that's all.) Now add the onion and fry for 3 to 4 minutes before adding the serrano chile and cooking for 1 more minute. Waiting to add the chile keeps it from turning soggy and preserves its bright green color. Decrease the heat to low.

CONTINUED

Drop the potatoes into the bowl of eggs and then pour the mixture over the onion and chile mixture. Salt the top with the remaining ½ tsp salt. For the first few minutes, help the tortilla cook by using a spatula to loosen the eggs from the side of the pan, allowing more of the raw egg to keep coming into contact with the hot metal, and jiggling it until the cake of eggs begins to set. Then place a lid on the skillet and let it cook for another 2 to 3 minutes with the lid on. You want the top surface to be still moist but not runny. Use a spatula to test whether the eggs can be lifted as one unit from the pan and to see if it's golden on the bottom. Once it is, take a plate, place it on top of the skillet, and swiftly invert the pan and plate together so that the whole tortilla gets transferred to the plate. Then carefully ease the tortilla back into the pan to cook it on the other side for 2 to 4 more minutes. I like tortilla Española on the runny side, but if you prefer yours firmer, cook it for the full 4 minutes.

Cut into wedges and serve with spoonfuls of the mayonnaise or salsa. Tortilla Española tastes good hot, cold, and at room temperature. The tortilla can be stored in a sealed container in the refrigerator for 3 to 4 days.

PASTEL DE ELOTE SAVORY CORN PUDDING

This savory cornbread makes a great side to go with a meat like the Costillar de Cerdo (see page 290). It can also be a simple vegetarian supper, accompanied by a soup or salad. Definitely use fresh corn on the cob. The best variety of corn is cacahuazintle, which has big white kernels. Look for the closest to this description that you can get. You can lay strips of roasted poblano peppers on top of the raw cornbread, as I do here, or stew strips of roasted pepper with crema and spread it on top of the baked dish once it comes out of the oven. Both ways are delicious.

―――――――――

Preheat the oven to 350°F / 180°C. Butter an ovenproof casserole dish, another pan that is at least 12 inches / 30.5cm square, or a large and deep skillet.

Place the corn, onion, cornmeal, eggs, butter, crema or crème fraîche, baking powder, salt, and pepper in the jar of a blender and puree thoroughly. Pour the contents of the blender into the prepared baking dish. Evenly distribute the cheese on top and then arrange the poblano strips in an interesting design.

Bake for 1 hour, then let rest for 5 to 10 minutes before serving.

MAKES 6 TO 8 SERVINGS

6 ears white corn, shucked and kernels removed
¼ white onion
1 cup / 140g medium-grind cornmeal
4 eggs
½ cup / 110g unsalted butter, softened
½ cup / 120g Crema Ácida (page 65) or crème fraîche
1 tsp baking powder
2 tsp sea salt
Pinch of freshly ground white pepper
1 cup / 80g grated sharp Cheddar cheese
4 roasted poblano chiles (see page 67), cut into strips

FIDEO SECO CON CHIPOTLE CHIPOTLE NOODLE CASSEROLE

MAKES 4 TO 6 SERVINGS

2 canned chipotle chiles in adobo,
    plus 2 Tbsp of the sauce
2 garlic cloves
4 Roma tomatoes, cored
2 Tbsp tomato paste
½ white onion
1 qt / 960ml water
Sea salt
½ cup /120ml safflower oil
1 lb 2 oz / 500g angel hair pasta,
    broken into 2- to 3-inch / 5 to
    7.5cm lengths
1 sprig epazote
1 cup / 80g shredded whole milk
    mozzarella or another mild
    melting cheese
1 recipe Crema Ácida (page 65)
    or crème fraîche
1 avocado, cut in half, pitted,
    peeled, and cut into about
    8 slices

Fideo seco, one of the most common dishes in Mexican home cooking, often gets translated as "dry noodle soup," which doesn't sound very appetizing, nor does it do this favorite comfort food justice. It's Mexico's answer to mac and cheese: a gloppy noodle casserole in which fried angel hair pasta gets cooked in a tomato-y chipotle broth on the stove top, then topped with melted cheese, sour cream, and avocado. It tends to be a favorite among children, but it's a taste that a lot of adults never outgrow, myself included. Different people make it differently, and some versions are soupier than others. I like to cook almost all of the moisture out of my noodles so I can press them briefly into a Bundt pan, and the whole thing holds the shape of the mold and can be cut it into slices like a cake. This was a popular dish at Barracuda, the diner that I ran in Mexico City for many years, a homey alternative to the burgers and hot dogs that were also on the menu.

———————

Place the chiles and adobo sauce, garlic, tomatoes, tomato paste, onion, water, and salt in the jar of a blender and liquefy.

In a Dutch oven or heavy-bottom saucepan, heat the oil over medium-high heat until it's shimmering but not smoking. Drop the noodle pieces into the hot oil and fry, stirring constantly, until the pieces turn golden. Pour in the contents of the blender and add the sprig of epazote. Simmer until the pasta absorbs most of the liquid, stirring every minute or two so that the noodles don't stick to the bottom of the pot. You really want them to absorb as much of the liquid as they can. Once most of the liquid has been absorbed, taste and add more salt, if needed. Turn off the heat and let the pot sit for about 2 minutes.

Coat a 10-cup / 2.4L Bundt pan with cooking oil. Invert the noodle mixture into the pan. Pack it in tightly. Invert the pan onto a cutting board and lift off the pan. (At this point, you can keep the fideo warm in a 200°F / 95°C oven for up to 20 minutes before serving.) Cut the noodle cake into slices and serve, topped with the cheese, crema or crème fraîche, and a slice or two of avocado.

BUÑUELOS DE BACALAO CODFISH FRITTERS

Bacalao is salted, dried codfish, which is extremely popular on the Iberian Peninsula. In order to eat it, however, you must reconstitute the dried fish. It sounds complicated, but it really just takes time. You soak the fish in water overnight, changing the soaking water a couple of times, which extracts the salt that was used to preserve it. The batter for these fritters is made like the flour-and-butter paste for choux pastry, but thickened with potato. I like them served hot with chipotle mayonnaise. I promise it's not that complicated.

———————

In a bowl of cold water, soak the codfish for 24 to 36 hours, changing the water twice, or until a pinch of fish tastes only mildly salty (not saltier than you can comfortably eat). Ideally, you'll need to add salt after preparing the paste; it's always best to be able to salt to taste than to make something saltier than people enjoy eating.

Place the codfish in a medium saucepan, add fresh water to cover, and bring it to a boil over high heat. Decrease the heat and simmer for 20 minutes, or until the fish turns soft. Taste the fish again at this point.

While the codfish is cooking, bring a small saucepan of water to a boil and add the potato. (Leave the skin on the potato while it boils to preserve the starch.) Let it cook for 15 to 20 minutes. Test with a fork. Once it's soft, remove the skin (it should slip right off) and mash the potato in a small bowl.

Using a slotted spoon, transfer the softened codfish to a colander and let it cool until you can shred it with your hands.

MAKES 4 TO 6

10 oz / 280g dried salt cod
1 small Yukon gold potato
1 cup / 240ml water
1 Tbsp unsalted butter
1 cup /140g all-purpose flour
2 Tbsp chopped parsley leaves
1 garlic clove, diced
2 eggs
¾ cup / 180ml safflower oil
⅓ cup / 80g Mayonesa con Limón (page 62) or Mayonesa con Chipotle (page 62)

CONTINUED

In a medium saucepan over high heat, bring the water and the butter to a boil. Decrease the heat to low, add the flour all at once, and use a wooden spoon to stir it into the mixture until it's well combined. Keep stirring vigorously for 1 to 2 minutes, until the mixture forms a ball that begins to come away from the side of the pan. Remove the pan from the heat and stir in the potatoes, parsley, garlic, and codfish. Add the eggs one at a time, incorporating the first one fully before adding the second.

Line a plate with a brown paper bag. In a large heavy-bottom skillet over medium-high heat, heat the oil until it's shimmering but not smoking. Use a spoon to form uniform balls of the batter (about 1 Tbsp each) and ease them into the hot oil, gently turning and frying until they turn golden brown. Transfer them to the plate to drain.

Serve warm, with the mayonnaise on the side.

EMPANADA GALLEGA TUNA IN PUFF PASTRY

MAKES 4 TO 6 SERVINGS
AS A MAIN COURSE OR
MORE AS A PASSED APPETIZER

1 tsp unsalted butter
2 sheets store-bought frozen
    puff pastry, thawed in the
    refrigerator overnight
1 Tbsp olive oil
1 white onion, diced
2 garlic cloves, diced
8 Roma tomatoes, cored and diced
1 bay leaf (preferably fresh)
4 (140g / 5 oz) cans albacore
    or other high-quality line-
    caught oil-packed tuna or 1 lb /
    910g tuna or salmon, cooked,
    deboned, and flaked
2 Tbsp coarsely chopped
    green olives
2 Tbsp capers, coarsely chopped
1 tsp sea salt (optional)
1 egg

Empanada Gallega is another popular dish that comes from the Iberian Peninsula. Like the codfish fritters (page 209), this empanada is a common offering in Mexican cantinas, which are casual neighborhood places where families and friends share light meals (similar to the tapas bars in Spain).

Look for puff pastry in the freezer section of a good supermarket. Let the pastry partially thaw before using. You want it to be pliable but not mushy. If you have the time, the best way to thaw it is to place it in the refrigerator overnight. Roll it out lightly, just until it's the right shape and size to fit your baking vessel. This empanada is an easy starter or main course.

———————

Butter the bottom of your casserole dish. I use a 12 x 16-inch / 30.5 x 40.5cm ovenproof baking dish, but you can use another approximate size. On a lightly floured work surface, roll each sheet of puff pastry to the dimensions of your baking dish. Place one of the rolled-out sheets of puff pastry in the bottom of the dish. Cover the other sheet with a damp dish towel.

Preheat the oven to 425°F / 220°C.

In a large Dutch oven or heavy-bottom saucepan, warm the oil over medium heat until it's shimmering but not smoking. Add the onion and garlic and sauté until they are translucent but not browned. Add the tomatoes and bay leaf. Bring to a boil, then decrease to a simmer and let the sauce cook for 3 to 4 minutes. Remove the bay leaf and discard.

Drain the tuna and add it to the sauce, along with the olives and capers. Turn off the heat. Taste and add more salt if needed. It may not, due to the fact that the tuna, olives, and capers are already quite salty.

Spread your tuna filling across the bottom layer of puff pastry. Now take the second sheet of rolled-out puff pastry and place it on top of the casserole, crimping the edges to seal it to the baking dish.

Whisk the egg in a bowl and brush over the pastry so that the crust will be shiny after it bakes. Prick the top with a fork to vent steam as the filling bakes.

Bake for 10 minutes, until the pastry puffs. Then decrease the heat to 375°F / 190°C and bake for 10 to 15 minutes more, or until the pastry looks golden brown.

Serve immediately. Once cooled to room temperature, the casserole can be stored in a sealed container in the refrigerator for 2 to 3 days and eaten cold or gently reheated.

Torta de Atún at SALON COVADONGA, Puebla 121, Roma Norte

4 PLATOS FUERTES

MAIN DISHES

Platos *fuertes* translates literally to "strong dishes" and includes all entrées heavy enough to not be preceded by first courses (which isn't to say that you shouldn't have one, just that you won't need one). In Italy, the equivalent would be a *secondo*, which is the second bigger course in a meal—typically a meat dish—that often follows a lighter pasta first course.

As in Italy, Mexican primeros also include most rice and pasta dishes, whereas platos fuertes tend to feature fish or meat. For instance, the vegetarian version of Fideo Seco con Chipotle (page 208) gets categorized as a primero, while the Fideo Costeño (page 247), which features chunks of seafood nestled in the noodles, becomes a fuerte.

Of course, as any vegetarian knows, a dish without meat can be perfectly filling and hearty, and there are plenty of seafood dishes that get categorized as primeros because they're considered relatively light—such as ceviches and tostadas—and things to start meals, not meals in and of themselves. That said, I could be perfectly happy eating a selection of tostadas for a meal or a large bowl of ceviche with freshly fried tortillas . . . So I guess what I'm saying is, as in any art, knowing the rules doesn't mean you have to follow them slavishly. It all depends on you, whom you're serving, and the occasion.

Mexico has a lot of popular renditions of what you might call casseroles. These are great dishes to serve a crowd: things that can be made ahead of time and often taste even better when reheated. Enchiladas are one obvious example that traveled north long ago and have already found their way into many a non-Latino repertoire. But we have many similar dishes in Mexico—such as Pan de Cazón (page 253), in which tortillas get layered with cooked fish and a red salsa, or Pastel Azteca (page 286), which treats tortillas like the noodles in a lasagna—that deserve to be tried.

Among my favorite fuertes are guisos. *Guisos* means "stews," often served as taco fillings or used to fill enchiladas or roasted peppers. A lot of times, that's what I do with leftovers. I'll make something like chicken in salsa verde and eat it as a plated entrée with rice the first night, then take what's left and use it to make tacos or Pastel Azteca the second, giving my cooking a second life and ensuring that there's something delicious to serve for dinner when I don't have time to start a meal from scratch.

Some of these fuertes, including Camarones al Ajillo (page 235), come together in less than 15 minutes. Others, like the moles, require more of a time commitment. But I think it's worth making a mole for a very special occasion, like a birthday or holiday meal. While there are a fair number of steps involved, none of them is particularly difficult, and the whole dish is completely done before anyone arrives. Although if you have an open kitchen or accessible grill and enjoy cooking while chatting with company, other dishes in this section—like the ones featuring shellfish—are great for entertaining, too, since they come together quickly but definitely taste best served immediately.

Nothing in this section is overpoweringly spicy because I never want a guest at my table to feel as if their mouth is on fire if that's not something they enjoy. In fact, at Contramar we even came up with our now famous two-colored fish, one side painted with a red salsa of medium heat, the other side with a green salsa that has no spice whatsoever, to serve a table of "mixed" palates so everyone could eat from the same dish and leave happy. The secret to entertaining well is paying attention to your guests, making sure that everyone can share the food you took the time to make for them and that everyone feels particularly cared for. And if someone *wants* to feel as if their mouth is on fire? Well, that's what salsas are for.

COGOLLOS ASADOS Y FRIJOLES ROJOS
GRILLED LITTLE GEMS AND RED BEANS

Grilled Little Gem lettuce makes the perfect base for this tart bean salad, since the lime vinaigrette seeps into the crevices of the lightly charred lettuce leaves that cradle the beans. Normally vinaigrettes call for a higher ratio of olive oil to acid, but this one gets a lot more kick from equal amounts of lime juice and oil, plus ample garlic, salt, and parsley. When the cooked red beans marinate in this vinaigrette, they soak up a lot of flavor. At Cala, this dish comes with warm tortillas that you can use to scoop it up into tacos, which I highly recommend. Even committed meat eaters will find this vegetarian main dish satisfying. And if you have leftovers, all of these components keep for several days, making this an easy workday meal to reassemble. This recipe yields at least 3 cups / 800g of red bean salad, but I usually find it's not worth cooking dried beans to make a smaller quantity.

Make the red bean salad first, since the beans need to cook for about an hour and then marinate for another hour once dressed. Any small red bean that holds its shape could work, from adzuki beans to the Mexican red beans available at Mexican supermarkets. Plan on serving each person one head of Little Gem lettuce. It takes just a few minutes to grill the lettuce, which should be done right before you serve them to make sure they keep their crispness.

Cook the beans, following the instructions on page 84. Remember that the cooking time depends on the shape, type, and freshness of the beans. Start checking the beans for doneness after 45 minutes, since you don't want them to overcook. They should be soft but not mushy, creamy inside but still able to hold their shape when you gently pinch them. At the very end of the cooking time, add 3 tsp of the salt to the cooking water and turn off the stove. Let the beans cool in the pot of water for about 20 minutes. Add ice cubes if you need to speed up the process. If you cook the beans in a pressure cooker, don't use the quick-release valve or the beans may burst. Set them to a natural pressure release.

In a large bowl, whisk ¾ cup / 180ml of the oil with the lime juice and the remaining 1 tsp salt. Add the garlic and parsley. Cover and set aside.

MAKES 4 TO 6 SERVINGS

2 cups / 360g dried small red beans

4 tsp sea salt, plus more as needed

¾ cup / 180ml plus 1 Tbsp extra-virgin olive oil

¾ cup / 180ml freshly squeezed lime juice

2 large garlic cloves, finely minced

½ cup / 10g flat-leaf parsley, finely chopped

4 to 6 heads Little Gem lettuce, rinsed and damaged outer leaves discarded

8 to 12 Tortillas de Maiz (page 72)

CONTINUED

Once the beans are cool, drain them. I encourage you to reserve the broth, which makes a simple and delicious soup or can be added to another soup as a base. Don't rinse the beans under cold water. Cooked beans are delicate and, like potatoes, will absorb whatever they come into contact with. Cold water will probably make them fall apart and will reduce their flavor when cooked, which you definitely don't want. In this case, you also want them to soak up the flavor of your lime vinaigrette.

Transfer the beans to the bowl of vinaigrette and stir gently. Let the beans marinate for at least 1 hour and up to 4 hours before serving. (After 4 hours, lime juice oxidizes and starts tasting a little metallic and unpleasant.)

Cut the lettuce heads in half lengthwise, brush their cut sides with the remaining 1 Tbsp oil and sprinkle with salt.

Warm the tortillas on an ungreased comal or in a skillet over medium heat and place them in a basket or other container with a lid to keep warm.

Heat a grill pan or cast-iron skillet over high heat. When you lay the heads of lettuce face down on it, you should hear a sizzle. Let them cook for about 1 minute before flipping. Cook for about 1 minute on the other side. Press lightly with a spatula. You want them to wilt slightly, and—if using a grill pan—for the cut surface of each head of lettuce to have nice dark lines. But they should also hold their shape and remain crisp and sweet.

Serve the lettuce cut-side up, topped with a scoop of bean salad and dressing from the bottom of the bowl, passing the tortillas at the table.

GUISOS

Mexicans eat a lot of guisos, which don't exactly exist as a category in the United States (outside of Mexican restaurants). In addition to translating to "stew," a guiso can also be a "ragout" or "braise," and all of these definitions apply.

Guisos are a practical way to feed a crowd. A lot of times, they begin as a way of extending leftovers. For instance, you might make a pork mole for a dinner party and then eat some of the remaining sauce with bits of shredded meat over roasted vegetables or on warm tortillas for an easy taco lunch the next day. But guisos don't have to become tacos. You can eat them as is, over rice, as tamale fillings, or rolled into enchiladas. And many of the salsas in the basics chapter can be used as the base for guisados—such as tongue in morita chile salsa or chicken in salsa verde.

Whether you're cooking ahead for a busy work week or planning an easy menu to entertain a crowd, guisos are a great way to go, because they're the kind of dish that tends to taste better the longer it cooks and that can be made ahead and reheated without sacrificing any flavor.

PAPAS CON RAJAS Y CREMA ÁCIDA
POTATOES WITH ROASTED POBLANO CHILES AND MEXICAN SOUR CREAM

MAKES 4 TO 6 SERVINGS

5 large poblano chiles, stemmed,
    seeded, and veins removed
    (or not, depending on how spicy
    you want this to be)
2 large Yukon gold potatoes or
    another waxy potato, cut into
    ½-inch / 12mm cubes
1 Tbsp sea salt, plus more as
    needed
1 Tbsp safflower oil
1 large white onion, thinly sliced
1 cup / 240g Crema Ácida
    (page 65) or crème fraîche

This is an extremely popular vegetarian guisado and one of my personal favorites: it's a combination of roasted poblano chiles, cubed boiled potatoes, onions, and crema, cooked into a savory concoction that can be used all in sorts of ways. It makes a divine taco filling and a heavenly topping for Pastel de Elote (page 207), elevating an otherwise simple cornbread to a casserole that can easily be a dinner table centerpiece. It's meatless but very hearty, thanks to the potatoes and crema. For a saucier guisado, rajas con crema, omit the potatoes. In that case, I'd double the amount of roasted poblanos.

———————

Begin by roasting and peeling your chiles, following the instructions on page 67. Once you have removed and discarded the skin and seeds, cut them into rajas, or strips, about the width of fettuccine.

In a small saucepan, cover the potatoes with 2 inches / 5cm water and add the salt. Bring to a boil over medium-high heat, then decrease to low and simmer for about 5 minutes. Remove one of the potatoes and taste it. The piece should be soft but not falling apart, still holding its cube shape. Cubed like this, they will cook quite quickly, so be attentive. Once they have the right texture, drain the potatoes and set aside in a medium bowl with a lid or cover the pan with a plate to keep them warm.

Using the same comal or skillet in which you toasted your chiles, heat the oil over medium-high heat until it's hot but not smoking. Add the onion and sauté until it's translucent but not browned.

In a saucepan, combine the potatoes, chiles, onion, and crema or crème fraîche. Bring to a boil, then turn off the heat and let it sit for 5 to 10 minutes. As the mixture cools, the starches will absorb some of the melted cream and help it firm up. Taste and add more salt if needed. Serve as you wish!

These potatoes can be stored in a sealed container in the refrigerator for up to 2 days.

CHILES RELLENOS

Mexican cooks love to stuff all sorts of peppers with all kinds of fillings. When roasting any fresh chile, the method for roasting and then peeling them is the same as the one given on page 67, so you should feel free to use that as a template and experiment. Because they're large and robust, poblano chiles are the most common chile to stuff and the one that most people in the United States associate with this dish. But like all chiles, the spiciness of poblanos can vary a lot from one pepper to the next and one farmer's crop to the next. Poblanos in Mexico tend to be significantly hotter than the ones in the United States, where they're usually quite mild.

If you like your food spicy, then I suggest that instead of stuffing fresh poblano chiles you try stuffing ancho chiles, which are smoked and dried poblanos. Anchos sold in the United States are usually imported from Mexico, so they're likely to be spicier; plus, drying the chile intensifies its flavor. Stuffing dried peppers is actually easier than stuffing fresh ones, since you don't have to roast and peel them, which is the most laborious part of the process. Instead you simply soak them until they're soft enough to hold the fillings, then proceed as you would with the fresh version of the dish—scooping out their seeds, stuffing, breading (if you want), frying, and then cooking them in sauce.

If you really like food that sets your mouth on fire, you could also try roasting and stuffing manzano chiles. That's a chile that doesn't joke around. For something a bit milder but most likely more fierce than poblanos, try roasting large jalapeños and stuffing them with a melty cheese or simply with beans. In the following recipes, I'll offer a few of my favorite stuffed chiles, but as with all of the dishes in this book, let the ingredients that look best guide you and don't be afraid to experiment.

Chiles Rellenos at TACOS DON JUAN, Calle Juan Escuita 35, Condesa

CHILES RELLENOS CON FRIJOLES REFRITOS Y QUESO
CHILES STUFFED WITH REFRIED BEANS AND CHEESE

MAKES 4 TO 6 SERVINGS

4 to 6 poblano chiles
1 white onion, chopped
2 garlic cloves
8 Roma tomatoes, cored and cut in
    half, or 1 large (28 oz / 795g) can
    of whole tomatoes
1 cup / 240ml water
1 Tbsp olive oil
2 tsp sea salt, plus more as needed
1 cup / 240g Frijoles Refritos
    (page 85)
1 cup / 80g shredded whole-milk
    mozzarella or good queso
    Oaxaca
2 eggs
1 cup / 240ml rice bran oil,
    safflower oil, or any vegetable
    oil with a high smoke point

In this version of chiles rellenos, the roasted poblano chiles are filled with refried beans and whole-milk mozzarella before they're battered in whipped egg, lightly fried, and cooked to perfection in a bubbling pot of tomato sauce. While roasting, battering, and frying the chiles require some delicacy, once these are on the stove and simmering in their sauce, they can keep cooking for as long as needed, making them a great make-ahead dish for a dinner party.

If tomatoes are out of season and unappealing, feel free to use canned whole tomatoes (which are better than bad fresh tomatoes) instead.

You should serve chiles rellenos with any of the variations of Mexican rice (see pages 77-79), which will sop up the delectable sauce.

_____

Follow the process for roasting poblano chiles (see page 67), being extra careful not to tear the peppers as you peel them, since you want them as intact as possible for stuffing. While they are "sweating" in a sealed container, make your tomato sauce.

Place the onion, garlic, and tomatoes in the jar of a blender. Add the water and liquefy.

Heat the oil in a large Dutch oven or heavy-bottom stockpot over high heat. Once it's shimmering but not smoking, suspend a fine-mesh strainer over the pot and pour the liquefied tomato sauce over the hot oil. While it's not strictly necessary to strain the sauce (and if you're not fussy, you could skip this step), it creates a more refined sauce, allowing you to eliminate the tomato seeds but still retain their flavor. Add the salt and bring the sauce to a boil, then immediately decrease to the lowest simmer. Taste and add more salt if needed.

Once your chiles have sweated and are cool enough to handle, after about 10 minutes, carefully remove their charred skins. Make a neat vertical slit from the stem end to the tip of each pepper and pull out the seeds, being as gentle but as thorough as possible. Because you will be stuffing the chiles, make an effort not to tear them open. Leftover pepper seeds will taste bitter and unappealing so do try to remove every one.

Using an electric stand mixer fitted with the whisk attachment or a medium bowl and a whisk, whip up your eggs for 3 to 5 minutes, until they hold firm peaks. You want them quite stiff and foamy.

Place your roasted chiles on a plate, slit-side up. Inside each pepper, place 1 to 2 Tbsp of the refried beans and top with 1 to 2 Tbsp of the cheese. If you want, you can close each pepper using a toothpick, which you gently thread through the flesh near the slit. (Just remember to remove them before serving or your guests could get an unpleasant surprise.) Remember not to overstuff your chiles, as you don't want them bursting and losing their fillings in the pot.

In a medium heavy-bottom skillet, warm the oil over medium-high heat until it registers 375°F / 190°C on an instant-read thermometer. Gently dip each stuffed chile into the whipped egg, very carefully flipping it over so that both sides get well coated and using a spatula to spread the egg onto the top side. Then lower the battered chile into the hot oil and let it fry for about 2 minutes per side, flipping it carefully. You'll know it's done when it turns golden and puffs up. Then remove the chile with a slotted spoon, letting any excess oil drip back into the pot, and carefully place the chile in the hot tomato sauce. Repeat with each stuffed chile until they are all in the pot of tomato sauce. Don't worry about crowding them. Once the chiles are fried, they will hold their shape in the pot and can withstand jostling.

Bring the tomato sauce back to a boil and then decrease to a simmer and cook the chiles for a minimum of 5 minutes so that all of the peppers are cooked through and hot. Feel free to leave them simmering on the lowest heat for longer if you're still fixing the rest of your dinner or waiting for guests to arrive. You really can't overcook chiles.

ANCHO RELLENOS DE QUESO DE CABRA / ANCHO CHILES STUFFED WITH GOAT CHEESE VARIATION

If you want to make chiles rellenos using ancho chiles, soak 4 to 6 anchos in very hot water for about 1 hour until they soften. Then pat them dry, pull off their stems, remove their seeds, and proceed with stuffing and frying them according to the directions above, substituting a soft chèvre for the mozzarella. The freshness of the goat cheese makes a great counterpoint to the smoked chiles.

TORTAS DE CHILES RELLENOS
CHILES RELLENOS SANDWICHES

4 to 6 bolillos (Mexican sandwich
   rolls) or 1 large ciabatta
   or baguette, cut into 4 to
   6 sandwich-size pieces
½ cup / 120g Frijoles Refritos
   (page 85)
4 to 6 Chiles Rellenos (page 226)
1 large avocado, cut in half, pitted,
   peeled, and sliced
1 recipe Cebollas Rojas Encurtidas
   (page 39) or Salsa Brava
   (page 45), made with red onions

What do you do with leftover chiles rellenos? If you are guessing—put
it on a taco?—you're right. You certainly *could* do that. But my favorite—
because it takes me back to a delicious childhood memory—is to make a
torta (a Mexican sandwich) out of them. This was one of the things that the
guys who worked construction on our house in Tepoztlán used to eat for
their almuerzo, the late-morning meal which they were always willing to
share with my brother and me or whoever was around. They worked up
an appetite and the meals they brought from home, or that their wives or
moms would deliver hot around 10 or 11 AM, were some of the best things
I remember having tasted. When I make chiles rellenos, I always throw
extra in the pot so that I'll be able to enjoy some on a torta or, yes, in a
taco the next day.

Cut your bread in half. Spread a thin layer of beans (about 1 tsp) on both
cut sides. Top with a chile relleno, slices of avocado, and pickled red onions
and serve.

CHILES EN NOGADA CON MARISCOS
SEAFOOD-STUFFED CHILES WITH WALNUT SAUCE

There's a legend surrounding chiles en nogada, maintaining that they were first made by the nuns in Puebla to serve to Agustín de Iturbide, the first president of Mexico. According to this legend, the red pomegranate seeds scattered on a creamy white walnut sauce that is poured over a roasted green chile—represent the colors of the Mexican flag. But this legend, it turns out, cannot be true. The flag at that time was white and blue, not green, white, and red. Nevertheless, the myth persists, and this dish is always served in September when we celebrate Mexican independence, which is also when the key ingredients in this dish are all in season (which is likely the real reason that chiles en nogada came to be served at this time in the year). The walnuts that arrive in the markets in Mexico are "green," which means that they have been freshly picked and are unroasted so the nutmeats are a little soft and milky when they are blended. Although I love the walnut sauce that comes with this dish, flecked with the bright pomegranate seeds, the truth is, I've never cared for the typical chiles en nogada, in which the filling is made of pork, pineapple, and other dried fruits and can be too sweet for my taste. Everyone who makes this dish has their own traditional recipe. After I was invited by a good friend at a market in my neighborhood to taste a seafood version, I adapted it to make this recipe for Contramar. So my version features marisco—minced crab, shrimp, and octopus.

Green walnuts are only available in September and October and—in the United States—only for sale at some farmers' markets (or nut stands if you live near nut orchards). If you can't find them, get the freshest, best-quality walnuts that you can because old ones can taste a bit rancid. At a well-stocked natural foods store, you should be able to sample the ones in the bulk bins before you buy them.

For this recipe, make sure that you roast the chiles well before stuffing them. Unlike other chiles rellenos, these will not continue cooking in the sauce, so their skins need to be cooked all the way through, not just blistered.

MAKES 4 TO 6 SERVINGS

Walnut Sauce
1 cup / 240g Crema Ácida
    (page 65) or crème fraîche
1 cup / 120g shelled walnuts,
    the freshest you can find
2 tsp sea salt
1 Tbsp sherry

Filling
1 cup / 240ml olive oil
1 large white onion, minced
1 tart apple (such as Granny Smith
    or Pink Lady), peeled, cored,
    and diced
½ cup / 70g dried cranberries,
    chopped
1 cup / 200g cooked crabmeat,
    well cleaned (see page 161)
1 cooked octopus (see page 247),
    chopped into ½-inch / 12mm
    pieces
1 cup / 325g cooked chopped
    large shrimp
1 tsp sea salt, plus more as needed

4 to 6 large poblano peppers,
    roasted and peeled (see
    page 67)
2 eggs
1 cup / 240ml rice bran oil,
    safflower oil, or any vegetable
    oil with a high smoke point
Seeds from 1 pomegranate
½ cup / 10g parsley leaves, minced

CONTINUED

To make the sauce: In a blender combine the crema or crème fraîche, walnuts, salt, and sherry and blend on low speed (so you don't inadvertently make a nut butter), until everything is well combined and really creamy.

To make the filling: Warm the oil in a large heavy-bottom skillet over medium heat until it's shimmering but not smoking. Add the onion and fry it until it's translucent but not browned, then add the apple and cranberries and cook for another 3 to 4 minutes, giving the apple time to soften. Add the crabmeat, octopus, shrimp, and salt and cook, stirring constantly, for only 1 to 2 minutes, just until everything is heated through. Taste and add more salt if needed.

Following the same process outlined on page 67, cut through each roasted and peeled chile and remove all the seeds and big veins. Stuff each chile with ½ to 1 cup / 140 to 280g of filling, depending on the size of the chile. Don't overstuff them. If you want, you can close each pepper using a toothpick, which you gently thread through the flesh near the slit. (Just remember to remove them before serving or your guests could get an unpleasant surprise.)

Place each chile on an individual plate. Cover each chile with 3 to 4 Tbsp of the walnut sauce. Scatter 1 Tbsp of the pomegranate seeds and 1 tsp of the parsley on top of each.

Serve immediately.

SUSTAINABLE SEAFOOD

The fresh fish served on the beach in Zihuatanejo inspired me to open Contramar, and I've been cooking predominantly seafood at my restaurants ever since. But I was also raised to understand the importance of sustainability, and there's no doubt that the ocean's ecosystem is one of the most fragile ones, and that we must be mindful of our consumption of seafood and try not to do harm to the planet in the way that we eat.

When I got my start in Mexico, I was determined to use only Mexican fish on the menu at Contramar, but I would also only use tuna when it was legal to be caught; this meant that sometimes we couldn't serve our signature tuna tostadas. Twenty years later, in California, the mercury levels in tuna are high, and it's a controversial fish that should only be line-caught at certain points in their reproductive cycle. As a result, I decided to make the tostadas at Cala using a beautiful trout from a Northern California farm on the border between Oregon and California, where they feed their fish the by-products of pistachios grown nearby plus algae and other plant-based foods, which gives their flesh a silky richness, much like what you find in tuna and salmon from the ocean. The trout tostadas are slightly different than the tuna version from Mexico City, but just as good, and reflect my philosophy on using the best local or regional, in-season, and sustainable ingredients rather than slavishly following a recipe.

There are a lot of misconceptions about seafood. First of all, don't assume that farmed fish is necessarily bad. Domestically, in the United States at least, there are sustainable fish and shrimp farms with ecologically sound operations that don't use antibiotics and are organic. What you should avoid are imported Asian farmed shrimp, for example, because they're known for using a lot of antibiotics and pesticides that pollute waterways, just to start with. But domestic bivalve shellfish, like clams, oysters, and mussels, are typically "farmed" in suspension systems—mesh bags hanging in the ocean—with no chemicals used. They glean plankton and other nutrients from the water. And because their little bodies work like filters, they actually help clean the water in which they live, which makes it even more important that they come from clean ocean water and that they are not fed anything they wouldn't have in their natural state.

Also, don't assume that you have to use a particular fish or shellfish just because it's the one specified in a recipe. As always, you can substitute creatively, looking to what's available and fresh and beautiful near you. I can't give you a printed list of fish to choose from, because good food is a moving target, since the ocean and its populations keep changing. I follow the Slow Food principles: *buono, pulito,* and *giusto* (good, clean, and fair). For instance, pan de cazón, a dish from Campeche, Mexico, that I love, is traditionally made with dogfish, which is baby shark. For a long time, shark has been an endangered species in the United States, and so I have made this recipe with cod and other firm-fleshed white fish. Recently, some species in the San Francisco Bay Area have rebounded and are no longer on the prohibited list, so we can now use dogfish at times. I have learned from my mentors to live life like a progressive adventurer while regarding nature like a conservationist. Make sure you research the best sustainable options in your area and do your part for the future of the species and our whole ecosystem.

When buying fish, more than any other ingredient, you should shop with your senses, just as you do when cooking. The freshest fish is often the most sustainable, because it tends to have been caught locally, hopefully, in clean waters. If possible, buy your fish at a market where there are human beings behind the fish counter who can answer your questions about it. They should know where it was caught and when. They should also be willing to let you take a whiff of it to make sure it has no fishy smell. Finally, don't assume that just because a fish was frozen, it's bad. Sustainably caught fish can be frozen immediately after being pulled out of the ocean and not lose much in terms of flavor—although this will probably not be the fish you want to serve or eat raw, as the consistency does suffer alterations when frozen, especially if it's not a very fatty fish. Octopus is almost always sold frozen in the United States, as are soft-shell crabs.

Seeking out sustainable seafood means that you're investing in people and businesses with a stake in protecting the ocean and its biodiversity. And as always, what's better for the planet also tastes better on the plate.

While I often make larger quantities of other meat and vegetable dishes so that I can enjoy the leftovers, I typically purchase only the amount of seafood that I think my guests and I can eat. Fresh seafood is best eaten on the day it's cooked (or served raw, in the case of ceviches and aguachiles). Some seafood dishes are okay the next day, but they will never be as good as on the day you made them.

CAMARONES AL AJILLO PRAWNS SAUTÉED WITH GARLIC

This is basically a Mexican scampi. These rich and flavorful prawns come together in less than 15 minutes, but guests at a dinner party will never know how easy they were to throw together. The only tricky part is paying close attention when you fry the garlic and guajillo chiles. Garlic can burn quickly, so remove it from the oil as soon as it turns golden. In that same oil, you want to flash-fry the rings of guajillo for even less time than you did the garlic, just getting them crispy and releasing some of their flavor into the oil, which you will then use to cook the prawns. Definitely serve this dish over rice to soak up all of the great flavor from the garlic- and chile-infused olive oil.

MAKES 4 TO 6 SERVINGS

3 guajillo chiles, stemmed
   and seeded
½ cup / 120ml olive oil
5 garlic cloves, thinly sliced
1½ lb / 650g raw giant (18- to
   20–count) whole prawns, shelled
   and deveined, with heads on
1 Tbsp sea salt
1 recipe Arroz (page 77)

Using kitchen shears, snip the chiles into skinny ⅛-inch / 3mm-wide rings.

Heat the oil in a medium heavy-bottom skillet over medium heat. You don't want the oil to be too hot when you drop in the garlic since it fries so quickly. Drop all of the garlic slices in at once and then agitate them continuously as they fry so that they don't stick together. Be sure to remove them from the oil when they are golden, not brown. If they're still white, they will stay limp, but if they're too dark, they will taste bitter, so pay attention and find that sweet spot when they're just finished. Remove them with a slotted spoon in batches, taking out the most golden ones first and spreading them out in a single layer on a plate.

Decrease the heat slightly. Into this same oil, drop the chile rings and don't take your eye off them for a second, since that is just about how long they take to fry. The moment you can smell them and they start to change color, pull them all out at once using your slotted spoon and spread them on another plate to dry.

Increase the heat to medium-high and add the prawns to the infused oil, followed by the salt. Sauté the prawns, stirring constantly, for 2 to 3 minutes, just until they turn pink. Turn off the heat, return the fried garlic and chiles to the pan, and toss to incorporate.

Serve the prawns over a scoop of rice.

ARROZ VERDE CON CAMARONES
PRAWNS WITH GREEN RICE

MAKES 4 TO 6 SERVINGS

1 qt / 960ml water
7 oz / 200g washed spinach or kale
1 Tbsp sea salt
½ cup / 120ml olive oil
1 large white onion, chopped
3 garlic cloves, chopped
2 cups / 400g Arborio or
    Calasparra rice
1 sprig epazote
2 Tbsp salted butter
8 to 12 large prawns, shells on
Juice of 1 lime

It's very Spanish to serve shrimp this way, adding green things (in this case spinach) to the water in which the rice is cooked, and using this as a base for buttery prawns freshened up with a squeeze of lime. It's easy enough to be a weeknight dinner but tasty enough for company, too.

_____

In the jar of a blender, blend the water with the spinach and salt.

Warm the oil in a saucepan over medium heat. Add the onion and garlic and sauté. Add the rice to the pan and let it fry until the grains are clear. Stir in the spinach water. Bring the contents of the pan to a boil. Add the epazote, then decrease the heat, cover the pan, and simmer for 15 minutes.

As soon as you decrease the heat and place the lid on the pan, melt the butter in a large skillet over medium-high heat. When the butter is bubbling but not brown, add the prawns and sauté for about 1 minute per side. Keep warm.

After 15 minutes, the majority of the liquid in which the rice is cooking should have been absorbed. Remove the epazote sprig, place the buttery shrimp on top of the rice, and cover the pan for a final 5 minutes to finish cooking. Taste the rice and if it is already very close to cooked, re-cover the pan, turn the stove off, and let it steam for 5 minutes.

Squeeze the lime juice over the pan and serve immediately.

CAMARONES A LA VERACRUZANA
VERACRUZ-STYLE SHRIMP

MAKES 4 TO 6 SERVINGS

3 Tbsp / 45ml olive oil

1 white onion, diced

2 serrano chiles, stemmed, seeded, veins removed (or not, depending on how spicy you want this to be), and sliced into rings

2 garlic cloves, minced

5 Roma tomatoes, cored and diced

1 bay leaf (preferably fresh)

1 tsp sea salt, plus more as needed

¼ cup / 60ml Castelvetrano olive brine

1½ lb / 650g cooked bay shrimp

15 Castelvetrano olives, pitted and coarsely chopped

2 Tbsp capers, chopped

Juice of ½ lime

2 Tbsp minced flat-leaf parsley leaves

1 recipe Arroz (page 77)

Veracruz has one of the largest and oldest ports in Mexico, and a vast and complex gastronomic tradition. Many of the seafood dishes that come from there include imported ingredients that traveled into the country by boat from Europe, like the olives and capers that flavor these shrimp. Make sure that you buy olives in brine, since a splash of this goes into the dish, too. I like to break up the olives with my hands so that the chunks are big and irregular. I also drop them in at the very last minute rather than cooking them, to preserve their firmness and freshness rather than letting them stew. I usually serve this with white rice, but feel free to substitute Arroz Verde (page 79) for an extra pop of color and flavor.

_____

Heat the oil in a medium heavy-bottom skillet over medium-high heat until it's shimmering but not smoking. Add onion and chiles at the same time (the onion keeps the chiles from burning) and sauté until the onion is translucent but not browned. Then add the garlic and cook for 1 more minute, until you can smell it.

Decrease the heat to medium and add the tomatoes, bay leaf, and salt. Simmer until the tomatoes begin to break down and turn saucy—about 10 minutes. Then add the olive brine and the shrimp and cook for just 1 to 2 minutes. Since the shrimp are already cooked, you are really just heating them in the sauce. Cooking the shrimp any longer will make them overcooked and tough.

Turn off the heat and add the olives, capers, and lime juice. Taste and add more salt if needed. Garnish with the parsley.

Serve the shrimp immediately, with a scoop of rice to soak up the sauce.

JAIBA SUAVE A LA PLANCHA
SAUTÉED SOFT-SHELL BLUE CRAB

A soft-shell crab is a crab that has outgrown its shell (molting like a snake) but has not yet grown a bigger one. Fishermen used to have to catch them at that exact moment, but nowadays they have developed the ability to grow them in tanks, monitoring their molting. Soft-shell crab is still a luxury, however. The thin, edible shell adds richness and flavor to whatever dish you eat them in. If you have only eaten soft-shell crab as sushi, you're missing out. This Mexican preparation treats it like the grilled chicken or carne asada that you'd find in a taco. You sauté it in butter, chop it up, and serve it with warm tortillas, onion, cilantro, and any salsa you like. It's simple yet unexpected, and such a treat. A good fish market will usually have a box of soft-shell crabs in the freezer, already cleaned. Just defrost them and then sauté them whole before chopping them up.

In a skillet over high heat, melt the butter until it's bubbling and turning golden. Add the crabs and salt. Turning them over fairly regularly, sauté them until all of the butter has cooked out of the pan. Place the crabs on a cutting board and chop them up into bite-size pieces. Arrange the crab pieces on a serving plate, sprinkle them with the cilantro and onion, and serve with the tortillas and salsa.

MAKES 4 TO 6 SERVINGS

1 Tbsp unsalted butter
3 fresh or frozen and thawed
    soft-shell crabs, rinsed and
    patted dry
½ tsp sea salt
2 Tbsp minced cilantro leaves
2 Tbsp minced white onion
4 to 6 Tortillas de Harina (page 72),
    warmed
1 recipe Salsa Brava (page 45) or
    another salsa of your choosing

ALMEJAS A LA MEXICANA MEXICAN-STYLE CLAMS

3 Tbsp / 45ml olive oil

½ white onion, chopped

3 garlic cloves, crushed

1 serrano chile, stemmed, seeded, veins removed (or not, depending on how spicy you want this to be), and minced

1 tsp sea salt

2 oz / 60ml mezcal

2 cups / 325g chopped Roma tomatoes

6 lb / 2.7kg clams, soaked in cold water in the refrigerator for 30 minutes then drained

3 Tbsp / 5g minced cilantro or parsley leaves, or a combination

1 recipe Arroz (page 77) or crusty bread

Fresh clams steam in the juices of a brothy salsa Mexicana, and then the dish gets sprinkled with minced cilantro. I like to add mezcal to the mix; the alcohol cooks out, but a delicious hint of its smokiness lingers. This should definitely be served with rice to absorb the succulent broth.

———————

In a medium Dutch oven or heavy-bottom pot, warm the oil over medium-high heat until it's shimmering but not smoking. Add the onion, garlic, and chile all at once; the onion keeps the garlic and chile from burning. Sauté for 3 to 4 minutes, until everything has softened. Add the salt, mezcal, tomatoes, and clams and stir frequently until the liquid returns to a simmer. Place a lid on the pot and let the clams simmer in the broth for about 5 minutes, steaming until they open. Any clams that don't open should be discarded.

Scatter with cilantro or parsley and serve over a scoop of rice or with a hunk of bread.

MEJILLONES AL CHIPOTLE MUSSELS IN CHIPOTLE SAUCE

Mussels are a wonderfully sustainable seafood. They are plentiful, repro-duce quickly, and improve the water quality by filtering it through their bodies. Not only that, they're also inexpensive and absolutely delicious cooked in this rich and aromatic broth of white wine, chipotles, and crema. If you want your dish to be spicy, blend whole chipotles from the can with crème fraîche. For less heat, use only the adobo sauce from the can of chipotles.

If you've never cooked mussels before because they seem fancy or you assumed they'd be difficult to cook, you're in for a happy surprise. They couldn't be simpler or quicker to make. Just be sure to wash them well. Use an abrasive sponge to scrub off their beards, the little tendrils by which they were attached to the rocks. As soon as mussels are done cooking, they open up. That's when you remove them from the heat. This should take only a couple of minutes. For an extra pop of flavor, serve with warm garlic toast.

MAKES 4 TO 6 SERVINGS

¼ cup / 60ml olive oil
1 cup / 140g finely minced shallots
1 tsp sea salt, plus more as needed
2 garlic cloves, pressed or mashed
    with a mortar and pestle
1 cup / 240ml white wine
1½ cups / 360ml shrimp stock or
    Caldo de Pescado (page 89)
4 lb / 1.8kg mussels, well scrubbed
    so that no grit or beards remain
¼ cup / 60g Crema Ácida
    (page 65) or crème fraîche
2 Tbsp adobo from canned
    chipotles in adobo or 2 whole
    chipotles
Chopped parsley
Crusty bread

Heat the oil in a large heavy-bottom stockpot over medium-high heat until it's shimmering but not smoking. Add the shallots and cook until they're translucent but not browned. Add the salt, then add the garlic and sauté for just 1 minute, until you can smell it. Add the wine, bring to a boil, and let boil for about 2 min-utes before adding the stock. Return to a boil, add the mussels, and cover the pot. As soon as the majority of the mussels open, which should take only a few minutes, turn off the heat. Any mussels that don't open should be discarded.

Combine the crema or crème fraîche and adobo or chipotles in a small bowl. Stir the chipotle mixture into the broth.

Serve the mussels immediately in individual bowls, dividing the sauce evenly over the mussels. Garnish each portion with a scattering of parsley. Enjoy with a hunk of bread.

PESCADO A LA TALLA
CONTRAMAR'S SIGNATURE RED AND GREEN GRILLED RED SNAPPER

MAKES 4 TO 6 SERVINGS

Green Sauce
4 garlic cloves
2 cups / 40g parsley leaves
½ cup / 120ml safflower oil
Pinch of ground cumin
1 tsp sea salt

Safflower oil
1 whole red snapper, butterflied,
    or 4 (8 oz / 230g) boneless red
    snapper fillets, with skin on
Sea salt
1 cup / 240ml Adobo de Chiles
    Rojos (page 58)
1 recipe Salsa Roja Asada (page 48)
    or another red salsa of your
    choosing
1 recipe Salsa Verde Cruda
    (page 43) or another green salsa
    of your choosing
1 recipe Tortillas de Maiz (page 72),
    warmed
1 recipe Frijoles Refritos (page 85)
Additional salsa of your choosing
Lime wedges

My family has two kinds of eaters: those who love chiles with wild abandon and those who really don't. As you might be able to guess, the Mexican side likes their food hot; the Italians, not so much. But for a close family, Pescado a la Talla is the perfect solution. In its traditional presentation, a whole red snapper is butterflied and split down the middle so that you can grill the fillets on both sides of the fish at once. Two different salsas—a mild green parsley one and my hotter red adobo—are painted onto the two sides of the fish. The cooked fish is brought to the table on one platter. Everyone shares the same meal, but the spice lovers don't have to compromise and those who prefer things milder don't have to suffer. Both sides of this fish are delicious, and it looks spectacular, too. This has become one of our most popular fuertes at Contramar, where the waiters gingerly remove the flesh from the bones at the table and serve it with warm tortillas and refried black beans.

If you don't have a fishmonger who can butterfly a whole snapper for you, buy four fillets instead and cook two of them with the red sauce and two with the green, in a grill pan or on a grill. You want the grill marks because they sear the sauce into the flesh of the fish. Both sauces can be made a day ahead and stored in separate sealed containers in the refrigerator.

——————

To make the green sauce: Place the garlic, parsley, oil, cumin, and salt in the jar of a blender and puree until smooth.

Once you are ready to cook your fish, heat a grill to medium or a grill pan over medium heat. Brush the cooking surface with oil so that the fish won't stick.

Clean your fish well, then pat it dry. Using a sharp knife, crosshatch the flesh on the diagonal, making cuts about ½ inch / 12mm deep and 1 inch / 2.5cm apart. Sprinkle with salt. If using fillets, spread two of them with ½ cup / 120ml of the red sauce each and the other two with ½ cup / 120ml of the green sauce, being careful to coat the entire surface and get the sauce into the crosshatched knife marks. If using a butterflied whole fish, spread the red sauce on one half of the fish and the green sauce on the other half, carefully covering the whole surface area and working the sauce into the knife marks.

Grill the fish, skin-side down, until it's almost cooked through, 7 to 10 minutes. Using a spatula, carefully flip it over and cook the flesh side until it has char marks and easily releases from the grill or pan. Place it flesh-side up on a platter or onto individual plates. Serve with the warm tortillas, a bowl of refried black beans, whatever salsa you wish, and wedges of lime.

FILETE DE ESMEDREGAL CON VERDOLAGAS Y NOPALES EN SALSA VERDE

SEA BASS, PURSLANE, AND CACTUS WITH SALSA VERDE

MAKES 4 TO 6 SERVINGS

Salsa Verde with Purslane

1 lb / 455g small tomatillos, papery husks removed and discarded, rinsed

1 large white onion, cut in half, half left intact and the other half chopped

2 garlic cloves

3 or 4 serrano chiles, stemmed, seeded, and veins removed (or not, depending on how spicy you want this to be)

1 tsp sea salt

Pinch of freshly ground black pepper

3 Tbsp / 45ml vegetable oil

1 lb / 910g purslane, well rinsed and leaves cut from the stems

4 to 6 cactus paddles, dethorned

Olive oil

4 to 6 (6 oz / 170g) sea bass fillets

1 tsp sea salt

Generous pinch of freshly ground black pepper

1 recipe Frijoles Refritos (page 85)

It's very a Mexican thing to braise pork and grilled cactus under a thick layer of salsa verde and serve it with sautéed purslane. My friend Guillermo taught me this version and I adapted it for Contramar, using sea bass instead, and it soon became a favorite fuerte. The tart tomatillo salsa and grilled cactus really balance the sweet and flaky white fish. You may be more familiar with purslane, or *verdolagas* as we call it, than you realize. This succulent grows like the weed that it is, in many parts of North America (including lots of backyards). It's also available in the produce section at most Latin markets and many farmers' markets, prized by cooks in the know for its bright lemony taste. Note that grilling cactus means that you don't have to cure it in salt to de-slime it, as the grilling process will have the same effect.

———————

To make the salsa: Begin by placing the tomatillos in a Dutch oven or heavy-bottom skillet, together with the half intact onion, garlic, and serranos. Add enough water just to cover and bring to a boil. Decrease the heat and simmer for 10 minutes. Pour the contents of the Dutch oven into the jar of a blender, add the salt and pepper, and liquefy.

Warm the vegetable oil in a large skillet over medium heat. Add the chopped onion and sauté until it's translucent but not browned. Then add the salsa from the blender and simmer for 10 minutes. In the last minute, add the purslane and stir to combine and heat through.

While your salsa is simmering, grill your cactus paddles. Heat a grill to medium or a grill pan over medium-high heat. Score the cactus paddles by slicing thin crosshatched lines across each flat surface. Rub them with the olive oil to keep them from sticking and then place them on the hot grill or grill pan, and cook for 6 to 7 minutes on each side. Place the grilled cactus on the bottom of a baking dish large enough to accommodate them.

Preheat the oven to 350°F / 180°C.

Arrange the sea bass fillets on top of the grilled cactus. Season with the salt and pepper. Cover with the salsa and bake for 25 to 30 minutes.

Serve hot, with the refried beans.

FIDEO COSTEÑO NOODLES WITH SEAFOOD

Fideos, or noodle casseroles, are super popular in Mexico. The most basic one, Fideo Seco con Chipotle (page 208), is a homey and easy comfort food. Fideo costeño ("coastal" fideo) is a much more elegant and grown-up version of the dish, a menu staple at Contramar that is mostly enjoyed as a full meal, which includes seafood.

As in the original fideo, broken pieces of angel hair pasta get treated like the rice in a paella: briefly fried until they turn golden, then simmered in a seafood stock blended together with tomato, onion, and garlic, most of which gets absorbed into the simmering noodles. Then you nestle succulent chunks of cooked octopus, whole shrimp, and steamed clams into the noodles, spread it all in a casserole dish, and broil it to crusty goodness. Served with a generous dollop of mayonnaise, this is still comfort food, but comfort food at its most refined.

While you could make this dish with any cooked seafood you like, I think that octopus makes it extra special. There is a lot of debate about how to cook octopus, which is basically one huge muscle and is quite tough if it's not tenderized. Some people advocate using extreme measures like slamming it against a wall. I find this impractical (and I've had less than great results). A simpler solution is to let it simmer and braise for a couple of hours, enough time for the meat to toughen up and then gradually relax to the desired softness. If you have a pressure cooker—a tool I couldn't live without—you can reduce a 2-hour simmer to 20 minutes, and the octopus comes out tender and perfect. One thing to note is that most octopus for sale is frozen (or was previously frozen), and that's actually a good thing, since the freezing process begins tenderizing the meat. It also means that your octopus will have been well cleaned, saving you that step. This recipe calls for ¼ cup / 65g of salt in the cooking water for the octopus, because you want the water to have the saltiness of the sea.

MAKES 4 TO 6 SERVINGS

Octopus
1 (2 to 2½ lb / 910g to 1.2 kg) fresh or thawed frozen whole octopus, rinsed
4 scallions, crowns discarded
1 tomato, punctured with the tines of a fork (so that it doesn't explode in the pot)
1 garlic clove
2 bay leaves (preferably fresh)
4 sprigs thyme
¼ cup / 65g sea salt

3 cups / 720ml Caldo de Pescado (page 89)
3 or 4 Roma tomatoes, cored
1 garlic clove
½ white onion
1 tsp sea salt
2 Tbsp safflower oil
7 oz / 200g angel hair pasta
12 steamed clams
6 oz / 120g shrimp, shelled and deveined
1 lime, cut in half
1 recipe Mayonesa con Chipotle (page 62)

CONTINUED

Begin by cooking your octopus: Put the octopus, scallions, tomato, garlic, bay leaves, thyme, and salt in a large stockpot and add water to cover by about 2 inches / 5cm. Bring to a boil, then decrease the heat and simmer with the lid on for 2 hours. If using a pressure cooker, cook under high pressure for 20 minutes. Once the octopus is cooked, it will have shrunk to about 50 percent of its original size and will puncture easily, since the flesh will be tender. The skin should come off easily but the suckers less so.

Remove the octopus from the pot and let it cool until you can handle it. Starting with the tentacles, pull off any loose skin, which should slip off like a sock, and discard. You don't need to worry about getting all of it off, just the parts that come off easily. Chop the body and tentacles into bite-size pieces and set them aside.

In the jar of a blender, combine the stock, tomatoes, garlic, onion, and salt and liquefy.

In a Dutch oven or heavy-bottom saucepan over medium heat, warm the oil until it's shimmering but not smoking. Add the pasta, breaking the noodles into 2-inch / 5cm lengths as you drop them into the hot oil. With a wooden spoon or spatula, stir them continuously as they fry to a golden color. Pour the contents of the blender over the fried noodles. Bring to a simmer and continue to cook until the noodles are very soft and most of the liquid is absorbed, about 8 minutes. Don't worry if it's still a bit soupy. This is a wet casserole, and more of the moisture will cook out in the final broiling step.

Preheat the broiler.

Pour the cooked noodles and their sauce into a paella dish or a large, shallow casserole dish. Tuck the chunks of cooked octopus, the steamed clams, and the raw shrimp into the top of the noodles. You could also use steamed mussels or other seafood if you prefer—it all tastes delicious. Broil for 3 to 4 minutes, until the top is just crusty and a little browned.

Finish with a squeeze of lime, a dollop of mayonnaise, and a scattering of parsley and serve immediately.

ARROZ NEGRO BLACK RICE

MAKES 4 TO 6 SERVINGS

½ cup / 120ml olive oil
1 white onion, minced
1 garlic clove, pressed or mashed
    with a mortar and pestle
1 green bell pepper, diced
1 red bell pepper, diced
1½ cups / 150g cleaned and
    quartered cremini or white
    mushrooms
¾ lb / 340g squid, cleaned and
    cut into rings
1 oz / 30ml sherry, tequila, or
    mezcal
2 tsp sea salt
2 cups / 480ml Caldo de Pescado
    (page 89)
2 Tbsp squid ink
2 cups / 400g bomba or
    Arborio rice
¼ tsp ground nutmeg
2 jalapeños, stemmed and minced
1 recipe Mayonesa con Chipotle
    (page 62) or Mayonesa con
    Limón (page 62)

This is essentially a squid paella, made black by the squid ink that gets added to the stock near the end of cooking. While this is a traditional Spanish dish, this recipe originally came to me from a fishmonger at the Mercado de San Juan, who shared it with the mother of a friend. The Mercado de San Juan is a really good produce market in downtown Mexico City. It used to be the only place where you could find extraordinary things from Spain and Italy, like imported prosciutto or bottles of squid ink. Chefs would go there, as well as the cooks of fancy ladies, like the one who made it for my friend's mother. These days, delicacies like squid ink are more readily available. Aside from this one ingredient, everything in this dramatic showstopper of a dish is easy to come by and inexpensive, making this a great one to wow guests at a dinner party who may never have seen—or tasted—black rice. While it's satisfying as is, you could also add a little minced Soppressata or Spanish chorizo for an even more filling fuerte.

———————

Warm the oil over medium heat in a Dutch oven or paella pan. Once it's shimmering but not smoking, add the onion and fry for 3 to 4 minutes, until it looks translucent but not browned. Then add the garlic, bell peppers, and mushrooms, and fry for an additional 1 to 2 minutes. Once you can smell the garlic and the mushrooms have softened, throw in the squid, and add the sherry, tequila, or mezcal and the salt. Cook everything for 4 to 5 minutes. While this mixture cooks, bring your stock to a boil in a small saucepan.

Add the boiling stock to the pot with the vegetables and the squid. Decrease the heat to low, add the squid ink, and simmer to dissolve it into the stock. Add the rice and the nutmeg and continue to simmer for 20 minutes, until almost all of the liquid has been absorbed into the cooking rice. You shouldn't stir it, but you can use a spoon or spatula to nudge the broth under the rice occasionally.

In the last 5 minutes of the simmering time, preheat the broiler.

Once the rice has just absorbed the broth but is still quite moist, remove the pan from the stove top and place it under the broiler for 2 minutes, just to crisp the top.

Sprinkle with the parsley and jalapeño and serve immediately, passing the mayonnaise at the table.

PAN DE CAZÓN FISH AND TORTILLAS IN RED SALSA

MAKES 4 TO 6 SERVINGS

Tomato Sauce

2 Tbsp olive oil

1 white onion, coarsely chopped

1 habanero chile, stemmed, seeded, veins removed (or not, depending on how spicy you want this to be), and chopped

1 garlic clove, chopped

4 Roma tomatoes, cored, blanched in boiling water for 30 seconds, peeled, and chopped or 4 canned whole tomatoes

1 Tbsp tomato paste (optional; use only if the tomatoes are at all pink)

½ tsp sea salt, plus more if needed

Pinch of freshly ground white pepper

2 cups / 480g Frijoles Refritos (page 85)

1¼ lb / 575g Pescadillas filling (page 200)

¼ cup / 60ml safflower oil

8 to 12 Tortillas de Maiz (page 72)

6 habanero peppers

1 recipe Cebollas Rojas Encurtidas (page 39)

This dish from Campeche is kind of like a deconstructed enchilada or an individual lasagna, because you get a stack of layered fried corn tortillas, separated by a savory fish filling and refried beans, all smothered in a hot red salsa and served with pickled red onions and avocado. The filling is the same one used in Pescadillas (page 200). Make it ahead of time so that it's ready when you're ready to assemble this dish, which is plated individually and makes an impressive dinner that will delight any seafood lover, who probably has never enjoyed fish this way before.

To make the sauce: Warm the olive oil in a skillet over medium heat until it's hot but not smoking. Add the onion and chile and cook until the onion is translucent. Add the garlic and cook for 1 minute more, just until you can smell its fragrance. Add the tomatoes, tomato paste, salt, and pepper and simmer over low heat for about 5 minutes, until it reduces a bit. Taste and add more salt, if needed.

In separate pans, warm the refried beans and pescadillas fillings over low heat.

Once your filling, tomato sauce, and beans are all hot and you're ready to serve this dish, heat the safflower oil in a skillet over medium-high heat until it's shimmering. Line a plate with a brown paper bag. Fry the tortillas one at a time in the oil, flipping them so that each side gets golden and they puff slightly. Place them on the plate to drain.

On the ungreased comal or in a skillet over high heat, cook the habanero peppers until blistered on all sides, about 3 minutes.

To serve, place a tortilla on a plate and spread it with 1 to 2 Tbsp of the beans. Top with 1 to 2 Tbsp of the filling. Place another fried tortilla on top of it and ladle the sauce over. Garnish with a sprinkling of pickled onions and a padron pepper and serve immediately.

WHAT WOULD DIANA DO?

Even before I was friends with Diana Kennedy, I thought of her as "Diana," because she had been such a presence in my home since I was a child. My mother grew up in Italy and the United States, so she didn't know about cooking Mexican food. After she married my dad, one of his sisters gave her Diana Kennedy's books. Even though we lived in Mexico, those were the recipe books we had for Mexican food. When we wanted to see how something in Mexican cooking was done, we always checked to see what Diana would do.

I met Diana for the first time when she came to Contramar, not long after we opened. Her publisher was in the same neighborhood, and he decided to bring her in for lunch, and she loved it immediately. She said it was so full of life, which is exactly how I would describe her. We got along right away. It was like meeting family. She's a person who's interested in everything—of course food, but also science, history, the environment—and she loves a real conversation, not chitchat that hovers at the surface. It wasn't long before I got to know her very well.

Diana's life would make a great movie. She was born in England, and served in the forestry service during World War II, when she was still in her teens. After that she emigrated to Canada and then traveled to Haiti, where she met a *New York Times* correspondent with whom she moved to Mexico based on "a half-baked promise of matrimony"; eventually, they married. They moved to New York for a few years, but after her husband died she returned to Mexico, where she has been living for more than fifty years, traveling all over the country, interviewing people, and writing down their recipes. A lot of these recipes would have been lost if not for the nine cookbooks in which she faithfully compiled them.

Diana disagrees when people call her "the Julia Child of Mexican cooking." "I'm the Mick Jagger of Mexican food, because I wear leather pants" she

likes to say. Some people find her intimidating, but I love how frank and unapologetic she is. I'll never forget the first time she invited me to her house in Michoacán. I brought my brother, and both of us immediately felt so at home. She had the same solar-powered oven as we had in Tepoztlán, the same low-flush toilets and cisterns to collect rainwater. My brother and I ended up tucked into bed with her, all of us watching a movie.

It's still Diana's books I turn to when I want to check how to make something traditional. In my own Mexican cooking, I walk a line between tradition and innovation. On the one hand, I believe that recipes exist to be followed. If people have always done something a certain way, because it works, and it still tastes good, then why mess with it? I don't believe in a lot of hacks, especially because doing things the right (or traditional) way isn't that difficult. On the other hand, innovation happens every time someone enters the kitchen, especially for experienced cooks. Good cooks add their own variations to recipes for various reasons, maybe because they want to feature a special ingredient, to use something up that might otherwise go bad, or to play around a little.

It's important to me to be creative, to take risks in the kitchen, but also to be respectful of the traditions I'm playing with so that the dishes don't get lost in the innovation. That's why I owe Diana such a tremendous debt, not only for the reference library that she's provided with her cookbooks, but also for her friendship and honest evaluations of my cooking. Diana truly has no filter. She cannot hold back. Her opinion of tasting menus? "They're for people who are bored and not very hungry." And when she pronounces a dish, "sophisticated," her mouth puckering as if she just sucked on a lemon, no one could mistake it for a compliment. But she's just as generous when she loves something, and she doesn't mince words or talk about "flavor profiles" or anything pretentious like that. When Diana likes a dish I cook, she calls it "delicious," and that's all I need to hear to know that I got it right. Diana means the world to me. We relate in absolute respect and love for each other. Honesty and "no suffering in silence" is our motto. She always pushes me in new directions and makes me go places that are important in my life and in my cooking.

TAMALES

Tamales might seem intimidating to make if you've never made them before, but don't feel daunted. You don't need origami skills to wrap them up. In Mexico, some tamales are wrapped in corn husks and others in banana leaves. It really depends on where in Mexico a particular tamal originated. Seafood tamales, from the coastal regions, tend to use banana leaves because those trees grow nearby. Vegetarian and meat tamales tend to be wrapped in corn husks. In the United States, you can almost always find corn husk wrappers at Mexican markets. To use them, simply soak them in a big bowl of warm water until they're soft, then squeeze out the excess moisture. Banana leaves are also available at a lot of Asian markets as well as at Mexican ones (and are also used to steam things in Southeast Asian cuisines). They are stocked in the freezer section and thaw out very quickly. They don't need to be soaked; just cut them into pieces that are the right size for your tamales. I usually cut them to be about the size of a small place mat, unless I'm making pibipollo (page 264), which is one big tamal made with uncut leaves.

In terms of wrapping strategies, you don't need to follow a diagram to the letter. What matters most, no matter which kind of tamal you're making, is that you keep all of your fillings tightly bundled up so that the masa doesn't escape while they're steaming. The masa that I use in tamales is the same as the one I use to make tortillas. This means you can use fresh masa if you have access to it, or mix your own from masa harina and water. To this mixture, you will add lard and/or butter, depending on the recipe, and possibly some other seasonings as well. When you add in fat, you want to mix it extremely well so that it gets really fluffy. The more air and fat you manage to whip into your masa, the lighter the tamale will taste.

To make the kind of tamal you have probably eaten in restaurants, you spread a small rectangle of masa—about 3 x 4 inches / 7.5 x 10cm and ½ inch / 12mm thick—on the wrapper and place 2 Tbsp of filling in the center of the masa. When you roll or fold it up, the masa will surround and encase the fillings. To ensure that it's tightly contained, feel free to use a few wrappers, one on top of another. When you are enveloping a tamal with a cut piece of banana leaf, fold it up like an envelope around the masa and fillings. The wrapped tamales will be rectangular and fairly flat; this means you can stack them up in your steamer. With tamales wrapped in

corn husks, stand them on end, with the open part of the wrapper facing up, so that the fillings stay contained at the bottom and steam comes out of the top. Some people like to take the extra step of cutting a corn husk into ribbons and using them to tie up the tops of the tamales. This is a good idea, though not essential.

It doesn't really matter what size or shape your tamales are. What does matter is that each of the tamales is the same size as the others that you're steaming simultaneously. It's like pasta—if you try to cook angel hair pasta with penne, it won't work because pastas of different sizes need to cook for different amounts of time. Tamales of the same size will also cook for the same amount of time. Whenever you steam tamales, you should take one out after 20 minutes to see if it's done. When you unwrap it and cut into the masa, you should be able to slice through it neatly, both halves staying more or less intact. If the masa oozes at all, wrap it back up and steam for another 5 minutes, then test again.

One of the best things about tamales is that, aside from seafood ones that should be eaten right away, you can steam them until they're cooked, then refrigerate them until you're ready to eat them and resteam them right before serving. The second time around, you're just getting them hot, so you don't have to worry about masa oozing out or nailing the timing.

And as with tacos, tostadas, enchiladas, you can really put anything in a tamal that strikes your fancy. Pumpkin and cheese, leftover carnitas, pineapple and walnuts (in a sweet tamal). Once you get the basic idea down, experiment with fillings to your heart's content. The method doesn't change, and most fillings are tasty inside steamed masa.

TAMALES DE MEJILLÓN MUSSEL TAMALES

MAKES 10 TO 12 TAMALES

1 package banana leaves
4 cups / 1kg fresh masa or 4 cups
    / 520g masa harina mixed with
    2 to 2½ cups / 480 to 600ml
    water (as directed on page 72)
¼ cup / 50g lard
2 Tbsp unsalted butter
2 tsp sea salt
½ cup / 10g parsley leaves, minced
Zest of 1 lemon
1 Tbsp olive oil
1 leek, trimmed, cut in half
    lengthwise and thoroughly
    washed
36 large mussels or 50 smaller
    ones, well scrubbed so that no
    grit or beards remain

This recipe is my adaptation of a delicious dish from Oaxaca, where there are lots of tichindas (tiny mussels that thrive in brackish waters), which people have traditionally cooked inside tamales. In my version, as in the original, you press whole mussels, shells and all, inside seasoned masa, and wrap everything in a banana leaf to cook. Once it's done, you have to go on a treasure hunt for the mussels in the masa. Because the masa gets flavored with serrano chiles and garlic, you don't need to serve these tamales with any condiments.

———————

Cut your banana leaves into 24 place mat–size rectangles. Then run each one swiftly over the flame of your burner. You're not looking to toast them, but the heat of the fire loosens the fibers and makes the leaves more pliable.

In the bowl of a stand mixer fitted with the paddle attachment, combine the masa, lard, butter, and 1 tsp of the salt and beat on medium-high speed for 3 to 4 minutes, until it gets much fluffier. The more air you can whip into the masa, the better, since this keeps the tamales light-tasting. Fold in the parsley and lemon zest.

Oil a comal or skillet and heat it over medium-high heat. Sprinkle the remaining 1 tsp of salt on the cut side of the leek and place it cut-side down on the hot comal or skillet. Once it begins to soften, flip it over and cook the other side. When it has cooked through and looks translucent, take it off the stove and cut it into 1-inch / 2.5cm pieces.

Spread 2 heaping Tbsp of the masa mixture in the center of one of your prepped banana leaves, using the back of a spoon or a spatula to paint a rectangle about 3 inches / 7.5cm wide by 4 inches / 10cm long and ½ inch / 12mm thick.

Place as many mussels as fit over the strip of masa, followed by a few pieces of grilled leek. (Divide your leek so that each tamal gets an equal amount.)

Now it's time to fold the banana leaf. Don't worry that there isn't masa on top of the mussels and leeks. Once you fold it and it steams, it will all mix up. You just want to make sure that the mussels are well embedded in the masa. Fold the leaf around the mussels as if you were making an envelope or wrapping a package. Once it's wrapped, place the whole package facedown on top of another cut banana leaf and wrap that around the original package. Again, it isn't important exactly how you wrap it, just that it is completely wrapped up so that the masa doesn't ooze out in the steaming process. Repeat this process until you have packaged 10 to 12 tamales.

Place a few inches of water in the bottom of a steamer. Put all of the tamal packages in the steamer basket, not stacked in a single tower but arranged in layers of three or so, as flat as possible, with room for a little steam to rise in between them. Turn on the heat, cover the pot with a lid, and bring the water to a boil, then decrease it to a simmer. Steam the tamales for 20 to 25 minutes, monitoring about halfway through the process to make sure that there is still a good inch or two of water at the bottom of the pan and adding more water if necessary.

To check if the tamales are thoroughly cooked, open the top parcel and see if the masa is firm to the touch. It shouldn't be wet and soupy anymore. Try cutting into the center with a knife to ensure that the masa has the consistency of firm polenta and doesn't ooze at all. As soon as the tamales are ready, remove them from the heat and serve them while they're still hot. If you're not quite ready to eat them, you can keep them warm in the pot with the heat off and a lid on for up to 30 minutes.

While most tamales can be steamed, then refrigerated, and then steamed again, these are an exception, because the mussels should be eaten hot, shortly after they first open.

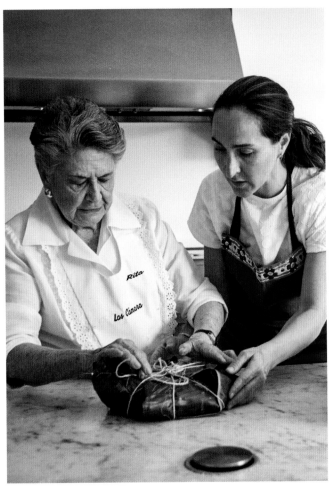

PIBIPOLLO HUGE PORK AND CHICKEN TAMAL

A traditional Mayan dish, *pibipollo* translates to "buried chicken," because the chicken is essentially buried in what amounts to one giant tamal, the masa seasoned with achiote so that it looks bright red, the whole thing steamed inside a package of folded-up banana leaves. It's made with both chicken and pork, the two meats stewed to a savory, shredded goodness, so even though you can't tell what you're getting in any bite, you just know it's delicious. This is a great dish to feed a crowd. It's filling, amply seasoned but not spicy, and the presentation is neat, like a giant present that you unwrap at the table. Served with black beans and salsa, this makes a memorable meal.

For shredded pork and chicken of the consistency you want at the center of a pibipollo, a slow cooker is best (though you can approximate a slow cooker using a stockpot filled with water at a very low temperature). You can cook them together, leaving them both in for 6 to 8 hours to ensure that the pork cooks thoroughly, or you can start with the pork and then add the chicken in the last hour if you want to make sure that it doesn't get too mushy.

The last step in the process, once you've steamed your pibipollo, is to remove the banana leaf in which it steamed and bake it in the oven to brown the masa slightly. After steaming it, you can refrigerate it until you're ready to bake and serve. (You just increase the baking time slightly.)

To cook the meat: Place both meats in a slow cooker if you have one, and cover with at least 6 cups / 1.4L water plus 1 Tbsp of the salt, the whole onion, bay leaf, cloves, and avocado leaf. Cook at a very low simmer for 5 to 6 hours, until the meat is soft and stringy. If you are doing this in a heavy-bottom stockpot on the stove, I suggest beginning with the pork plus the water, salt, onion, and aromatics, simmering it for about 20 minutes, then adding the chicken for another 20 minutes. Once the meat is completely tender and falls apart when you prod it with a fork, turn off the stove and let the meat cool until you can handle it. Strain the meat from the cooking liquid, reserving the liquid and discarding the onion and aromatics.

In the jar of a blender, liquefy the whole epazote leaf, achiote, vinegar, garlic, the 2 whole Roma tomatoes, 1 Tbsp of the salt, and 1 cup / 240ml of the reserved liquid in which the meat cooked.

MAKES 6 TO 8 SERVINGS

½ lb / 230g chicken breasts
    or thighs
½ lb / 230g boneless pork
    shoulder
2½ Tbsp sea salt
2 white onions, 1 left whole and
    1 minced
1 bay leaf (preferably fresh)
2 cloves
1 avocado leaf
¼ cup / 5g epazote leaves,
    1 large leaf left whole and the
    remainder minced
1 box achiote (annatto) seeds
2 Tbsp white vinegar
1 garlic clove
3 Roma tomatoes, 2 left whole and
    1 cored and minced
1 cup / 240ml reserved pork/
    chicken cooking liquid
4 cups / 1kg fresh masa or 4 cups
    / 520g masa harina, mixed with
    2 to 2½ cups / 480 to 600ml
    water (as directed on page 72)
1 cup plus 2 Tbsp / 250g lard
1 package banana leaves, plus
    kitchen twine for binding
1 recipe Cebollas Rojas Encurtidas
    (page 39)

CONTINUED

In the bowl of your stand mixer fitted with the paddle attachment (or in a very large bowl, using your hands), combine the liquid from the blender with the masa, the remaining ½ Tbsp salt, the minced onion, the minced tomato, the minced epazote, and 1 cup / 220g of the lard and mix on low speed. It will be a very liquidy, sticky mixture.

To prepare your banana leaves, run each one swiftly over the flame of your burner. You're not looking to toast them, but the heat of the fire loosens the fibers and makes the leaves more pliable. Spread a leaf with a 9-inch / 23cm pie-size circle of the masa mixture. Place the shredded meat in the center and then distribute an equal amount of the masa mixture on top of the meat to cover it. Wrap the large tamal with a banana leaf, then wrap it in another one and continue until the parcel is tightly enveloped. Use your string to bind the parcel.

In order to steam your pibipollo, place a large steamer basket at the bottom of a heavy-bottom stockpot and add a few inches of water. Place the parcel in the basket, cover, and bring the water at the bottom of the pot to a slow boil over medium heat. Leave the lid on and steam for about 40 minutes. In the last 10 minutes of this steaming time, preheat the oven to 350°F / 180°C.

Once the tamal has steamed and the masa is no longer falling apart, place it on a baking sheet or in a casserole dish it can fit in. Partially unwrap the parcel so the top of the pibipollo is exposed. Dab the top with the remaining 2 Tbsp of the lard and put it in the oven for 10 minutes if it is still hot from being steamed, 20 minutes if it was cold. It's perfectly fine to steam the pibipollo ahead of time and do this last baking step right before serving.

Slice into your pibipollo as you would a pie and serve hot, with the pickled onions.

PULPO A LAS BRASAS CON SALSA NEGRA
GRILLED OCTOPUS WITH BLACK SALSA

MAKES 4 SERVINGS

1 cooked octopus (see page 247)
2 to 4 Tbsp Salsa Negra (2 Tbsp
    per 1 lb / 455g of octopus;
    page 56)

If you've made the delicious Salsa Negra (page 56), then you have some (or a lot) left over. The truth is, you can't really make a small quantity of salsa negra. It requires a lot of garlic, fried at such low heat that it's really caramelized. And because it's such a rich salsa with an intense taste, a little goes a long way. That means that once you've made a batch, you'll want to multipurpose it. The good news is that it keeps for up to three months in the refrigerator, so you can use it in lots of dishes. This is an incredible (and incredibly easy) way to enjoy it: rubbed over a whole cooked octopus that is very briefly grilled, just to give the sauce the chance to cook into the meat. If you have your salsa negra ready and a cooked octopus (which only takes 20 minutes in a pressure cooker), you can grill this in 10 minutes and serve a real feast. I would serve the grilled octopus with mashed potatoes or with slices of oven-roasted sweet potato, because I love octopus with potato, and both nicely offset the boldness of the salsa.

You can also prepare grilled octopus using either the green or red sauces from the Pescado a la Talla (page 244) or the charred chile adobo that I use on the pork tenderloin for Costillar de Cerdo en Recado Negro (page 290). In other words, if you have a cup of good salsa left over from one of these other fuertes, why not get a second life out of it and use it as the coating for this delicious grilled octopus?

———————

Coat the octopus in the salsa negra, rubbing it all over. Oil your grill and heat it to high or oil a grill pan and place it over high heat. Place the octopus on the heated grill or grill pan and let it cook on each side for a few minutes. You are not cooking the meat, just heating it through and giving it a chance to absorb and cook the sauce a little more.

When the octopus has nice grill marks and the heat of the grill has fused the sauce with the octopus, transfer it to a cutting board and let it rest for 5 to 10 minutes. Chop into pieces and serve warm. It's best eaten on the day it's cooked.

TINGA DE POLLO SHREDDED CHICKEN IN TOMATO-CHIPOTLE SAUCE

MAKES 4 TO 6 SERVINGS

6 Roma tomatoes, cored and
    cut in half
4 garlic cloves
1 cup / 240ml Caldo de Pollo
    (page 88; or use the chicken-
    poaching water plus a few
    aromatics and vegetables)
2 canned chipotles in adobo,
    plus more if desired
2 tsp sea salt, plus more as needed
¼ cup / 60ml safflower oil
3 large white onions, slivered
2 poached boneless, skinless
    chicken breasts (see page 88),
    finely shredded

This is a really classic and easy guiso, served at many taquerias. The ratio of onions to chicken is high in this dish, because traditionally a tinga is a way of extending chicken, using the less expensive onion to stretch out the meat. In addition to being economical, stewed onion also adds texture to this dish. Instead of stewing the chicken in the tomato and chipotle sauce, you add the shredded meat at the very end. It tastes as complex as if you had braised it for a long time, but it comes together really fast if you already have the poached chicken. (In a pinch, you could even use rotisserie chicken.) Using your fingers, shred the chicken breasts as finely as possible to create a soft contrast to the crunch of the fried onions. You don't even have to use chicken. They serve a delicious tinga vegetariana in the Polanco district in Mexico City at a certified kosher taqueria, and it's nothing but onions stewed in the red chipotle sauce.

————————

In the jar of a blender, combine the tomatoes, garlic, stock, chipotles, and 1 tsp of the salt and liquefy.

Over high heat, warm the oil in a large heavy-bottom skillet or medium saucepan. Add the onions, making sure they sizzle when they hit the pan. You want them to cook at a high enough heat that they are frying and not caramelizing, so they retain a slight crunch rather than becoming soft and sweet. Add the remaining 1 tsp salt and cook until the onions are golden brown.

Pour the contents of the blender into the pan of onions and bring to a boil. Decrease the heat and simmer for 5 to 10 minutes, until the sauce has thickened. Add the chicken and cook briefly, just until the chicken has absorbed some of the sauce and heated through. Taste and add more salt if needed.

Tinga de pollo tastes great as a taco topping, an enchilada filling, or served on its own with rice and beans. It can be stored in a sealed container in the refrigerator for up to 5 days, and in fact, it tastes even better reheated than when it's first made.

Tinga de pollo taco at TACOS HOLA, Amsterdam 135, Hipódromo Condesa

POLLO EN SALSA VERDE CON CILANTRO
CHICKEN IN TOMATILLO SALSA WITH CILANTRO

MAKES 4 TO 6 SERVINGS

¼ cup / 60ml safflower oil, plus
    more if needed
1 garlic clove
1 whole chicken, cut into 6 pieces
3 Yukon gold potatoes, peeled or
    not, cut into large (1- to 2-inch /
    2.5 to 5cm) chunks
½ white onion, finely diced
2 cups / 480ml Salsa Verde
    (page 50)
1 cup / 20g cilantro leaves, finely
    chopped
1 recipe Arroz (page 77)

This chicken, stewed in salsa verde, was one of the staple weekday dishes cooked by Victoria, the lady who helped around our house when I was a child. It was always a favorite of mine, but I couldn't get her recipe because she never used one—or measured anything that went into her pot, for that matter. I loved to watch her spear a garlic clove on the prongs of a fork, swivel it through the scalding oil at the base of her pot, and then remove it, using that oil to brown the chicken. I watched her enough times to be able to re-create this dish. I like to make a big pot on a Sunday when I don't have much going on and then I reheat it on weeknights when I get home too tired to cook. I always eat it with white rice. The perfume of jasmine rice mixes well with the aroma of the fresh cilantro that you add to the chicken at the end.

——————

Warm the oil in a 4 qt / 3.8L Dutch oven or heavy-bottom stockpot over medium-high heat. Skewer the garlic clove on the tines of a fork and swivel it through the hot oil. The oil should be hot enough that the garlic sizzles and turns golden. Once this happens, remove the garlic and set it aside (don't throw it away).

Add 2 or 3 chicken pieces, skin-side down, to the hot oil. Don't overcrowd the pan. You are not cooking the chicken through, just searing it, allowing the skin to brown slightly, which brings out the flavor when it stews. The chicken skin will stick at first, but will release fairly easily once it's done searing. Using tongs or a slotted spoon, flip each piece of chicken to sear the other side. Then remove the seared chicken and set aside on a plate while you continue to sear the rest of the pieces on each side. Set it all aside while you cook the potatoes.

Using the hot oil in the bottom of the pan (add a bit more, if needed), brown the potato chunks just as you did the chicken, adding them in a single layer and allowing them to turn golden on each side before flipping them. You are not cooking the potatoes through, just searing them; this also helps bring out their flavor and keeps them from falling apart in the stew. Once they're a light golden color, remove them and set them on a plate.

Now take that clove of garlic that you used to swivel in the oil before you cooked your chicken and slice it fairly thinly. Add the sliced garlic to the oil in the pan, along with the onion, and sauté until soft and lightly browned. Strictly speaking, you could skip this step, since the salsa has plenty of flavor, but I really like the texture of the minced onion.

Add the salsa to the pot, along with the chicken pieces and potatoes. Bring it to a boil, cover, decrease the heat, and simmer for about 30 minutes. Cut into a thick piece of chicken and chunk of potato to confirm they're cooked through.

Sprinkle the cilantro over the stew. To serve, scoop the rice into bowls and spoon the stew over the rice. The tinga can be stored in a sealed container in the refrigerator for 3 to 5 days.

LENGUA CON SALSA CHILE MORITA
BEEF TONGUE IN MORITA CHILE SALSA

MAKES 4 TO 6 SERVINGS

1 (3 to 4 lb / 1.4 to 1.8kg) beef
    tongue
1 bay leaf (preferably fresh)
1 Tbsp coriander seeds
1 Tbsp black peppercorns
2 chiles de árbol, stemmed,
    seeded, and torn in half
2 or 3 sprigs thyme or
    1 Tbsp dried
2 or 3 sprigs oregano or
    1 Tbsp dried
2 Tbsp sea salt
4 garlic cloves
1 Tbsp safflower oil
½ white onion, minced
1 recipe Salsa de Chile Morita
    (page 55)

If you're feeling a little more adventuresome than chicken, here's a great dish. Anyone with an aversion to tongue just because of what it is should overcome their squeamishness and try it, because once you've tasted this meltingly rich and tender meat, it's impossible to imagine why you resisted to begin with. It also couldn't be easier to cook. You just let it simmer for a few hours, then slice or shred it, and serve it with hot Salsa de Chile Morita or another salsa of your choice.

To cook the tongue: Preheat the oven to 325°F / 165°C. Place the tongue in a small to medium heavy-bottom stockpot, in which it just fits snugly. Add the bay leaf, coriander, peppercorns, chiles, thyme, oregano, salt, and garlic, then cover with water. Bring to a boil and then place aluminum foil or an oven-safe lid on the pot and put it in the oven for 3 to 4 hours. After 2 hours, check the temperature of the cooked tongue with a meat thermometer; when the meat is done the temperature should be 160°F / 70°C. You can also test for doneness by seeing if the light skinlike covering on the tongue peels away easily. You want it to be tender but retain its shape rather than shredding when you slice it. Keep cooking until it reaches this temperature and consistency. Alternatively, if you have a slow cooker, it's a great way to cook a tongue. You can cook it on the low setting overnight, and in the morning (after 8 to 10 hours), it will be perfect.

When the tongue is done, remove it from the cooking water and let it cool on a plate or baking sheet. Reserve the liquid in which the tongue has cooked, since it makes a rich and savory base for picadillo (page 296). Once cool, freeze to use later.

Peel away the tongue's skinlike covering and the rough patch beneath the tongue, where it was attached. Slice the tongue crosswise into ¼-inch / 6mm-wide slices.

In a large skillet over medium-high heat, heat the oil until it's shimmering. Add the onion and sauté until it's translucent but not browned. Add the salsa and bring it to a simmer. Add the sliced tongue and stir until it's coated and hot. If you didn't overcook the tongue, it won't fall apart. (Even if you did, it will still taste great.)

Serve over rice or use as a filling for tacos or tortas. Store leftovers in a sealed container in the refrigerator for up to 3 days. To reheat, warm in a saucepan over low heat.

Taco at TACOS DON JUAN, Calle Juan Escuita 35, Condesa

MOLE

The word *mole* comes from the Nahuatl word *molli*, which means "sauce" or "paste" and refers to dishes that combine a variety of roasted chiles, nuts, seeds, tomatoes, broth, and other ingredients, all ground to a smooth and unctuous paste that goes into a sauce served over protein or vegetables. In the old days, and in rural villages still, this grinding was done by hand in a metate (a rough stone mill), which is probably one of the reasons many people think making mole is laborious. But now with great blenders, the most difficult part of mole making has been reduced to the push of a button.

While moles are not hard to make, most do have a lot of ingredients that have to be handled in a variety of ways. The trick is not to skip any of these ingredients—because each matters—and to go through the steps of coaxing the maximum flavor out of everything. You toast and soak chiles. You roast and grind spices, tomatoes, onion, and garlic. You fry raisins or prunes and sometimes bread or crackers, too. But in the end, everything gets blended together, and as the concoction simmers, all of those flavors meld into a sauce that tastes as rich and nuanced as its many components. In a good mole, you can't really pick out particular flavors anymore, although your mouth can tell how much is going on.

A mole can serve as the base for just about any kind of meat or vegetable. And while the sauce will taste good right after you make it, it'll be even better the next day, when the flavors have fully emerged. They can be served as a stew over rice or used to make enchiladas. Whichever way you go, they're bound to be a hit at parties, which is when I remember eating mole as a child. In Tepoztlán, women from town would always make mole for occasions when a crowd needed to be fed. To me, red mole made by our late neighbor Estela forms the standard against which I judge other moles (and they never quite measure up).

There are so many ingredients in this dish that when I set out to re-create it, I couldn't remember them all, and my first guess tasted off. I knew that Herlinda and Laura, the women who help out at my parents' house, still make the mole in the traditional Tepoztecan way. So I called Laura and she

gave me her list of ingredients, which included Ritz crackers and Abuelita chocolate—the round disks of chocolate sold at Mexican markets. I don't like to cook with processed foods, but I trusted these ladies, and as soon as this sauce started simmering, I could smell that my trust had paid off.

This mole also has no fewer than seven kinds of nuts and seeds, plus raisins, plantains, and a variety of spices in small quantities that are nonetheless important for what they bring to the finished product: a refined sauce in which you can taste the complexity but nothing overwhelms the balance of the flavors as they meld together into something velvety, and unmistakably special.

People in Mexico use different kinds of chiles and nuts for their moles. Mine uses only the chile mulato. Like the ancho, it's a smoked poblano but darker, not especially spicy, and delicately smoky. This is part of what makes my mole a great party food. When serving a crowd, you don't want something so spicy that it could turn off guests who can't handle heat.

Unlike the other recipes in this book, for the Mole Rojo (page 283) I've written the recipe to serve 10 to 12. You can certainly cut it in half, but I really think that if you're going to take the time to make this dish, then you should do it for a party. This sauce is rich enough that you could eat a cup ladled onto rice and be quite satisfied. It needs no other garnish or accompaniment, though hot tortillas are always welcome on the side.

I've asked you to sear your chicken and then add it to the sauce to finish cooking. If you make it this way, I recommend serving each piece of chicken over white rice. Another option is to use poached chicken and shred it as you would for a tinga (see page 268), so that it's thoroughly incorporated into the sauce. This is what I'd recommend if you intend to use this as a filling for tacos or enchiladas.

Before you tackle this dish, read through the steps and prepare your ingredients. Nothing you'll be doing is difficult; there are just a lot of steps. Your goal is to get maximum flavor out of the ingredients by toasting the ones that need toasting, soaking the ones that need soaking, frying the ones that need frying, and eventually blending everything together. Have a big bowl ready to hold the components as you toast and fry them. Making the mole is no more difficult than making a smoothie, which certainly wasn't true back when people had to do all of the grinding by hand!

POLLO O PUERCO EN MOLE VERDE
CHICKEN OR PORK IN GREEN MOLE

MAKES 4 TO 6 SERVINGS

2 Tbsp olive oil

1½ lb / 650g skin-on chicken thighs or boneless pork shoulder, cut into 1- to 2-inch / 2.5 to 5cm cubes

2½ cups / 300g pumpkin seeds

1 white onion, quartered

2 garlic cloves

4 serrano chiles, stemmed, seeded, and veins removed (or not, depending on how spicy you want this to be)

6 cups / 1.4L Caldo de Pollo (page 88)

2 cups / 40g cilantro stems and leaves

2 lb / 910g green beans, cut into 1-inch / 2.5cm pieces

2 Tbsp sea salt, plus more as needed

1 recipe Arroz (page 77) or cooked egg noodles

Growing up in Italy, my mom never learned to love spicy food the way the rest of us do. That's why this is her favorite mole, because it's so mild. Unlike the red mole on page 281, which contains seven kinds of nuts and seeds, this one has only pumpkin seeds, which have a less pronounced flavor than some other nuts but make the sauce thick and rich. The green color comes from an abundance of cilantro as well as from a few serrano chiles. The leftovers from this green mole are outstanding served on fettuccine, as the sauce clings perfectly to the noodles. This is a tradition that we began in my house because my dad makes the best fresh pasta, and has done so ever since I can remember. In fact, this recipe turns out so well that I've made mole verde to use as pasta sauce. It's not that crazy, especially since it's a relatively quick and easy sauce to make (at least compared to the red mole).

———————

Warm the oil in a large skillet over medium-high heat. Once the oil is shimmering, sear the chicken or pork in batches, being careful not to crowd the pan. (Normally you salt meat when you sear it, but you don't want to salt a green mole until the last minute because salt can cause it to turn watery.) Sear the meat on all sides, until it is noticeably browned but not cooked through. Transfer the seared meat to a plate and set it aside while you make the sauce.

In a dry skillet over medium-high heat, toast the pumpkin seeds until they turn golden brown, being careful to stir them regularly so they don't burn.

In the jar of a blender, grind the pumpkin seeds. Add the onion, garlic, and chiles and pulse to puree. Add 3 cups / 720ml of the stock with the cilantro, and pulse to liquefy. Pour the contents of the blender into a large Dutch oven or heavy-bottom pot and turn the heat to medium-low. Cook, stirring, until the sauce is simmering, about 15 minutes. Add the chicken or pork, cover the pot, and cook over low heat for about 45 minutes, until the sauce is thick and the meat is tender and beginning to fall apart. Add the green beans and the salt and cook for 10 to 15 minutes more. Taste and add more salt if needed.

Serve with the rice or over the egg noodles. The mole can be stored in a sealed container in the refrigerator for 3 to 5 days.

MOLE ROJO DE TEPOZTLÁN RED MOLE FROM TEPOZTLÁN

The night before a big party in Tepoztlán, our late neighbor Estela would be assisted by a bunch of other ladies in making a humongous vat of this mole and a towering stack of tortillas. The parties in Tepoztlán go on and on. People just come to the house whenever and stay for hours, and there's a bottomless pot of mole for everyone to enjoy. Just as there are so many components in a mole, each adding its own unique flavor to the finished sauce, every person who comes to one of these parties brings their unique personality to the mix. Although the finished sauce is flavorful, it won't burn anyone's mouth and will appeal to guests regardless of whether or not they like spicy food.

———————

First, lightly toast the chiles by placing them on a hot, ungreased comal or in a skillet over medium heat, turning them constantly as they heat up and begin to release their fragrance. Before they turn brown, remove them from the heat and submerge them in a bowl of water to let them soak and soften while you prepare everything else.

Next, you are going to toast all of the spices on your hot, dry comal or in an ungreased skillet. You should do this in batches because they have different toasting times, beginning with the ones that will toast the fastest: the anise and cumin. As soon as you can smell these toasted seeds, take them off the comal or skillet and place them in a spice grinder. Now do the same with the peppercorns, allspice, cloves, and cinnamon stick. After they're toasted, add them to your spice grinder and grind the spices together. Dump the ground spices into a large bowl. You will be frying things in batches that you will be adding to this bowl. Eventually, all of this will go into the blender, but for now, you need a place to store the mole ingredients as you prepare them to be blended together.

Now sear the chicken that you are going to cook in the sauce. Melt 4 Tbsp / 50g of the lard in a Dutch oven or large heavy-bottom skillet over medium-high heat. When the lard has melted completely and is shimmering, place as many pieces of the chicken in the pot as you can fit without crowding. The goal here is to brown each piece, so be sure they're not overlapping. Sprinkle them lightly with salt and flip them over so that both sides get seared. When they look golden, using tongs, transfer them to a platter and repeat with the rest of the chicken pieces, adding more lard to the pan as needed. The chicken should be just seared and not be cooked though at this stage because it will continue cooking in the mole sauce.

MAKES 10 TO 12 SERVINGS

9 oz / 255g mulato chiles, stemmed and seeded
Pinch of aniseeds
Pinch of cumin seeds
2 black peppercorns
2 allspice berries
2 cloves
½ cinnamon stick
4 to 6 Tbsp / 50 to 75g lard
2 whole chickens, cut into serving-size pieces
¼ cup / 30g pine nuts
3 Tbsp / 30 g pumpkin seeds
Scant ¼ cup / 30g black raisins
3 Tbsp / 30 g almonds
¼ cup / 30g hazelnuts
3 Tbsp / 30 g peanuts
¼ cup / 30g pecans
3 Tbsp / 30 g sesame seeds
6 Ritz or other rich-tasting crackers
1 corn tortilla
2 slices fluffy white bread (dinner roll or ciabatta)
½ white onion, coarsely chopped
2 Roma tomatoes, cored and quartered
1 very ripe (black) plantain, peeled and cut into chunks
1 large garlic clove
5 oz / 140g semisweet chocolate
¼ cup / 60ml water
6 cups / 1.4L Caldo de Pollo (page 88)

CONTINUED

Once you're finished searing the chicken, keep whatever grease and drippings remain in the Dutch oven or skillet to fry other things. You want about ½ inch / 12mm of shimmering oil in the bottom of the pan, and you will have to add more lard as needed. You are going to be frying the nuts and seeds in batches because, depending on their sizes, they will cook at different rates. You are looking for each thing to turn golden but not dark brown.

Begin with the pine nuts, pumpkin seeds, and raisins. Once you can smell the fragrance of these nuts and seeds and they look golden, remove them with a slotted spoon and place them in the big bowl with the spices. Now fry the almonds, hazelnuts, peanuts, and pecans until they are fragrant and golden and then add them to the big bowl. Fry the sesame seeds by themselves, being extra careful to monitor them the whole time and moving them around with a wooden spoon or spatula as they fry because they can burn quickly. Add the sesame seeds to the big bowl.

Remember to add more lard to the pan when you need it, since the nuts and seeds will likely have soaked it up. Once the added lard has melted and is shimmering, fry the Ritz crackers very briefly, because they burn fast, then the tortilla, and finally the bread, placing it all in the big bowl with all of the previously toasted and fried ingredients. Add more lard if needed and fry the onion, tomatoes, plantain, and garlic until everything is golden and a bit stewy, then add it all to the big bowl.

In a small saucepot, combine the chocolate with the water and heat until the chocolate melts. Turn off the heat while you blend your sauce ingredients.

Due to the amount of volume here, you are going to need to blend your sauce in batches. Know that from this point on, everything is getting blended together and then simmered, so the order in which you blend things doesn't much matter. You want a ratio of about 1:1 of stock to solid ingredients. I would suggest blending a couple of cups of solids at a time (4 cups / 960ml total, including the stock). When the contents of the blender are liquefied, dump it into your largest stockpot and then repeat the process. Finally, blend the soaked chiles with the remaining stock and add this to your pot, along with the melted chocolate, and stir well to combine.

Bring the mole to a simmer over medium-low heat. Drop the chicken into the pot and cover. Let it simmer for 20 to 25 minutes, then serve. The mole can be stored in a sealed container in the refrigerator for 3 to 4 days or frozen for up to 3 months.

ENCHILADAS DE POLLO EN MOLE ROJO
CHICKEN ENCHILADAS IN RED MOLE

Red mole makes an excellent enchilada filling, which is my favorite way to use the leftovers. Take whatever pieces of chicken remain, remove the meat from the bone, and shred it finely. If you happen to have a lot of sauce but less chicken in your mole, you can add more chicken by poaching and shredding a couple of chicken breasts (see page 88) or even by shredding a chicken breast from a store-bought roasted chicken. What really matters is the sauce.

_____

Preheat the oven to 350°F / 180°C.

Remove the cooked chicken from the mole. Take the meat off the bone and shred it finely.

Coat the bottom of a 9 x 13-inch / 23 x 33cm baking dish with mole about ⅜ inch / 1cm deep. Pour off about 1 cup / 240ml of the mole into a shallow bowl.

In a skillet over medium heat, heat the oil until it's shimmering. Fry one tortilla at a time, flipping after about 1 minute so that both sides are golden. Once heated, use tongs to dip both sides of the tortilla in the bowl of mole.

Lay the tortilla on a plate and fill with about 2 Tbsp of the shredded chicken. Roll it into a cigar shape and place in the pan. Repeat with each tortilla until the pan is full. Cover with the remaining mole and sprinkle with the cheese.

Cover the pan with aluminum foil and bake for 15 minutes. Then remove the foil and bake for an additional 5 minutes, until the top is bubbling and lightly browned. Serve with the pickled onions, avocado, and cilantro.

MAKES 4 TO 6 SERVINGS

3 cups / 720ml leftover Mole Rojo de Tepoztlán (page 281)
¼ cup / 60ml safflower oil
12 to 18 Tortillas de Maiz (page 72)
1 cup / 80g shredded queso Oaxaca, queso Chihuahua, or whole-milk mozzarella (optional)
1 recipe Cebollas Rojas Encurtidas (page 39)
1 avocado, cut in half, pitted, peeled, and sliced
¼ cup / 5g minced cilantro leaves

MOLE AMARILLO CON CHOCHOYOTES
YELLOW MOLE WITH MASA DUMPLINGS

MAKES 4 TO 6 SERVINGS

6 guajillo chiles, stemmed, seeded, and torn into strips
1 cup / 240ml water, plus more if needed
1 cinnamon stick
2 allspice berries
½ tsp cumin seeds
1 tsp dried oregano
2 Roma tomatoes, cored and cut in half
2 tomatillos, papery husks removed and discarded, rinsed
1 white onion, cut in half
2 garlic cloves
1 hoja santa leaf, torn into pieces, or packed ¼ cup / 5g cilantro leaves and ¼ cup / 5g minced parsley
3 Tbsp / 45ml safflower oil
5 cups / 1.2L vegetable stock (see page 31)
1 cup plus 3 Tbsp / 310g fresh masa or 1 cup plus 3 Tbsp / 155g masa harina
2 Tbsp unsalted butter, softened
1 tsp sea salt
2 Yukon gold potatoes, cut into 1-inch / 2.5cm cubes
2 small yellow squash, cut into 1-inch / 2.5cm rings
1 lb / 455g green beans, cut into 1-inch / 2.5cm pieces on the diagonal
1 recipe Arroz (page 77)

This is one mole that's quite speedy to put together. It's called a yellow mole because it was traditionally made with the yellow chilhuacle chile, which grows in one region of Oaxaca. This chile is expensive to produce and difficult to find even in most parts of Mexico, so people have found different hacks to approximate the yellow color, such as using saffron or a pinch of achiote. I don't think this cosmetic fix is necessary. Guajillo chile works well in this sauce instead of the chilhuacle, although expect the mole to look more orange than yellow. I have made this recipe vegetarian, since the masa balls that cook in the sauce give it substance, so instead of making them with lard I use butter. But feel free to add meat if you'd like. It would be delicious with shrimp or shellfish, in which case I'd use seafood stock instead of vegetable stock, and I'd let the seafood simmer in the mole for just a few minutes at the end. You can also adapt this recipe to use other vegetables that are in season. In the winter, butternut squash and mushrooms would be delicious instead of the summer squash and green beans.

———————

Place your chile strips in an ungreased comal or skillet over medium-high heat and toast them lightly to bring out their flavor. Remember that you just want to heat them up, not brown them, so move them around and take them off the comal as soon as you can smell them, before they smoke or smell burnt. This should take only 1 to 2 minutes. Once the strips are lightly toasted, place them in the jar of a blender together with the water and let them soak and soften while you toast the rest of the spices.

Add the cinnamon, allspice, and cumin seeds to the hot comal and move them around as they toast. After 1 to 2 minutes, when you can smell them, remove the cinnamon stick and set it aside. Grind the toasted allspice and cumin seeds in a spice grinder and add them to the blender, or, if your blender is strong enough to pulverize them, skip the spice grinder and add them whole. Add the oregano.

Now roast the tomatoes, tomatillos, onion, and garlic on the comal or in the skillet over medium-high heat, flipping them over every minute or so until they are lightly charred all over and the tomatoes are slumping and releasing their juices. This should take about 5 minutes. Then add them to the blender. Toss in the hoja santa leaf or cilantro and parsley and liquefy.

In a 4- to 6-qt / 3.8 to 5.7L Dutch oven or heavy-bottom pot, warm the oil over medium-high heat until it's shimmering but not smoking. Holding a strainer over the pot, pour the contents of the blender through the strainer into the hot oil. Fry the contents of the blender, stirring constantly, until your sauce has turned a darker red and absorbed the oil. Then add the stock and the 3 Tbsp / 50g of the fresh masa or 3 Tbsp / 25g of the masa harina and the reserved cinnamon stick. Whisk the sauce while it comes to a boil and begins to thicken slightly. Then decrease the heat slightly and simmer for about 15 minutes, stirring the sauce with your whisk every 5 minutes or so to make sure it doesn't clump or stick to the bottom.

Meanwhile, place the remaining 1 cup / 260g fresh masa in a bowl. Alternatively, place the remaining 1 cup / 130g masa harina in a bowl, add ¾ cup / 180ml water, and knead until the masa harina has the consistency of stiff cookie dough. Add the butter and salt and continue kneading for another few minutes, until the butter is well incorporated. Divide the dough into 1-inch / 2.5cm pieces, rolling them into balls and pressing each ball between your thumb and finger so that it's lightly dimpled. Set these dumplings aside.

Add the potatoes to the simmering sauce and cook for 10 minutes. Then add the squash, beans, and masa dumplings and cook for 10 minutes more, until the dumplings are set.

Serve hot, spooned over rice.

PASTEL AZTECA TORTILLA AND CHICKEN CASSEROLE

MAKES 4 TO 6 SERVINGS

2 poached chicken breasts (see
    page 88)
1 qt / 960ml Caldo de Pollo
    (page 88)
2 canned chipotle chiles in adobo,
    plus 2 Tbsp of the sauce
2 garlic cloves
4 Roma tomatoes, cored
2 Tbsp tomato paste
½ white onion, chopped
2 tsp sea salt
2 Tbsp olive oil
12 Tortillas de Maiz (page 72)
1½ cups / 120g shredded toma,
    a blend of sharp Cheddar
    and whole-milk mozzarella, or
    another good melting cheese
½ cup / 120g Crema Ácida
    (page 65) or crème fraîche
Minced cilantro

Pastel Azteca is a cross between lasagna and enchiladas. Instead of noodles, we use tortillas, layered with shredded chicken, cheese, and sauce and then baked until bubbly and golden. This tends to be a universal crowd-pleaser because, frankly, what's not to like? The following recipe should be treated as a template. You can make it as is—using poached chicken and a chipotle sauce—but really this is a great way to use up things in your fridge. I call for toma cheese, but if you have a different cheese that melts well, such as a whole-milk mozzarella or even a Cheddar that you could mix it with, that will work perfectly, too. Instead of chicken, you could make a vegetarian version with sautéed mushrooms or braised greens. It's a delicious vehicle for Papas con Rajas y Crema (page 222). Instead of red sauce, a salsa verde or salsa de chile morita would also be delicious in a pastel azteca. Serve with soupy black beans on the side.

_____

Using two forks, finely shred the chicken.

Oil a lasagna pan or similar low-sided casserole dish and preheat the oven to 350°F / 180°C.

In the jar of a blender, combine the stock, chiles and adobo sauce, garlic, tomatoes, tomato paste, onion, and 1 tsp of the salt and liquefy.

In a medium saucepan over medium-high heat, heat the oil until it's shimmering but not smoking. Pour the contents of the blender over the hot oil and bring to a boil, then turn off the heat.

Ladle about one-quarter of the sauce over the bottom of the prepared lasagna pan or casserole dish. Add 4 tortillas to the bottom of the pan, arranging them in one layer. Distribute one-quarter of the chicken over the tortillas. Top with one-quarter of the cheese. Repeat to make two more layers of sauce, tortillas, chicken, and cheese, until you have used up all of your ingredients, being sure to finish with cheese as your top layer.

Cover the pan with aluminum foil and bake for 15 minutes. Then remove the foil and bake for an additional 5 minutes. As soon as it's bubbling on the sides and the cheese is golden brown, it's ready to eat. Place a spoonful of crema ácida or crème fraîche and a scattering of minced cilantro on each helping.

Pastel azteca can be eaten immediately while hot, or it can be stored in a sealed container in the refrigerator for 3 to 5 days and tastes great as leftovers.

POZOLE BLANCO HOMINY AND PORK SOUP

In Tepoztlán, there's a popular street food stall that people go to late at night for steaming bowls of pozole blanco, a slow-cooked stew made from pork and hominy. It's another typical party food in Mexico, because it's festive, feeds a crowd, and everything is ready ahead of time. Mexican pozole blanco is typically made with the head of a pig. The cartilage makes the broth deliciously gelatinous, and people are given crunchy bits of the ears to enjoy. This isn't such a popular taste in the United States, so here I use stew meat from the pork shoulder or butt. You can tell a good pozole blanco by the clarity of the broth. The key is to skim the foam that rises to the top of the pot when the pork comes to a simmer. If you don't skim, the broth will turn brown. (It'll still taste good, but it will look muddy.)

You'll need a few hours for the whole corn kernels to "flower," or soften and expand in boiling water with a little "cal," or calcium oxide, which is the same lime that nixtamalizes the corn to make masa. (If you're not familiar with powdered lime, its real name is calcium oxide, and it's a fine white powder sold in Mexican markets with the dried spices.) While that's happening, your pork will be simmering in another pot, and eventually you'll combine the two. Not much else goes into this soup, but at the table, diners pick and choose from bowls of minced onion, radishes, shredded cabbage, and sliced avocado to garnish their individual servings. Most people go for a generous squeeze of lime, but it's up to you if you want to add a pinch (or more) of ground chile.

Often in Mexico, pozole is left to simmer softly overnight in a pot with a lid on. The longer it slow-cooks, the better it will taste. Once your guests arrive, you'll have nothing to do but enjoy eating with them.

Place the corn in a large stockpot and fill it with water to cover the corn by 3 inches / 7.5cm. In a separate cup, stir the powdered lime with a few tablespoons of water until it dissolves.

Add the dissolved lime to the pot with the corn kernels, bring the water to a boil over high heat, then decrease the heat, and simmer, covered, for 20 to 30 minutes. The corn should be yellow, and the outer skins will now slough off, though they tend to dissolve, so you may not notice them. Drain the hominy in a colander and rinse under cold water until it's cool enough to handle. Now it's up to you if you want to remove the pedicel—the darker-colored nub that connected the kernel to the cob. To do so, you need to use a paring knife or your fingernail

CONTINUED

1 lb / 455g (about 2 cups) dried pozole corn, preferably white and not red

1 Tbsp powdered lime (calcium oxide)

2 lb / 910g bone-in pork shoulder, cut into several large pieces

3 Tbsp / 45g sea salt, plus more to taste

1 white onion, minced

3 garlic cloves, halved

8 radishes, thinly sliced

¼ head white cabbage, shredded

1 or 2 avocados, cut in half, pitted, peeled, and thinly sliced

3 or 4 limes, cut into wedges

12 Tortillas de Maiz (see page 72), fried and broken into pieces, or good quality tortilla chips

Ground chiles de árbol

to nick off each one. This takes time, but it will result in a more refined pozole with a more uniform texture. Rinse out your large soup pot. Refill the pot with water and return the hominy to the pot. Bring to a simmer, cover, and cook for about 2 hours.

While the hominy is cooking, place the pork in another stockpot and cover with 10 to 12 cups / 2.4 to 2.8L water, or enough to cover the pork by at least 5 to 6 inches / 13 to 15cm. Bring the water to a boil over high heat. Within a few minutes, you will notice a lot of gray foam rising to the surface of the roiling water. You want to skim this off, using a slotted spoon, as soon as you can. If you leave it in, it will tint the soup so that it's no longer blanco, or white. You may need to skim the foam off a few times before the pork stops releasing it. Once the broth is clear and foam free, add the salt, half the onion, and the garlic. Decrease the heat to low, cover, and simmer very gently for 3 to 4 hours, until the meat is visibly falling apart.

Check to make sure that the corn is soft enough and simmer for up to 30 minutes longer, if needed. Taste and add more salt if needed. Drain the hominy and add the cooked kernels to the pork soup.

At this point, you can serve the soup right away or chill it overnight, which will lead to a more complex flavor when you reheat it the next day.

Ladle the pozole into big bowls, leaving enough room for guests to add the remaining onion and the radishes, cabbage, avocados, limes, tortilla chips, and ground chile as they wish.

Pozole can be stored in a sealed container in the refrigerator for 3 to 4 days.

Pozole, in Tepoztlán

COSTILLAR DE CERDO EN RECADO NEGRO
GRILLED PORK TENDERLOIN IN CHARRED-CHILE ADOBO

MAKES 6 TO 8 SERVINGS

8 cascabel chiles, stemmed
    and seeded
3 ancho chiles, stemmed
    and seeded
3 guajillo chiles, stemmed
    and seeded
3 pasilla chiles, stemmed
    and seeded
6 Fresno chiles, stemmed, cut in
    half, seeded, and veins removed
    (or not, depending on how spicy
    you want this to be)
6 garlic cloves
4 Tortillas de Maiz (page 72), plus
    more, warmed
1 tsp dried oregano
½ tsp cumin seeds
3 cloves
1 tsp allspice berries
2 cups freshly squeezed orange
    juice
½ cup / 130g sea salt
2 (1 lb / 455g) pork tenderloins,
    trimmed and silver skin removed
1 recipe Guacamole (page 60)
1 recipe Salsa Roja Asada (page
    48), Salsa Verde (page 50), or
    another salsa of your choosing
Lime wedges

A recado negro is a black mole. In the recipes before this one, you've been asked to pay close and careful attention while roasting your dried chiles to make sure they never get blistered or burned. To make a recado negro, however, you do just the opposite, and char them until they're nearly crumbling to ash. That's where the flavor in this dish comes from. The good news is, you can't ruin it as a result of inattention. The blacker and more pungent your paste, the better. But just be sure to open your windows before you let your spices char, or you'll set off your smoke alarm!

Preheat the oven to 500°F / 260°C.

On a rimmed baking sheet, toast the cascabel, ancho, guajillo, and pasilla chiles until completely blackened—about 5 minutes. Transfer to a large bowl and cover with cold water. Let them soak and soften for about 30 minutes, then drain.

While the chiles are soaking, toast the Fresno chiles, garlic, and tortillas on the same rimmed baking sheet that you used to roast the dried chiles for 12 to 15 minutes, until blackened and charred.

On an ungreased comal or in a small skillet over medium-high heat, toast the oregano and cumin seeds, agitating constantly, for 1 to 2 minutes. When you can smell their toasted fragrance, transfer them to a small bowl. In the same comal or skillet, char the cloves and allspice for about 4 minutes, until black and ashy.

In the jar of a blender, puree the softened dried chiles, fresno chiles, garlic, toasted tortillas, oregano, cumin seeds, cloves, allspice, orange juice, and salt. Place the tenderloins in a large bowl and pour the contents of the blender over the meat, submerging it completely. Cover and refrigerate for at least 6 hours or up to 12 hours.

Heat a grill to medium or a grill pan over medium-low heat. Grill the pork, turning it once after the first 20 minutes, until a meat thermometer inserted into the thickest part of the meat reads 145°F / 63°C; this should take 35 to 45 minutes total.

Let the meat rest on a cutting board for 15 minutes before slicing thinly. Serve with the warmed tortillas, guacamole, salsa, and lime.

COCHINITA PIBIL SLOW-COOKED PORK IN ACHIOTE

Cochinita Pibil is a very Yucatecan way of slow-cooking pork after marinating it in orange juice and achiote paste and wrapping it in banana leaves. In the Yucatán they use naranja agria—a species of orange that is more bitter than the common Valencia oranges, but the sweetness of regular oranges is fine. After it slow-cooks, the pork should be falling apart and shreddy. It's a very popular dish that gets eaten every which way, including served with beans and tortillas, used in tamales and tacos, and as a main dish with rice. Feel free to cook this and use it as you'd like. My favorite is to put the leftovers on a torta (sandwich) with refried beans, avocado, and pickled onions. In fact, I often make cochinita pibil just so that I have enough to use in this way for days to come.

MAKES 4 TO 6 SERVINGS

3 or 4 large banana leaves
3 Tbsp / 40g achiote (annatto) seeds
Juice of 2 oranges
2 Tbsp sea salt
1 (2 lb / 910g) bone-in pork shoulder or butt

Prepare the banana leaves by running them swiftly over the flame of your burner. You're not looking to toast them, but the heat of the fire loosens the fibers and makes the leaves more pliable.

Grind the achiote seeds in a mortar and pestle or a spice grinder. Add the orange juice and salt. It should make a very liquidy paste. Rub the pork shoulder all over with it and marinate it in the refrigerator for at least 1 hour but preferably overnight.

When you are ready to cook it, preheat the oven to 200°F / 95°C.

Wrap the marinated pork in the banana leaves, enveloping it entirely like a parcel, and place in a baking dish. Bake for 6 hours. Then remove the banana leaves, increase the oven temperature to 350°F / 180°C, and bake for an additional 30 minutes so that it develops a nice crust.

Leftover cochinita pibil can be stored in a sealed container in the refrigerator for up to 4 days.

PUERCO O POLLO AL PASTOR
MEXICO CITY'S UBIQUITOUS ACHIOTE-MARINATED PORK OR CHICKEN

If there is one dish associated with Mexico City, it would have to be tacos al pastor. These are to Mexico City what cheesesteaks are to Philadelphia and poutine is to Montreal. If you've ever walked around Mexico City, no doubt you've noticed people making and selling tacos al pastor. The bright red-tinted meat (usually pork but also chicken) rotates around and around on a gas-fueled grill, topped by a big chunk of roasting pineapple. Thin slices of this grilled meat get hacked off and served on tortillas with bits of the pineapple. If it reminds you of gyros and kebabs, there's a good reason. The story goes that we incorporated this dish into Mexican cuisine after an early wave of Arab immigration. Of course we had to Mexicanize it by making it more spicy and tropical.

While this is definitely street food, and few people have the equipment to rotate pork on a spit, you can get the basic taste of this dish by marinating and sautéing chopped pork or chicken. It's also a delicious marinade for vegetables such as eggplant or zucchini. Just be sure to serve it with cara-melized pineapple—that completes the dish.

_____

Rub the slices of meat with the salt and then place them in a bowl, cover with the adobo sauce, and marinate in the refrigerator for at least 1 hour or preferably overnight.

When you're ready to continue, begin by making the caramelized pineapple chunks. In a skillet over medium heat, cook the pineapple with the sugar, stirring constantly so that it doesn't burn, for about 5 minutes, until the chunks are translucent but not falling apart. Remove from the heat and let them cool slightly while you cook the pork.

Heat the oil in a large skillet over medium-high heat until it's shimmering. Add the pork in its marinade and cook at a low simmer for 5 to 7 minutes. You want some of the marinade to cook off so that it's not too wet.

On an ungreased comal or in a small skillet, warm the tortillas and place in a basket or a box with a lid to keep warm.

Serve the pork and pineapple with the tortillas and bowls of the onion, cilantro, and salsa to spoon on as garnishes.

MAKES 4 TO 6 SERVINGS

2 to 3 lb / 910g to 1.4kg pork tenderloin, cut into thin (almost bite-size) slices, or 2 to 3 lb / 910g to 1.4kg boneless, skinless chicken breasts, cut into thin slices

2 Tbsp sea salt

1 cup / 240ml Adobo de Chiles Rojos (page 58)

1 cup / 100g small chunks pineapple

1 Tbsp granulated sugar

2 Tbsp safflower oil

8 to 12 Tortillas de Maiz (page 72)

1 small white onion, finely minced

½ cup / 10g cilantro leaves, minced

1 recipe Salsa Verde (page 50)

ALBÓNDIGAS EN SALSA DE CHILE MORITA
MEATBALLS WITH MORITA CHILE SAUCE

MAKES 4 TO 6 SERVINGS

Meatballs
1 lb / 455g ground beef
1 lb / 455g ground pork
5 oz / 140g chicharrónes, ground
    with a mortar and pestle or
    finely chopped
¾ cup / 90g minced onions
2 eggs
2 garlic cloves, chopped
½ cup / 10g parsley leaves,
    chopped
½ tsp sea salt
2 Tbsp olive oil

Salsa de Chile Morita for Meatballs
1½ cups / 360ml vegetable oil
2 dried moritas chiles
8 Roma tomatoes, cored
1 white onion, chopped
1 garlic clove, chopped
1 Tbsp sea salt
Pinch of freshly ground black
    pepper
1 tsp dried oregano
½ cup / 120ml olive oil

Instead of spaghetti and meatballs, try these Mexican meatballs with rice. Traditionally, albóndigas are often served in a soup, but I love them simmered in this sauce, made smoky by morita chiles, which are dried and smoked jalapeños. This dish is not that spicy, however, and goes perfectly with rice and avocado. In addition to ground beef and pork, these meatballs include pulverized chicharrónes, which are fried pork rinds. I'm able to find them behind the meat counter at Mexican markets near me, but if you can't find them, feel free to use the chicharrónes that come in bags like potato chips. Crushed and added to the ground meat, they will work just fine. Serve these with rice, black beans, tortillas, and avocado.

──────────

To make the meatballs: In a large bowl, combine the ground beef and pork, chicharrónes, onion, eggs, garlic, parsley, and salt until well combined. Form the mixture into 2½-inch / 6cm balls.

Line a plate with a brown paper bag. Heat the olive oil in a skillet over medium-high heat. Once it's shimmering, gently drop the meatballs into the skillet and sear them on all sides, just to get them browned (but not cooked all the way through). If needed, do this in batches. Once seared, remove them from the oil and place them on the plate while you prepare the salsa.

To make the salsa: Pour the vegetable oil into a Dutch oven or other heavy-bottom pot over high heat. Fry the chiles, with their stems still on, for 1 to 2 minutes. As soon as they puff up, remove them from the oil (but keep the oil in the pan and turn off the heat). Once they're cool enough to handle, remove their stems and shake out and discard their seeds. Place the fried chiles in the jar of a blender.

Place the tomatoes in the same pot with the oil in which you fried the chiles and cook over medium-high heat, until their skins brown and they slump. Carefully transfer them with the slotted spoon to the jar of the blender with the chiles.

Add the onion and garlic to the pot and sauté until translucent, pour them and the remaining oil from the pot into the blender. Add the salt, pepper, oregano, and olive oil and puree everything together.

Pour the blended sauce into your Dutch oven or pot. Bring it to a boil over medium-high heat, then decrease to a simmer. Add the seared meatballs and simmer for about 20 minutes.

The meatballs can be stored in a sealed container in the refrigerator for up to 4 days.

PICADILLO GROUND BEEF HASH

MAKES 4 TO 6 SERVINGS

2 Tbsp lard
½ lb / 230g ground beef
2 tsp sea salt
½ white onion, minced
1 carrot, minced
2 garlic cloves, minced
Pinch of ground cumin
1 cup / 240ml beef stock (see page 303) or tongue broth (reserved from braised tongue, page 272)
1 Tbsp Adobo de Chiles Rojos (page 58; optional)
1 Tbsp Salsa Negra (page 56; optional)

Nearly every culture seems to have a staple dish made from seasoned and stewed ground beef. In Italy, there's the Bolognese. In Mexico, we have picadillo. This is no doubt the origin of the "seasoned ground beef" that went into the first incarnation of US tacos. For extra richness, I start by searing chunks of ground beef in lard, then simmer the meat with minced carrot and onion in a tongue broth. Beef broth works, too, but tongue stock imparts an added depth. If you happen to have any salsa adobo (see page 58) or salsa negra (page 56) in your refrigerator, adding a spoonful of one (or both) at the end will bring more layers of flavor.

Picadillo makes a great guiso for tacos, and it's also a wonderful filling for Chiles Rellenos (page 226).

_____

In a medium skillet over medium-high heat, heat the lard until it's bubbling. Drop quarter-size pieces of ground beef into the pan and let them sear, turning the chunks over with a spatula so they brown on all sides. Add 1 tsp of the salt. Once the chunks of beef are browned (but not thoroughly cooked), use a slotted spoon to transfer them from the pan to a plate. Don't rinse out the pan.

In the same pan used to sear the beef, fry the onion and carrot. Once the onion is golden and the carrot has softened, add the remaining 1 tsp salt, the garlic, and cumin and cook while stirring for about 1 minute, until you can smell the spices toasting. Return the meat to the pan. Add the stock and use a large wooden spoon or potato masher to break the meat into smaller pieces. Cover the pan and let it simmer for about 10 minutes so that the flavors meld together. Remove the lid and cook for another 2 minutes, until most of the liquid has been absorbed and/or has evaporated.

As a final step, stir in the salsa for added flavor, if desired.

Store in the refrigerator for up 3 days. To reheat, warm in a skillet over low heat.

COSTRADA DE ARROZ
BAKED RICE AND GROUND BEEF CASSEROLE

MAKES 6 TO 8 SERVINGS

¼ cup / 55g unsalted butter

Rice
1 qt / 960ml water
½ white onion, sliced
3 garlic cloves
2 jalapeños
1½ tsp saffron
1 tsp sea salt
2 cups / 400g white rice
    (preferably medium grain)

Picadillo
2 Tbsp safflower oil
½ white onion, chopped
½ large red bell pepper, chopped
1 lb / 455g ground beef or pork or
    a combination of the two
Healthy pinch of freshly ground
    black pepper
Pinch of ground cloves
Pinch of ground cinnamon
1 Tbsp raisins, coarsely chopped
2 Tbsp slivered almonds
1 garlic clove, chopped
4 or 5 Roma tomatoes, cored and
    chopped
1 Tbsp coarsely chopped parsley
    leaves
⅓ cup / 40g chopped olives
    (preferably Castelvetrano)
1 Tbsp capers, chopped
2 Tbsp sweet sherry
2 Tbsp apple cider vinegar

1 tsp sea salt, plus more as needed
½ cup / 100g granulated sugar
7 eggs

This savory rice casserole is something that my father's sisters always made for big family get-togethers. This is a recipe from Campeche, in the south of Mexico, where the Cámara family comes from. Beating sugar into eggs, which you blend together with saffron-infused rice, gives the casserole a crispy crust that also lends the dish its name. A savory picadillo gets nestled between two layers of rice.

———————

Preheat the oven to 375°F / 190°C.

Use the full ¼ cup / 55g of butter to thoroughly coat the base and sides of a 9 x 13-inch / 23 x 33cm baking dish. This will help form the crust.

To make the rice: In a 4- to 6-qt / 3.8 to 5.7L Dutch oven or other heavy-bottom pot, combine the water, onion, garlic, jalapeños, saffron, and salt. Bring to a boil over high heat, add the rice, and cover. When the water returns to a boil, decrease the heat so that it barely simmers. Cover and cook for 18 to 20 minutes. Then remove the lid and discard the jalapeños, onion, garlic, and whatever saffron threads may have settled on top of the rice, so that only the rice remains. Gently fluff the rice with a fork and set aside to cool.

While the rice is cooling, make the picadillo: Heat the oil in a large skillet over medium-high heat until it's hot but not smoking. Add the onion and bell pepper and sauté until soft, about 5 minutes. Add the ground meat and break it up with a wooden spoon as it cooks. Once it has browned, add the black pepper, cloves, cinnamon, raisins, almonds, garlic, tomatoes, parsley, olives, capers, sherry, vinegar, and salt. Keep cooking, stirring frequently, until all of the liquid has been absorbed, 10 to 12 minutes. Taste and add more salt if needed.

In a large bowl, combine ¼ cup / 50g of the sugar and the eggs and whisk well. Pour the cooled rice into the bowl and combine with the eggs and sugar. Spoon half of this rice-egg mixture into the buttered casserole dish and press down. Bake for 15 minutes, until the top is set. Remove from the oven and spread the picadillo mixture over the crust of rice. Pour the remaining rice-egg mixture on top of the picadillo and spread evenly, using a spatula. Sprinkle the remaining ¼ cup / 50g sugar on top.

Return to the oven and bake for 7 to 9 minutes, until the top is just turning golden brown. If you want it darker, you can broil it for the final 1 to 2 minutes. Let it cool for 5 minutes before cutting into squares and serving.

Store in a sealed container in the refrigerator for up to 3 days.

CAMOTE A LAS BRASAS CON SALSA NEGRA Y TUÉTANO
CHARRED SWEET POTATOES WITH BLACK SALSA AND ROASTED BONE MARROW

At Cala, we roast bones and emulsify the marrow into our salsa negra to serve with these charred sweet potatoes. We were inspired by the restaurant El Bajío's black sauce, but we've made our adaptations of this unctuous and unique dish that has become a customer favorite. That's why I didn't want to leave it out of this cookbook, although I recognize that the process of scraping out the roasted bone marrow, clarifying, and emulsifying it into the salsa is a bit of a headache and is not something that most people would want to tackle. Roasting bone marrow, however, is incredibly easy. Make sure to ask your butcher to give you grass-fed beef bones cut canoe style (lengthwise) rather than crosswise, since they are often cut to use in soups, and be sure to salt them a lot before you roast them to bring out the flavor. The marrow is then as soft as butter and can be spread on a warm tortilla before you load it up with roasted sweet potato and salsa negra. If I have adventuresome guests coming over, I like to serve this as a kind of cavemen's dinner party, placing one or two roasted bones on each plate alongside half a potato and passing the warm tortillas for people to assemble their own tacos.

MAKES 4 TO 6 SERVINGS

½ cup / 130g sea salt
2 or 3 large orange-fleshed sweet potatoes
4 pasture-raised beef femur bones, split lengthwise
1 recipe Salsa Negra (page 56)
1 recipe Salsa Brava (page 45)
1 recipe Tortillas de Maiz (page 72), warmed
Lime wedges

Preheat the oven to 425°F / 220°C.

Sprinkle ¼ cup / 65g of the sea salt on a plate. Wash the sweet potatoes well. While their skins are wet, roll them in the sea salt so they are as encrusted with salt as possible. Place them on a baking sheet, prick each one a few times with a fork, and bake for 50 to 55 minutes, until tender. Remove from the oven and let them cool while you roast your bones.

Sprinkle the remaining ¼ cup / 65g salt across the cut surfaces of the bones. It may seem like a lot, but this salt is what will bring out the meaty flavor of the roasting marrow. Roast the bones in the oven for 20 minutes, until well browned.

In the last 5 minutes before the bones come out of the oven, char the skin of each of your roasted sweet potatoes, holding them with tongs directly over the flame of your stove top burner and rotating them to char as much of the surface area as possible. You could also do this by placing the sweet potatoes directly on the coals of a grill. The goal is for the skins to get really blackened, but if you

CONTINUED

can't do this at home (if you have an electric stove, for example), this dish will still taste great even without the char.

Split the sweet potatoes in half lengthwise and place half on each plate, along with one roasted bone half. Place bowls of salsa negra and salsa brava on the table and pass a basket of warm tortillas so guests can scoop out the bone marrow, spread some on their tortilla, and top with a dollop of sweet potato and salsa. A few slivers of onion from the salsa brava add a delightful crunch and tang, in contrast to the potato's sweetness, and a squeeze of lime unites the flavors.

SALPICÓN DE RES SHREDDED STEAK SALAD

Many different cultures seem to have their own version of a steak salad. Salpicón de res is Mexico's. Flank steak has a lot of flavor, but as a lean meat, it can be tough. But simmering it for a long time as you do here really tenderizes the steak so that it can be shredded, and it absorbs the vinaigrette together with the romaine lettuce, tomato, and avocado. If you want your salad spicy, feel free to add minced serrano chiles.

I don't begin by salting the water in which I simmer my beef, since I believe that salt leaches the juices of the meat, which I want to retain. Less of the flavor stays in the steak this way. Instead, I add the salt near the end of the process, as I do when cooking beans.

In a Dutch oven or a stockpot, cover the flank steak with the water and add the bay leaves and garlic. Bring to a boil, then decrease the heat and let it simmer for 1½ hours. Add the salt and cook 30 minutes more, until the meat is tender enough to shred easily. Once the steak is tender, let it cool in the water until you can handle it. Then remove the meat from the broth (cool and freeze this broth for another purpose) and shred it.

In a large salad bowl, toss the shredded steak with the romaine, tomato, radishes, and onion.

In a small bowl, whisk together the oil, vinegar, oregano, and lime juice. Pour the vinaigrette over the salad and season with the finishing salt. Toss to coat everything well. Taste and add more finishing salt if needed. Add the avocados and toss gently, so that they don't get mashed. Serve immediately.

MAKES 4 TO 6 SERVINGS

2 lb / 910g flank steak

2 qt / 2L water

2 bay leaves (preferably fresh)

2 garlic cloves

2 Tbsp sea salt

2 heads romaine lettuce, washed and finely chopped

1 large or 2 small tomatoes, cored and finely chopped

6 radishes, thinly sliced

2 Tbsp minced white onion

½ cup / 120ml extra-virgin olive oil

¼ cup / 60ml champagne vinegar or sherry vinegar

1 tsp dried oregano

Juice of 1 lime

1 tsp Maldon sea salt or another finishing salt, plus more as needed

2 avocados, cut in half, pitted, peeled, and cut into ½-inch / 12mm chunks

5 POSTRES

DESSERTS

The truth is, and I know that this makes some people roll their eyes, most of the time I would rather have a perfect piece of fruit at the end of a meal than some heavy pastry. It's not that I don't love great pastry—of course I do—but a juicy mango or ripe peach in the summer, a crisp fall apple, or one of the tangerines or blood oranges that come into season in the winter—these are what appeal to to me on a day-to-day basis. Plus, I usually eat enough at a meal that I am quite full by the end of it.

But of course, life is punctuated by special occasions. Thank goodness! And one of the best and easiest ways to mark a special occasion is with a special dessert. I have to say that at Contramar, the desserts on our massive tray are pretty special. Our tray features everything from the traditional Mexican flan to the less traditional Nutella version and my most favorite in-season dessert of all: a bowl of puree made from zapote negro, which is a species of persimmon. There are also deliciously sweet, ripe mangoes and bowls of different types of berries, depending on the time of year. Then we have our staple billowy strawberry meringue cake that never fails to widen the eyes of children and adults alike. My mother religiously consumes one every time she eats at the restaurant. She got her sweet tooth from Nonna, who could eat more sugar than anyone I know.

The dessert menu at Cala features Mexican desserts that people outside of Mexico might not be familiar with, like buñuelos, which are light, crunchy fritters that we serve with homemade cajeta or jams and ricotta. I'm a huge fan of Mexican-inflected ice creams and sorbets because even when you're full, there's always room for a little scoop. While cooking outside of Mexico, I've figured out that certain key ingredients—chiles, citrus, nuts, syrups, and herbs—almost magically convert anything into a Mexican-tasting dessert.

And when you've got the time to make dessert—or you make the time—a dessert and coffee can be the perfect way to continue a meal. Dessert prolongs time spent together, providing something to linger over, savor, and remember.

BUÑUELOS MEXICAN FRITTERS

A common street food eaten late at night in a town square, buñuelos are flat disks of dough, fried and sprinkled with sugar, and often served with either fruit or piloncillo syrup. Sometimes they're called *buñuelos de viento*, because they can shatter from the wind alone. At Cala, we like to serve them for dessert as well as for brunch, in a stack, with lightly sweetened queso fresco and jam between the layers. Think of them like tortillas, in that they're a basic building block of the dessert world that you can add to and embellish as inspired. They're at their peak shortly after you fry them, when they're still just slightly warm. Make sure to sprinkle them with sugar immediately as they come out of the oil so that it sticks.

MAKES 20 FRITTERS

¼ cup / 55g butter, softened
3¼ cups / 450g all-purpose flour
1 cup / 240ml warm water
½ tsp salt
½ cup / 60g powdered sugar
1 qt / 960ml rice bran oil, safflower oil, or any vegetable oil with a high smoke point
Ice cream, for serving (optional)

In a medium bowl, knead the butter and flour with your hands until just combined. In a smaller bowl, combine the water and salt and stir to dissolve the salt. Add ½ cup / 120ml of the water to the flour mixture and knead by hand, gradually adding the rest of the water and kneading until smooth, about 5 minutes. Gather the dough into a ball and wrap snugly in plastic wrap. Set aside on the counter overnight or for at least 8 hours.

Flour your work surface and, using a rolling pin, press and roll out the dough until it's as thin as a tortilla, about ⅛ inch / 3mm. I use a 4 inch / 10cm round cookie cutter to cut out perfect rounds, but you could also use more fanciful cutters to create whatever shapes amuse you.

Spread the powdered sugar on a plate.

In a medium heavy-bottom pot with a candy or frying thermometer attached to the side, heat the oil to 350°C / 180°F.

Drop in the dough circles, working in batches so that you don't crowd the pot, and let them fry for about 1 minute. Once they are golden, using a slotted spoon, lift each one out of the oil, pausing to let the excess oil drain off, and then quickly place them on the sugar-covered plate, flipping them over so that each side gets coated. Using tongs, transfer the sugared buñuelos to cooling racks and continue with the rest of the dough.

Serve right away, with whatever ice cream strikes your fancy.

ARROZ CON LECHE RICE PUDDING

MAKES 6 TO 8 SERVINGS

1 cup / 200g Arborio rice
4½ cups / 1L plus 65ml water
1 cinnamon stick
1 can (12 oz / 354ml) evaporated
   milk
1 can (14 oz / 397ml) sweetened
   condensed milk
Ground cinnamon

Rice pudding is the homiest Mexican dessert, something everyone has a simple recipe for and that's a favorite comfort food for kids and adults; this is the reason it's not typically found on upscale restaurant menus. That's why I stubbornly wanted it on the menu at Contramar when we opened, in contrast to all of the glazed mousses and other imported fancy desserts that were the rage in restaurants at that time—as if dessert had to come from overseas to count as special. We make our arroz con leche special by using really good Arborio rice and a combination of evaporated and condensed milks. It's not inherently fancy, but no one complains! If you happen to have leftover conchas (see page 96) or feel like baking, I highly recommend slicing one in half and using it to make a rice pudding sandwich.

Place the rice in a bowl, cover it with water, and let it soak for at least 30 minutes. Discard the soaking water. Place the drained rice in a medium saucepan with the 4½ cups / 1L plus 65ml water and the cinnamon stick. Bring it to a boil over medium-high heat, uncovered, and then decrease to a simmer. Cook until the rice is tender, about 10 minutes.

Discard the cinnamon stick and stir in the evaporated milk and condensed milk. Increase the heat to medium-high and continue cooking until the mixture comes to a boil. Again decrease the heat to low and cook, uncovered, stirring constantly, until the mixture is thick—about 15 minutes. Place the mixture in a serving bowl and let it cool. Cover and refrigerate until you're ready to serve.

Serve cold, sprinkled with cinnamon.

FLAN DE NUTELLA NUTELLA FLAN

As a tiny child spending time in Italy, I was obsessed with Nutella. Every kid loves it, and it's a taste I've never outgrown. Back then, Nutella did not exist in Mexico, and I can still remember the excitement when it became available, how we searched for excuses to eat it. At Contramar, we shoved it into an ice cream, and it was delicious. So we decided to experiment by putting it into a flan, which is the most Mexican thing. Everyone loved it, and it has stayed on the menu ever since.

MAKES 8 SERVINGS

1 cup / 200g granulated sugar
3 Tbsp / 45ml water
½ cup / 120ml sweetened
    condensed milk
2 (12 oz / 354ml) cans evaporated
    milk
⅔ cups / 190g Nutella
4 eggs

_____

Preheat the oven to 325°F / 165°C.

To make the caramel for the bottom of the flan, place the sugar in a small saucepan and cover with the water. Simmer over medium heat, stirring occasionally, until the sugar has melted and the liquid is golden but not dark brown. Pour the caramel into a 9-inch / 23cm cake pan with 2½-inch / 6cm-high sides or a 10-cup / 2.4L Bundt pan. Set aside.

Bring a full kettle of water to a boil.

In the jar of a blender, pulse the condensed milk, evaporated milk, Nutella, and eggs. Pour the mixture into the prepared pan.

Place the cake pan in a roasting pan and fill the roasting pan with the boiling water to reach at least halfway up the outside of the cake pan. Bake for 1 hour.

Place the flan on a cooling rack to cool. When the flan has cooled to room temperature, refrigerate for at least 2 hours and up to 2 days.

Carefully place a serving plate over the cake pan and invert the pan and plate together so that the flan falls onto the plate. Pour the caramel that remains in the bottom of the cake pan over the top of the flan and serve. Store in a sealed container in the refrigerator for up to 2 days.

FLAN DE ZANAHORIA CARROT FLAN

MAKES 6 TO 8 SERVINGS

1 lb 2 oz / 500g carrots
¾ cup / 180ml whole milk
1 cup / 200g granulated sugar
⅔ cup / 185g unsalted butter,
    melted
6 eggs

Topping
¼ cup / 60ml cream
½ cup / 60g powdered sugar,
    sifted

This is my father's favorite dessert, which his mother used to make for his birthday every year when he was a boy, making everyone laugh because she was such a sophisticated baker, but he preferred this humble flan made from a puree of cooked carrots. Instead of using condensed milk, this one calls for a blend of milk, butter, and sugar. It's both rich and fresh tasting and has a unique flavor that a lot of people can't immediately identify as coming from the carrots. It's definitely a good dessert to serve when fruit isn't available.

———————

Preheat the oven to 350°F / 180°C.

Thoroughly scrub the carrots but don't bother peeling them. You are going to boil them, so if you need to cut them to fit comfortably in your pot, go ahead and do so.

Place the carrots in a medium pot. Cover with water and bring to a boil. Cook the carrots for about 15 minutes, until just soft. Pour them into a colander and let cool completely. Press out any excess water so that they aren't too heavy and waterlogged.

Bring a full kettle of water to a boil.

In the jar of a blender, combine the carrots, milk, granulated sugar, butter, and eggs and mix at high speed for about 30 seconds or until you have a smooth mixture.

Grease a 10½-inch / 26.5cm flameproof baking pan with butter. Pour the mixture into the pan. Place it in a roasting pan and fill the roasting pan with the boiling water to reach at least halfway up the outside of the baking pan.

Bake the flan for 1½ hours. Place the flan on a cooling rack to cool. When the flan has cooled to room temperature, refrigerate it overnight.

When ready to serve, place the flan pan on the stove over low heat and warm slightly. This will loosen the sides and help dislodge it. Carefully place a serving plate over the pan and invert the pan and plate together so that the flan falls onto the plate.

To make the topping: In the bowl of a stand mixer fitted with the whisk attachment, whip the cream and powdered sugar until soft peaks form. Slice the flan. Spoon the whipped cream over the top of the flan and serve.

"EL IMPOSSIBLE" CHOCOFLAN CON NARANJA
"THE IMPOSSIBLE" ORANGE-CHOCOLATE FLAN

MAKES 8 TO 10 SERVINGS

Orange Flower Caramel

1 cup / 200g granulated sugar

2 Tbsp orange flower water

Chocolate Cake

1 cup / 140g all-purpose flour

1 cup / 200g granulated sugar

2 Tbsp unsweetened cocoa
   powder

½ tsp baking soda

½ tsp baking powder

5 Tbsp / 70g salted butter

2 oz / 55g unsweetened chocolate

1 egg

1 cup / 240ml whole milk

Zest and juice of 1 large orange

Orange Flan

3 eggs

1 (12 oz / 354ml) can evaporated
   milk

1 (14 oz / 397ml) can sweetened
   condensed milk

1 cup / 240g Queso Fresco
   (page 64) or ricotta,
   well strained

Zest and juice of 1 large orange

1 Tbsp orange flower water

You start making this dessert by pouring chocolate cake batter into a Bundt pan, which is then topped with a raw flan, and somehow in the baking process, they trade places so when you take it out of the oven, the cake has done the impossible and risen to the top. How can this be? Because the cake batter is lighter than the flan, which settles to the bottom. But understanding the science behind the dessert doesn't make it any less fun to witness. I love a hint of orange with my chocolate, so I've added a bit to each part of this: orange flower water to the caramel, orange juice to the flan, and orange zest to the chocolate cake. This is perfectly delicious as is, but you could also serve it with a dollop of whipped cream, flavored with a bit more orange zest. If kumquats are in season, you could also make this even prettier by slicing a few of them very thinly and placing them in the caramel at the bottom of the pan.

———————

Preheat the oven to 350°F / 180°C and butter a 9-inch / 23cm cake pan with 2½-inch / 6cm-high sides or a 10-cup / 2.4L Bundt pan.

To make the caramel: In a skillet over medium heat, combine 1 cup / 200g of the sugar and the orange flower water. Stir as it melts and turns golden. You want it to be orange but not dark brown. Remove from the heat once it has turned orange and smells caramelized but not burnt. Immediately pour the caramel into the buttered cake pan and set aside. Note that it will harden into the bottom of the pan before going into the oven and then melt again in the baking process.

To make the cake: In a large bowl, sift together the flour, sugar, cocoa, baking soda, and baking powder.

In a small heavy-bottom saucepan over medium heat, melt the butter and chocolate, stirring constantly. Melting them at the same time keeps the chocolate from scorching and means you don't need a double boiler, but you should still pay attention and be sure to turn off the heat as soon as the butter and chocolate are melted. Remove the saucepan from the stove and set aside to cool slightly. After a couple of minutes, when the mixture is warm but not hot to the touch, whisk in the egg.

In a clean bowl, combine the milk and the orange juice and zest and let it curdle for a couple of minutes.

To your bowl with the dry ingredients, add the melted chocolate mixture, followed by the curdled milk. Stir until everything looks well incorporated and then pour your batter into the prepared Bundt pan on top of the caramel.

Bring a full kettle of water to a boil.

To make the flan: Put the eggs, evaporated milk, condensed milk, queso fresco, orange juice and zest, and orange flower water in the jar of a blender and liquefy. Carefully pour the contents of the blender on top of the chocolate cake layer in the cake pan.

Place the cake pan in a roasting pan and fill the roasting pan with the boiling water to reach at least halfway up the outside of the cake pan.

Bake for 1 hour. Remove from the oven and marvel at the magic that has taken place. Your chocolate cake is now on top and your flan on the bottom. Although you will be tempted to flip it immediately, let it cool for 1 hour (while your flan finishes setting). When cool, loosen the edges with a butter knife. Place a serving plate over the pan and invert the pan and plate together so that the flan falls onto the plate.

I recommend making this dessert on the day you intend to serve it. While it can keep in the refrigerator and still tastes good on the second or even the third day, it has a tendency to settle and get a bit heavy.

FLAN DE CAJETA CARAMEL FLAN

1 cup / 240g Queso Fresco
(page 64) or goat's milk ricotta
1 cup / 200g granulated sugar
2 tablespoons water
1 qt / 960ml goat's milk
Packed 1 cup / 180g light brown
sugar
6 eggs
1 cup / 240ml evaporated milk
1 cup / 240ml sweetened
condensed milk

Cajeta is the Mexican equivalent of the dulce de leche that's so popular deeper in South America or the *confiture de lait* enjoyed in France. To make dulce de leche, you slowly cook milk and sugar to a gooey caramel. But cajeta uses goat's milk, which adds a subtly grassy taste to the caramel. Making cajeta takes a long time and a lot of patience while stirring. The jarred cajeta that you can buy often contains added corn syrup and other artificial ingredients. To avoid this, without having to take the time to make my own cajeta, I use goat's milk ricotta in this flan, which gives the same complexity of flavor that you'd get from cooking cajeta from scratch. I love the goat's milk ricotta from Bellwether Farms in California. If you can't find goat's milk ricotta near you, it's easy to make your own using fresh goat's milk (which is more widely available) and the recipe for queso fresco. I like to make this flan in ramekins, but you can also make it in a Bundt pan if you prefer.

Preheat the oven to 350°F / 180°C.

Line a fine-mesh strainer with several layers of cheesecloth. Place the queso fresco in the strainer over a bowl and set aside to drain off the liquid while you make the caramel and the flan.

To make the caramel: Combine the granulated sugar and water in a saucepan and cook at medium heat until the sugar dissolves and the liquid turns a deep amber. Remove the pan from the heat as soon as the liquid darkens and immediately, being very careful, pour a spoonful of this very hot liquid caramel into each of 8 (¾ cup / 180ml) ramekins or a 10-cup / 2.4L baking dish.

To make the custard: Put the queso fresco, goat's milk, brown sugar, eggs, evaporated milk, and condensed milk in the jar of a blender and blend until well combined. Divide the contents equally among the ramekins or pour into the baking dish.

Bring a full kettle of water to a boil.

Place the ramekins or baking dish in a roasting pan and fill the roasting pan with enough of the boiling water to reach halfway up the outside of the ramekins or baking dish. If you have a cookie sheet or other metal tray that will fit inside the roasting pan, place this on top of the ramekins while they bake; this will ensure that they cook evenly. Bake for 45 minutes to 1 hour, until the flan is set but still slightly wobbly when you jiggle the baking dishes.

Remove the flans from the roasting pan and place on a cooling rack to cool. Serve warm.

TAMALES DULCES CON MANCHEGO Y ATE
SWEET TAMALES WITH MANCHEGO AND QUINCE PASTE

Some people like to finish a meal with a dessert, while others prefer a cheese course. And then there are those who like to have it all. These sweet tamales let you have your dessert and eat your cheese, too. Ate de membrillo, or quince paste, is commonly paired with manchego cheese. Here they are both nestled inside each tamal, providing a melting burst of sweet and sour with every bite. You can make your own ate by cooking down quince with sugar, similar to making jam, but fresh quince can be more difficult to come by than the paste that is widely available at Mexican, Spanish, and other specialty markets. If you want to play around with different fillings, you could also use chopped dried apricots with cheese.

_____

Begin by placing your corn husks to soak in a large bowl of warm water to soften while you prepare the ingredients.

Place the fresh masa or mixed masa harina in the bowl of a stand mixer fitted with the paddle attachment or, if you prefer to do this by hand with a whisk, in a large bowl. You want to whip up your masa to get as much air into it as you can, making it fluffy. The more it's worked, the lighter the tamales will taste. After beating it for 3 to 4 minutes, add the butter 1 Tbsp at a time and continue to whip it until it's well incorporated. Then add the sugar and mix for an additional 1 to 2 minutes.

Cut your manchego cheese and ate de membrillo into 12 equal logs, approximately 2 x ½ inches / 5cm x 12mm. They should look like half of a string cheese stick. It's not crucial that they be perfectly tidy and uniform as they will be tucked inside the tamales; you just want them to fit within the masa and for each tamal to have about the same amount of both cheese and quince paste.

Take your softened corn husks out of the water they've been soaking in, squeezing out any excess moisture. Open one up and place about 3 Tbsp / 55g of the masa mixture in the center of the husk. Use the back of a spoon or a spatula to spread it into a rectangle that's about 3 x 2 inches / 7.5 x 5cm and about ½ inch / 12mm tall. It doesn't need to be precise, just big enough to hold the fillings with enough corn husk on all sides so that you can wrap it up and no filling will ooze out. Place one log of manchego and one log of quince paste at the center of the masa and then bring the sides of the corn husk together, sealing the filling inside the masa. Now fold up the bottom of the corn husk so that the whole tamal is contained inside the corn husk, then roll it up from the side. The tamal should

CONTINUED

MAKES 12 TAMALES

30 corn husks
2 cups / 520g fresh masa or
   2 cups / 260g masa harina,
   mixed with 1 to 1¼ cups /
   240 to 300ml water (as directed
   on page 72)
5 Tbsp / 70g butter, softened
⅓ cup / 65g granulated sugar
6 oz / 170g manchego cheese
6 oz / 170g ate de membrillo
Crema Ácida (page 65) for garnish

be "closed" on the bottom and open on top. Use a second corn husk to bind it further. There really isn't a science to wrapping tamales. What's important is that the insides stay as tight as possible and that no masa comes out during steaming. Repeat this process with the rest of the masa and filling. If you want, you can cut one of the corn husks into ribbons and use these ribbons to tie up the tamales for extra insurance.

Once you've finished, place a steamer basket in a stockpot and add 2 to 3 inches / 5 to 7.5cm of water. Place all of your tamal packages in the pot and bring to a simmer. Cover the pot and let the tamales steam for 20 to 25 minutes, monitoring about halfway through the process to make sure that there is still a good inch or two of water at the bottom of the pan and adding more water if necessary. After 20 minutes, take one out and open it up to test if it's done. Cut into one with a knife to ensure that the masa has the consistency of firm polenta and doesn't ooze at all; the halves should cut cleanly and stay intact. Serve with a spoonful of the crema.

As with savory tamales, these can be cooked, stored in the refrigerator, and then reheated simply by steaming them again, and they will taste just as good as when they were freshly made.

MERECUMBÉ CON NATILLAS
SOFT MERINGUE RING WITH CUSTARD SAUCE

MAKES 8 TO 10 SERVINGS

7 large eggs, at room temperature and separated
2 ½ cups / 500g granulated sugar
1 tsp freshly squeezed lime juice
Pinch of cream of tartar

Natillas
4 ¼ cups / 1L plus 55ml whole milk
1 can (14 oz / 397ml) sweetened condensed milk
1 tsp vanilla extract
1 cinnamon stick or 1 tsp ground cinnamon
Pinch of sea salt
1 Tbsp cornstarch
1 can (12 oz / 354ml) evaporated milk

Seasonal fruit for serving

I love meringue in all forms. It's probably my favorite special-occasion dessert because it satisfies my sweet tooth without being too filling and is always enjoyed with fruit. I'm consistently amazed by the variety of textures that meringue can take, from crisp to gooey to cloudlike. My Tía Rita's merecumbé definitely falls in the cloud category. I treasure this signature recipe of hers, and I make it for very special occasions. The whipped egg whites get pressed into a ring pan on a base of caramelized sugar, then cooked for just 1 hour at a low temperature. The whole confection acquires a crispy edge but otherwise stays soft and spongy after you unmold it from the pan.

Natillas is a custard sauce, made from the yolks of the eggs you use to make your meringue, so nothing goes to waste. This sauce has the consistency of a crème anglaise but a Mexican flavor, thanks to the cinnamon. If you have a large platter with a deep enough rim, you can pour the custard sauce over the whole meringue ring and then scatter it with fruit. In the winter, I recommend using segments of clementine or tangerine. The tart citrus undercuts the sweetness of the caramel and richness of the custard sauce. In the summer, I serve it with berries or sliced stone fruit.

In Mexico, we use a smooth-sided, metal ring-shaped pan with fairly tall sides to make large flans. If you don't have one, a Bundt pan will work fine.

———————

Fill a large roasting pan with about 3 inches / 7.5cm of room temperature water, so that the water comes halfway up the outside of a ring pan or Bundt pan when it is placed in the roasting pan. Place the pan in the oven and preheat to 325°F / 165°C degrees.

In the bowl of a stand mixer fitted with the whisk attachment, whip the egg whites until soft peaks form. Add 1½ cups / 300g of the sugar, the lime juice, and cream of tartar. Resume whipping the whites on low-medium speed for about 5 minutes, while you make your caramel.

Pour the remaining 1 cup / 200g sugar into a 9-inch / 23cm round metal pan or a Bundt pan. Place the pan directly on a stove top burner over medium-low heat. Using oven mitts, hold the edges of the pan and tilt it continuously while the sugar at the bottom of the pan melts. Once the sugar has turned a dark caramel brown color and is totally liquid with no chunks, turn off the burner and let the pan sit there for a couple of minutes, until the melted caramel begins firming up. As the caramel firms, use a rubber spatula to smear it up onto the sides of the pan as evenly as possible, coating the entire interior surface.

Once the whipped egg whites and sugar have doubled in volume and form stiff, glossy peaks, turn off the mixer and pour about one-third of the meringue into the ring pan, on top of the caramelized sugar. As you fill the mold with the whipped egg whites, press the top of the meringue with the flat surface of a rubber spatula to compress it and squeeze out air bubbles. Repeat twice. Once you've put all of the meringue into the pan, it should reach the rim without puffing up over the edges. Place the filled pan in the water in the roasting pan and bake for 1 hour.

While the meringue is baking, make your Natillas: Heat 1 qt / 1L of the whole milk and the condensed milk in a Dutch oven or a large heavy-bottom saucepan over medium-low heat. Add the vanilla, cinnamon, and salt and stir. Bring to a gentle simmer. Do not let it come to a boil; you don't want the milk frothing up to the top of the saucepan.

Pour the remaining ¼ cup / 60ml of the milk into a small bowl or glass measuring cup and add the cornstarch. Stir to dissolve.

In the jar of a blender, blend the egg yolks together with the evaporated milk. Using a fine-mesh strainer, strain this egg yolk mixture into the saucepan. Whisk in the milk-cornstarch mixture. Continue to cook over low heat, stirring continuously, for about 5 minutes to firm up the custard. Once you've added the egg yolks, do not let the mixture come to a boil. This is meant to be similar to a crème anglaise. It should coat the back of a spoon but not be as thick as a custard. Once it reaches this consistency, turn off the heat and remove the cinnamon stick. Set on a cooling rack to cool before serving, refrigerating it if you'd prefer your custard chilled.

Right after you take the cooked meringue out of the oven, immediately slide the tip of a paring knife around the edge of the meringue to separate it from the pan before it cools and fuses to the pan. Place a serving plate on top of the pan and carefully invert the pan. It may take 5 to 10 minutes, but it will gradually loosen and release from the mold, dropping onto the plate with the caramel side up.

For a dramatic presentation—if your serving plate allows—you can pour the whole pot of cooled custard over the meringue, scatter it with fruit, and cut it into slices at the table. Alternatively, you could cut slices, put them on individual dessert plates, and pour about ½ cup / 120ml of the custard over each slice. Scatter with whatever fruit is in season, from tangerine segments to sliced persimmons and pomegranate seeds in the colder months or berries and sliced stone fruit in the warmer seasons.

PAVLOVA DE FRESAS CON PEPITAS
CRISP MERINGUE WITH STRAWBERRIES AND PUMPKIN SEEDS

MAKES 8 TO 10 SERVINGS

Meringue
5 cold egg whites
1 cup / 200g granulated sugar

Topping
1½ cups / 360ml heavy cream
14¾ oz / 420g strawberries, hulled
 and sliced, or mixed berries
2 Tbsp pumpkin seeds

My mother's favorite dessert at Contramar is the strawberry meringue cake, with layers of sugary meringue offset by unsweetened whipped cream and tons of sliced berries. For the restaurant version, the pastry chefs pipe long, skinny strips of meringue that we cut into pieces to decorate the outside edge of the "cake." Unless you're really skillful with a pastry bag and have time to make meringue pipettes, I recommend making this in a simpler Pavlova shape: one large round meringue disk, topped with cream and fruit and scattered with pumpkin seeds. It's a lot easier and no less delicious. For another variation, try a layer of lemon curd from the Torta de Limón Amarillo (page 324). I have also made a divine version but substituting passion fruit pulp for the lemon juice. These are nice alternatives when fresh berries aren't in season.

———————

Preheat the oven to 250°F / 120°C.

Line a baking sheet with parchment paper and draw a 10-inch / 25cm circle on it.

To make the meringue: Put the egg whites in the bowl of a stand mixer and chill in the refrigerator for 10 minutes. Using the stand mixer fitted with the whisk attachment, whip the egg whites while gradually raining in the sugar 1 Tbsp at a time, until firm peaks form. Continue to whip until the whites are glossy and stiff.

Pile the whipped egg whites onto the circle you've drawn on the parchment paper, smoothing the sides and the top with a knife or spatula. You want a shallow depression in the top of the circle; this will serve as the receptacle for your whipped cream and fruit.

Bake for 1½ hours or until completely dry (it should feel dry and crisp to the touch). Turn off the heat but leave it in the oven, allowing it to cool in there. Once the meringue is completely cool, remove the disk from the parchment paper. If you don't plan to serve it immediately, store it in an airtight container on the counter—do not refrigerate.

To make the topping: In a clean bowl for a stand mixer fitted with the whisk attachment, whip the cream on low speed for 1 minute, then increase to medium speed and mix for 6 more minutes until thick and airy.

Place the meringue on a serving plate and spread with the whipped cream. Top with the berries and a sprinkle of pumpkin seeds. Cut into wedges and serve. The Pavlova should be eaten right after it is assembled.

TARTA DE LIMÓN AMARILLO CON RICOTTA
LEMON AND RICOTTA TART

Piecrust
2 cups / 280g all-purpose flour
2 Tbsp granulated sugar
Pinch of sea salt
¾ cup plus 1 Tbsp / 180g unsalted
    butter, chilled and cut into little
    pieces
¼ cup plus 1 Tbsp / 75ml ice water

Ricotta Filling
1¼ cups / 300g full-fat ricotta,
    strained
2 Tbsp honey
Pinch of sea salt

Lemon Curd
⅔ cup / 130g granulated sugar
Zest of 1 lemon
⅔ cup / 160ml freshly squeezed
    lemon juice
½ tsp sea salt
3 eggs
1 egg yolk
2 tsp gelatin
2 tsp hot water
1 cup / 220g unsalted butter
1 Tbsp light brown sugar

This is my riff on a classic Italian Easter dessert. In Italy, the lemon in the traditional ricotta tart is a lot less pronounced—usually just a teaspoon of zest—although they also use honey as their sweetener. I like my lemon desserts a little more sour, so I've added a layer of tangy lemon curd to the top of this tart, which complements the creamy ricotta filling beautifully.

_____

To make the crust: Place the flour, granulated sugar, and salt in a food processor and pulse until the mixture is well combined. Add the butter, one piece at a time, then the ice water. Pulse until a ball of dough forms. Turn out the dough onto a piece of parchment paper. Roll the dough into a 9-inch / 23cm circle. (I like to use a rolling pin to roll it out gently on a piece of parchment paper, until it's approximately the size of the tart shell but slightly smaller, so that after chilling it, I only have to roll it a little bit more for it to fit inside the pan.) Cover the dough with a sheet of plastic wrap and chill it in the refrigerator for at least 2 hours.

After 2 hours, finish rolling out the dough by rolling the circle 1½ to 2 inches / 4 to 5cm larger. Fit it into a 9-inch / 23cm tart pan with a removable bottom. After fitting the dough into the pan, trim any excess from the sides so that it has a neat edge. Use a fork to prick the crust and then refrigerate for an additional 15 minutes while you preheat the oven to 325°F / 165°C.

Cover the shell with aluminum foil and scatter some dried beans on the foil to keep it from bubbling up. Bake it for 25 minutes. Then remove the beans and the foil and bake it, uncovered, for an additional 10 minutes. Remove from the oven and let cool.

While the crust is baking, make the ricotta filling and the lemon curd.

To make the ricotta filling: Combine the ricotta, honey, and salt in a bowl and mix with a rubber spatula or whisk until well blended. Chill until ready to use.

To make the lemon curd: Begin by vigorously whisking the granulated sugar, lemon zest, lemon juice, salt, eggs, and egg yolk in the top of a double boiler or in a bowl set over a pot of simmering water. Keep the heat low enough so that the eggs don't scramble and stir constantly until the curd is thick enough to coat the back of a spoon. Place the gelatin in a small bowl with the hot water. Stir until the gelatin "blooms," or dissolves into a fluff in the water, then whisk this into the pot with the lemon curd. Take the curd off the stove and whisk in the butter while it's still hot, whisking until it's melted and incorporated. Chill the lemon curd in the refrigerator for at least 1 hour.

When all the components have cooled, assemble the tart. Spread the ricotta mixture evenly in the tart crust. Chill in the refrigerator for 10 minutes. Whisk the lemon curd so that it's perfectly smooth. Pour the curd over the ricotta layer and return the tart to the refrigerator for 20 minutes. Right before serving, sprinkle the brown sugar over the top and torch it until the sugar forms a crackly surface similar to the top of a crème brûlée. You could also place it under a preheated broiler for 2 to 3 minutes but be sure you monitor it closely and don't wander away, because it takes only a few minutes to go from pleasingly crackly to scorched.

TARTA DE PLÁTANO CON DULCE DE LECHE
DULCE DE LECHE BANANA CREAM PIE

Barracuda was Mexico City's first proper US diner, an establishment dating back to the 1950s. When my partners and I took it over, it made the perfect setting for solo dining, with its long lunch counter and swivel stools. We restored it with a nostalgic vibe that people loved, extending to the menu, which included the burgers and hot dogs you'd expect in such a place. But inevitably, we Mexicanized some of the classics like this banana cream pie, which gets a thick spread of dulce de leche on a walnut crust and a layer of caramelized bananas under a cloud of whipped cream.

You can buy jarred dulce de leche at most Mexican markets, although it originated in Argentina. The Mexican version, cajeta, uses goat's milk to make the caramel, and it's also delicious. Either works here, though dulce de leche tends to be a bit thinner and easier to spread. You can also make your own dulce de leche by slowly reducing milk and sugar over very low heat to a sticky jam. No matter what you use, this pie will be delicious.

_____

To make the crust: In a food processor, grind the walnuts, being careful not to overprocess them so that they don't turn into nut butter.

In a medium bowl, combine the ground walnuts, cinnamon, cloves, ginger, baking powder, and flour.

In a stand mixer fitted with the whisk attachment, whip the butter and sugar until it's fluffy, scraping down the sides with a spatula and adding the egg yolk. Add in the dry ingredients from the mixing bowl and blend until it's incorporated and forms a ball.

Press the dough into the bottom of a 9-inch / 23cm springform pan or deep tart shell and chill in the refrigerator for at least 30 minutes.

Preheat the oven to 375°F / 190°C. Cover the nut crust with aluminum foil and bake for 20 minutes, then remove the foil and bake for an additional 5 minutes, until the crust looks golden brown. Remove the pan from the oven and set aside to cool.

To make the mousse: In a small bowl, sprinkle the gelatin into the warm water and let it soften. While it does, in the clean bowl of a stand mixer fitted with a clean whisk attachment, whip 1 cup / 240ml of the cream until soft peaks form.

MAKES 8 TO 10 SERVINGS

Walnut Crust
¾ cup / 90g walnuts
Pinch of ground cinnamon
Pinch of ground cloves
Pinch of ground ginger
Pinch of baking powder
1 cup / 140g all-purpose flour
5 Tbsp / 70g salted butter, softened
½ cup / 100g granulated sugar
1 egg yolk
6 Tbsp / 90ml dulce de leche or cajeta

Banana Mousse
2 tsp gelatin
2 tsp warm water
2 cups / 480ml heavy cream
2 large or 3 medium very ripe bananas
2 Tbsp sugar
Squeeze of lemon juice

Caramelized Bananas
2 Tbsp granulated sugar
2 large or 3 medium bananas, cut into ½-inch / 12mm diagonal slices
2 Tbsp butter
1 Tbsp ground cinnamon or cocoa powder

CONTINUED

In a food processor or blender, combine the bananas and 1 Tbsp of the sugar, until the puree is smooth and creamy. Into the mixer with the cream, add the softened gelatin, mashed bananas, and lemon juice, and whip for 1 to 2 minutes. Cover and refrigerate the mousse while you make the caramelized bananas.

To make the caramelized bananas: Place the remaining sugar on a small plate and roll each banana slice in it so that both sides of each slice are coated.

In a skillet over medium heat, add the butter and heat until it's bubbling. Fry the slices of banana in the butter, letting them caramelize on each side but being careful that they don't burn. The first side should take about 2 to 3 minutes, the second side 1 to 2 minutes. Once the bananas are cooked, remove them from the pan and place them on a plate.

Begin by spreading the dulce de leche or cajeta on the cool walnut crust. Spread it evenly but stop about 1 inch / 2.5cm from the outer edge of the crust. Arrange the caramelized banana slices in a layer on top of the dulce de leche. Spread with the banana mousse.

In a clean bowl of a stand mixer fitted with the whisk attachment, whip the remaining 1 cup / 240ml of the cream with the remaining 1 Tbsp of the sugar. Spread the whipped cream over the banana mousse.

Refrigerate the pie for at least 1 hour to set. To serve, dust the top with the cinnamon or cocoa powder before serving.

PASTEL DE CHOCOLATE Y NUECES SIN HARINA FLOURLESS CHOCOLATE-WALNUT CAKE

When Contramar first opened and while we were still figuring out how to run a restaurant and looking for desserts to put on the menu, we happened to taste this incredibly moist, rich, and delicious chocolate cake, made by a friend of ours. We asked if she'd be willing to make it for the restaurant, and she agreed, so we put it on the dessert tray. Twenty years later, it's still there, and it's newly popular, since it's naturally gluten-free because ground walnuts take the place of flour, which is why it's so moist.

———————

Preheat the oven to 350°F / 180°C.

In a food processor, grind the walnuts by pulsing them just until they look like coarse sand.

In a saucepan over very low heat, melt the butter with the chocolate chips and espresso, stirring constantly. As soon as the chocolate is melted, remove the saucepan from the heat, add the vanilla, and let it cool down.

Meanwhile, in the bowl of a stand mixer fitted with the whisk attachment, beat the eggs until they're light and fluffy—about 3 to 4 minutes—then add the brown sugar one spoonful at a time and continue mixing until they form stiff, glossy peaks.

Gently fold in the melted chocolate, trying not to lose volume from your beaten eggs. Little by little, add the walnut meal and salt, folding them in as gently as possible just until incorporated.

Grease a 9-inch / 23cm springform pan and line the bottom with parchment paper. Pour in the batter and bake for 40 to 50 minutes, or until the top and sides start to crack. The center will still look a little wobbly when you remove it from the oven, but this is fine. It tastes great when it's slightly runny, and it will set more as it cools. Place the cake on a cooling rack to cool.

When the cake has cooled completely, sprinkle with the cocoa or cinnamon, cut into wedges, and serve.

MAKES 8 TO 10 SERVINGS

1 cup / 120g ground walnuts
¾ cup / 165g unsalted butter
1 cup / 180g semisweet chocolate chips
2 Tbsp freshly brewed espresso
1 tsp vanilla extract
4 eggs
Packed ½ cup / 90g light brown sugar
½ cup / 100g granulated sugar
Pinch of sea salt
Healthy pinch of cocoa powder or ground cinnamon

HELADO DE CHOCOLATE CON PALANQUETA
DARK CHOCOLATE ICE CREAM WITH PUMPKIN SEED BRITTLE

This ice cream is seriously chocolatey—no messing around. Invest in the best-quality chocolate you can find. It really does make a difference to both the flavor and consistency of the ice cream, producing something that tastes a little chewy, like the gelatos of Italy. Do take the time to make the pumpkin seed palanqueta. Great food is so often about interesting contrasts of texture and flavors, and the crunch of the pumpkin seed brittle, plus a little hint of salt, really pairs beautifully with this decadent dark chocolate ice cream. It takes only about 5 minutes to make this pumpkin brittle, but make sure you have the necessary equipment before you get started. You will need two silicone baking-sheet liners. I use ones that measure 16½ x 24½ inches / 42 x 62cm. You'll also need a rolling pin and a candy thermometer.

_____

To make the ice cream: In a stand mixer fitted with the whisk attachment, beat the egg yolks and sugar until smooth and pale, 3 to 4 minutes.

Warm the milk in a large heavy-bottom stockpot over medium heat. When the mixture begins to simmer (but not boil), pour 1 cup / 240ml of the hot milk into the yolk-sugar mixture with the mixer running on low. Decrease the heat under the pot to the lowest setting. Pour the contents of the mixer bowl into the simmering milk while continuously whisking and scraping the bottom of the pot with a spatula. This keeps the eggs from scrambling while the custard forms. Once the steam begins to come off the surface of the mixture and it is thick enough to coat the back of a spoon, stir in the dark and milk chocolate and cocoa, stirring until fully incorporated. Once the custard is a uniform shade of brown, set a fine-mesh strainer over a clean bowl. Pour the custard into the strainer. Chill the bowl of custard for at least 2 hours. Churn in your ice cream maker, following the manufacturer's directions. Transfer to a container with a tight-fitting lid and place in the freezer to harden for 2 hours before serving.

To make the brittle: Line a baking sheet with a silicone liner. Scatter the amaranth seeds across the baking sheet.

In a small heavy-bottom saucepan over low-medium heat, combine the sugar and water and stir continuously for 3 to 4 minutes, until the sugar has melted completely and turned amber in color.

MAKES 6 TO 8 SERVINGS

Dark Chocolate Ice Cream
6 large egg yolks
¾ cup plus 2 Tbsp / 180g granulated sugar
2½ cups / 600ml whole milk
4 oz / 115g dark chocolate (75% cacao), finely chopped
4 oz / 115 milk chocolate, finely chopped
¼ cup / 20g cocoa powder

Brittle
3 Tbsp puffed amaranth seeds
¾ cup plus 2 Tbsp / 180g granulated sugar
1 Tbsp water
¾ cup / 100g pumpkin seeds
1½ Tbsp butter
1 tsp sea salt
1 Tbsp baking soda

CONTINUED

Decrease the heat to low. Add the pumpkin seeds, butter, and salt and continue stirring. Using your candy thermometer, take the temperature of the mixture. When it reaches 212°F / 100°C, stir in the baking soda and turn off the heat. Working quickly, pour the mixture on top of the liners over the amaranth. Place the second silicone liner on top and repeatedly roll over it with the rolling pin to spread the brittle as thinly as you can before it begins to cool and set.

Wait about 10 seconds, then remove the top silicone liner. Let the brittle cool for 2 to 3 minutes, then break it into pieces and serve with the chocolate ice cream. Leftover brittle can be stored at room temperature in a sealed container for up to 1 month.

SORBETE DE JAMAICA HIBISCUS SORBET

Agua de Jamaica is probably the best known agua fresca, made by steep-ing hibiscus flowers, which are deep fuchsia in color and have the acidity of lemons, and then sweetening the drink with plenty of sugar. You can buy bags of these dried hibiscus flowers inexpensively at Mexican markets and health-food stores. Get organic ones if you can. Mint is a delicious comple-ment to the flower, so we've added it to this sorbet.

_____

In a small saucepan over high heat, bring the water to a boil. Stir in the hibiscus and mint and then remove the pan from the heat and set aside to steep for 20 minutes. Place a fine-mesh strainer over a bowl. Pour the mixture through the strainer, pressing on the flowers and leaves to extract all of their flavor. Transfer the strained liquid to the saucepan and place over low heat. Add the sugar and salt. Stir until the sugar dissolves. If needed, return the liquid to a simmer to ensure that no granules remain.

Remove the saucepan from the heat and refrigerate for at least 3 hours, until the liquid is chilled. If you want to speed up this step, you can place the liquid in a small bowl that you nest in a larger bowl of ice water. Once cold, stir in the lime juice.

Churn in your ice cream maker, following the manufacturer's directions. Transfer the sorbet to an airtight container and place in the freezer to harden for 2 hours before serving.

MAKES 1 QT / 960ML

2½ cups / 600ml water
1½ oz / 40g organic dried hibiscus flowers
2 or 3 sprigs mint, leaves pulled from stems
¾ cup / 150g granulated sugar
½ tsp sea salt
1 Tbsp freshly squeezed lime juice

6 BEBIDAS

DRINKS

Good food and good drinks go together. It's part of the pleasure of lingering at the table. Many Mexicans love something sweet with their meals, and they often get that sweetness in the form of an agua fresca. For us, aguas frescas are the perfect beverage, taking advantage of the fruit that grows in abundance in Mexico throughout the year. Aguas frescas are made in the blender (which is why I keep a second blender jar that's never touched by chiles) by combining whole fruit or freshly squeezed fruit juice, along with sugar and water. This puree gets strained through a fine-mesh strainer, over a lot of ice, which keeps the flavor from oxidizing. Additional water is stirred into the pitcher, and then it's chilled before serving.

Horchatas are another popular cold drink often served alongside aguas frescas in the large glass dispensers you see behind the counter at a lot of taquerias. Horchatas are made not with fruit but with ground-up rice, nuts, or seeds and often with spices as well. They look and taste a bit milky, even though they don't contain any dairy.

On a hot day in Mexico, a frosty agua fresca is practically a necessity. But if you live someplace with distinct seasons, there's no reason to limit yourself to savoring them only in the summertime. San Francisco can be chilly year-round, but that doesn't stop anyone from ordering the set lunch at Tacos Cala, which includes one of three rotating flavors of aguas frescas and horchatas. Because we use whatever fruit is in season, we've come up with drinks to take advantage of the fall harvest as well as all of that gorgeous winter citrus. Of course, in the summer, we also make the classics, featuring melon, stone fruit, and berries. I frequently add spices and aromatics to mine, like ginger with grapefruit or pink peppercorns with pears (and that's unintentional alliteration, not a recipe requirement).

While I am giving you recipes for some of my favorite aguas frescas, the truth is that we seldom use precise recipes to make these drinks or go shopping for ingredients to make a particular one. That's because aguas frescas are a vehicle for fruit on the verge of going bad. Those three-day-old strawberries that are no longer pretty enough to plate? They're perfect for an agua fresca. The same with slumping peaches or nectarines that just need trimming before you throw them in the blender. As fruit ages, it gets sweeter due to enzyme breakdown. That is why older fruit tastes better than freshly picked fruit when you cook it in a pie—or blend it in an agua fresca. The extra sweetness may mean that you won't need to add as much sugar. As with salsas, where it's smart to add chiles and salt incrementally if you can, tasting until you're pleased with the results, it's wise to do the same with aguas frescas. The sweetness of the fruit you use is going to determine how much additional sweetener you want to add—that, and how sweet you like your drinks. So these recipes will give you a sugar range, and I recommend that you start with less and keep tasting and adding until you're happy with the sweetness.

Here are some of my personal favorites, all tried-and-true agua fresca recipes. But please don't be afraid to look in your fruit bowl to see what needs to be used up. And your veggie drawer, for that matter, since many popular aguas frescas combine fruits with green vegetables. Keep in mind that an agua fresca is not a smoothie; it should have a watery consistency. All of these recipes yield 6 to 8 cups / 1.4 to 2L, or 1½ to 2 qt, but you can always double them for a crowd. They're great to serve at large parties and delicious as the base for a cocktail.

When it comes to what kind of alcohol to pair with the food in this cookbook, you can certainly enjoy a good wine with any of it, but until recently wine wasn't readily available in Mexico and the idea of producing great Mexican wines wasn't even a notion. Mexico produces delicious beers and, of course, tequila, and mezcal, sotol, and raicilla. If you want to make a cocktail that isn't based on something more elaborate than a splash of hard liquor in an agua fresca, I've included the most popular cocktails from the bar at Cala. A lot of them, such as the margarita, are popular enough that their Spanish names have made their way into the English language. But just as with any of the more commonly known recipes in this book—from refried beans to tacos—when drinks like the margarita are made with the simplest and best available ingredients, carefully and precisely, they taste so much better than the ones made from convenient bottled mixes full of who knows what.

For those of you who are uncertain about the difference between tequila and mezcal, here's what you need to remember: all agave-based distilled spirits from Mexico are mezcales but in the state of Jalisco, a region called Tequila has been very clearly established under European principles of DOC, as they only use the blue agave typical of that region. Ideally, other DOC-designated regions will be established sooner rather than later. Approximately 85 percent of mezcal is produced in Oaxaca. Mezcal can be made from up to thirty different agaves (including the blue one). Tequila and mezcal are also produced differently. In general, the production of mezcal is done in smaller batches and with a less industrial process that involves smoking the plant in pits underground, which is why mezcal tends to have a smokier taste than tequila. But both can be extremely delicious. Try to sample tequilas and mezcals produced by some of the smaller purveyors who are working hard to produce these beverages in a way that's sustainable. Tequila and mezcal are meant to be sipped and savored, not thrown back as shots. When they are an ingredient in a Mexican cocktail, the drink should showcase—not mask—them.

Aguas frescas at MERCADO DE COMIDA, Av. Revolución (Av. 5 de Mayo), Tepoztlán, Morelos

AGUA DE JAMAICA HIBISCUS COOLER

MAKES 6 TO 8 SERVINGS
OR 2 QT / 2L

6 cups / 1.4L water
1½ oz / 40g organic dried hibiscus
    flowers
1 cinnamon stick
½ cup / 100g granulated sugar,
    plus more as needed
3 cups / 330g ice

This is made from the same hibiscus flowers that flavor the popular herbal tea. Unsweetened, it's as tart as cranberry juice and about the same color. In Mexico, Agua de Jamaica is a nearly ubiquitous drink, more popular than soda, with lunch in particular. It's very easy to make the concentrate by simmering hibiscus flowers in water (again like the tea). Once it cools, you add sugar and dilute it with more water and ice, and that's about it—although including some fresh mint is always welcome.

In a medium saucepan over medium-high heat, bring 5 cups / 1.2L of the water to a boil. Decrease the heat to low and, when at a simmer, add the hibiscus and cinnamon stick. Simmer for about 20 minutes. Once it's done, the flowers will all have settled on the bottom of the pot. Pour the mixture through a fine-mesh strainer into a bowl, discarding the flowers, and place it in the refrigerator to cool it down.

Once you're ready to serve it, stir the sugar and the remaining 1 cup / 240ml water into the concentrate. Taste and stir in more sugar if needed.

Fill a serving pitcher or glasses with the ice and then pour the agua fresca over the ice.

The agua fresca can be stored in a glass container (it tastes better when stored in glass than in plastic, and it has the tendency to stain plastic) in the refrigerator for 2 or 3 days.

Pictured (left to right): Agua de Jamaica (facing page);
Horchata de Almendra (page 350); and Agua de Piña,
Naranja y Albahaca (page 347).

AGUA DE LIMÓN WHOLE LIMEADE

MAKES 6 TO 8 SERVINGS
OR 2 QT / 2L

2 cups / 230g ice
6 cups / 1.4L water
2 whole organic seedless limes
(or, if not seedless, then cut
in half and seeded)
½ cup / 100g granulated sugar,
plus more as needed

This agua fresca (pictured on page 344) is one of my very favorite things to drink: whole limes briefly blended with water and sugar and then strained. You want to blend the fruit for as little time as possible, so you can taste the juice and skin of the lime but not the pith, which is bitter.

Whole limeade is delicious as is, but I also love it with a spoonful of chia seeds. They are native to Mexico, great for your digestion as well as fun to eat, and can be added to any of the other aguas frescas if you like their slippery crunch. Just add a spoonful or two of the seeds to the pitcher of agua fresca and let it stand for at least 15 minutes while the seeds soften. If you really like the taste and texture of chia and want to be able to add them without waiting, stir 3 Tbsp / 30g of chia seeds into a canning jar with 1 cup / 240ml of hot water, screw on the lid, and store it in the refrigerator. The seeds will turn gelatinous in an hour or so, and the jar of prepared chia will keep for up to 2 weeks, so you will always have them at-the-ready to spoon into a glass of agua fresca whenever you like.

Place the ice and 2 cups / 480ml of the water in your serving pitcher.

Place the limes (skin and all) in the jar of a blender, making sure not to include any seeds, and add the remaining 4 cups / 960ml of the water and the sugar. Blend briefly by pulsing a few times. Taste and stir in more sugar if needed.

Pour the mixture over a fine-mesh strainer into the serving pitcher. Chill until ready to serve.

The agua fresca can be stored in the pitcher the refrigerator for 2 or 3 days.

AGUA DE LIMÓN, PEPINO Y MENTA
CUCUMBER AND MINT LIMEADE

Lime, cucumber, and mint are frequently used in "spa water," because these three refreshing ingredients make natural companions. If you have access to a good market with interesting varieties of mint, I highly recommend using chocolate mint or cooling peppermint. Spearmint is grassier and tastes less of menthol, but it will still be delicious if that's what you have. You can play with the proportions in this drink (pictured on page 344) depending on whether you want this to be more or less minty and/or to taste more or less of cucumber.

_____

Place the ice and 2 cups / 480ml of the water in your serving pitcher.

Place the mint leaves in the jar of a blender with the lime juice, cucumber, sugar, and the remaining 4 cups / 960ml of the water and blend completely. Taste and stir in more sugar if needed.

Pour the mixture over a fine-mesh strainer into the serving pitcher. Chill. Garnish with the sprig of mint and/or float the slices of cucumber on top and serve.

The agua fresca can be stored in the pitcher in the refrigerator for 2 or 3 days.

MAKES 6 TO 8 SERVINGS
OR 2 QT / 2L

2 cups / 230g ice
6 cups / 1.4L water
10 to 20 mint leaves, plus 1 sprig, well washed
¼ cup / 60ml freshly squeezed lime juice
⅛ to ¼ English cucumber, peeled and 3 thin slices cut and reserved
½ cup / 100g granulated sugar, plus more as needed

Pictured in glasses (bottom left, center, top left): Agua de Limón, Pepino y Menta (page 343); Agua de Limón (page 342), Agua de Toronja y Jengibre (facing page).

AGUA DE TORONJA Y JENJIBRE
GRAPEFRUIT-GINGER DRINK

Asking me to choose a favorite agua fresca is like asking a parent to choose a favorite child. However . . . this is one that really pleases me, especially in the winter when the pretty pink color does as much to lift my spirits as vitamin C and ginger boost my immune system.

_____

Place the ice and 2 cups / 480ml of the water in your serving pitcher.

Place the ginger, remaining 4 cups / 960ml of the water, sugar, and grapefruit juice in the jar of a blender and blend on high speed, until well blended. Taste and stir in more sugar if needed.

Pour the mixture over a fine-mesh strainer into the serving pitcher. Chill until ready to serve.

The agua fresca can be stored in the pitcher in the refrigerator for 2 or 3 days.

MAKES 6 TO 8 SERVINGS
OR 2 QT / 2L

2 cups / 230g ice
6 cups / 1.4L water
1½ oz / 40g ginger, peeled and cut
  into rounds
½ cup / 100g granulated sugar,
  plus more as needed
1½ cups / 360ml freshly squeezed
  grapefruit juice

AGUA DE PERA Y PIMIENTA ROSA
PEAR AND PINK PEPPERCORN DRINK

MAKES 6 TO 8 SERVINGS
OR 2 QT / 2L

2 cups / 230g ice
6 cups / 1.4L water
2 pears, stemmed, cored, and
    peeled
2 Tbsp freshly squeezed lemon
    juice
¼ cup / 50g granulated sugar,
    plus more if needed
2 pinches of pink peppercorns,
    plus more for garnish

Pink peppercorns have a much fruitier, less sharp flavor than their black cousins, but the whisper of pepper is a delightfully unexpected complement to the fresh pears in this agua fresca, which provides a wonderful way to use the fall harvest. Play around with whatever varieties of pears you have access to, including the Asian apple pear. Be sure to strain this one, since the pear pulp has a gritty consistency, and you want the pink peppercorns integrated into the juice.

––––––––––

Place the ice and 2 cups / 480ml of the water in your serving pitcher.

Place the pears, lemon juice, sugar, 1 pinch of the peppercorns, and the remaining 4 cups / 960ml of the water in the jar of a blender and blend on high speed, until well blended. Taste and stir in more sugar if needed.

Pour the mixture over a fine-mesh strainer into the serving pitcher. Chill. Float the remaining peppercorns on the surface and serve.

The agua fresca can be stored in the pitcher in the refrigerator for 2 or 3 days.

AGUA DE PIÑA, NARANJA Y ALBAHACA
PINEAPPLE, ORANGE, AND BASIL DRINK

This is a particularly frothy agua fresca due to the pineapple, which foams when blended. I like to make and chill it for at least 30 minutes before serving, and then I use a spoon to skim off the head of foam just before I serve it.

_____

Place the ice and 2 cups / 480ml of the water in your serving pitcher.

Place the pineapple, orange, sugar, and the remaining 4 cups / 960ml of the water in the jar of a blender and blend on high until well blended. Add the basil and pulse until completely integrated and no small pieces remain. Taste and stir in more sugar if needed.

Pour the mixture over a fine-mesh strainer into the serving pitcher. Chill until ready to serve.

The agua fresca can be stored in the pitcher in the refrigerator for 2 or 3 days.

MAKES 6 TO 8 SERVINGS
OR 2 QT / 2L

2 cups / 230g ice
6 cups / 1.4L water
¼ pineapple, cut into pieces
1 orange, peeled
¼ cup / 50g granulated sugar,
    plus more as needed
3 to 4 fresh basil leaves (optional)

CON LIMÓN

As you cook through this book, undoubtedly you'll notice that lime appears as an ingredient in nearly every recipe within these pages. If you're not someone who has eaten or cooked a lot of Mexican food before, this might surprise you. We use lime so much that it's almost like another salt for us: a common enough ingredient that we don't notice when it's included as much we do when it's *not* there. A strong flavor, it's also a flavor enhancer—a bright note that highlights the other tastes in a dish. You often get a square of a lime with a taco. You get half a lime with a pozole and always with seafood. A squeeze of lime really wakes up a mellow soup like Caldo de Pollo (page 88). It's an essential part of "cooking" raw fish in a ceviche. And I can't imagine any seafood tostada without it.

Despite the fact that it's one of the key ingredients in my cuisine, I'm not going to steer you toward any particular or "exotic" kinds of lime. The lime that is most common in Mexico is just the standard lime, which is intensely green and thin skinned. It's not tiny like a key lime, it's just a little smaller than the standard lemon, and unlike lemon it possesses an additional taste and perfume that I can only describe as "limey." I'm sure you know what I mean. In Mexico (and in the States) limes are readily accessible and usually pretty inexpensive. I always buy organic limes. I usually squeeze them or roll them on the counter to see if they feel full. If they give a little, that's a good sign that they're going to be juicy. Plan on getting 2 Tbsp of juice per lime. So for ½ cup / 120ml of juice, you'll need 4 or 5 limes.

Ever since the Spaniards brought limes over five hundred years ago, they have been widely used. But in recent years, I believe we have started using limes more than before. This may be because as the world has become more globalized, Mexicans have become used to eating foods from different cultures, many of which are intensely flavored. Asian food, for example has become more mainstream in Mexico City, and it tends to include more acidic than the traditional western diet. Our palates have become accustomed to an acidity that limes lend. To use the salt analogy again—if you ate a low-salt diet, then after a while, salty food would not taste good anymore.

But if it's a flavor enhancer that you use regularly, you come to crave it, and food tastes bland without it. If you get used to your favorite dishes having an acidity, when you remove that something crucial appears to be missing.

Mexican cooking expert Diana Kennedy does not like lime on everything. For example, she dislikes lime in guacamole because, according to her research, it's not traditionally used. But people fix guacamole many different ways and I think a squeeze of lime really enhances the taste of raw avocado. I always crave a bit of acid with my fat.

There are few dishes that I don't think benefit from that hit of citrusy brightness. I am sure I got that craving from Mexican street and market food. But if you happen to disagree, then cut back or leave it out. Every palate is different and, luckily, lime is something that you add at the end (it's never cooked into a dish), so you can always adjust its usage to your own particular tastes.

HORCHATA DE ALMENDRA BLENDED RICE AND ALMOND DRINK

MAKES 6 TO 8 SERVINGS
OR 1 ½ QT / 1.4L

1 cup / 200g jasmine rice
½ cup / 70g almonds
2 cinnamon sticks
1 pinch of cardamom or 1 whole
    pod
1 vanilla bean, split lengthwise,
    or 1 tsp vanilla extract
1½ qt / 1.4L water
½ cup / 100g granulated sugar,
    plus more as needed
2 cups / 230g ice

Rice and nut and oat milks are super trendy right now, but they've been a thing forever in Mexico. Horchata is the original "rice milk," a staple beverage across Mexico and in other parts of Latin America, made from blending soaked rice with cinnamon and other spices, sugar, and often some nuts. This is an almond horchata (pictured on page 341), my personal favorite, although it's also fabulous with walnuts, a popular variation in Oaxaca. Experiment with whatever nuts you like, sticking to the ratio of two parts rice to one part nuts and soaking them together overnight.

———————

The night before you want to serve your horchata, cover the rice, almonds, cinnamon sticks, cardamom, and vanilla bean (or add the extract) with 3 cups / 720ml of the water and let soak overnight or for at least 8 hours in the refrigerator.

The next day, scrape the seeds from the soaked vanilla bean into the jar of a blender and discard the pod. Add the entire rice mixture, including the cinnamon sticks and cardamom pod, if using, and puree for about 3 minutes, until completely smooth.

Pour the mixture over a fine-mesh strainer into your serving pitcher, pressing on the solids to express all the liquid. Depending on how powerful your blender is, you may wish to repeat this process, returning the liquid to the blender and then straining it once more to filter out as much of the grit as possible, so that all you're left with is a creamy horchata. Once you're satisfied with the texture of your drink, add the sugar, the remaining 3 cups / 720ml of the water, and ice. Stir and taste. Add more sugar if needed. Serve the horchata over ice.

The horchata can be stored in the pitcher in the refrigerator for 2 to 3 days. Separation is normal. Just stir the horchata until it becomes uniform and creamy again before serving.

HORCHATA DE MELÓN BLENDED MELON DRINK

This drink (pictured on page 341) is really half horchata and half agua fresca, because it uses both the seeds and the flesh of the melon. Cantaloupe tastes great here and has a pretty color, but feel free to use honeydew as well. Blending the seeds in water gives this drink the creamy quality associated with an horchata, while the addition of sweet melon results in a pretty color. It can be hard to grind the melon seeds as finely as you want them to be, so I often blend and strain this a few times in a row until I'm satisfied that I've extracted as much of their flavor as I can.

MAKES 6 TO 8 SERVINGS
OR 1 ½ QT / 1.4L

2 cups / 230g ice
6 cups / 1.4L water
Seeds of 1 cantaloupe
    or honeydew melon
Flesh of ½ cantaloupe
    or honeydew melon
¼ cup / 50g granulated sugar,
    plus more as needed

Place the ice and 2 cups / 480ml of the water in your serving pitcher.

Place the seeds and flesh of the cantaloupe, the remaining 4 cups / 960ml of the water, and sugar into the jar of a blender and blend on high until well blended. Pour the mixture over a fine-mesh strainer into your serving pitcher, pressing on the solids to express all the liquid. Depending on how powerful your blender is, you may wish to repeat this process, returning the liquid to the blender and then straining it several times more to filter out as much of the grit as possible, so that all you're left with is a creamy, watery drink. Once you're satisfied with the texture, stir and taste. Add more sugar if needed. Serve the horchata over ice.

The horchata can be stored in the pitcher the refrigerator for 2 or 3 days. Separation is normal. Just stir the horchata until it becomes uniform and creamy again before serving.

MICHELADA BEER WITH LIME AND SALT

MAKES 1 COCKTAIL

1 Tbsp kosher salt
¼ lime
2 oz / 60ml freshly squeezed
    lime juice
Bohemia or other Mexican beer,
    very cold

A michelada is not a cocktail but a cerveza preparada, a cold beer enjoyed with lime and salt. (See Pepitas Preparadas, page 142, for a similar treatment of toasted sunflower seeds with lime and salt, which incidentally would be a great snack to accompany your michelada.) Some people like to add tomato juice (or Clamato juice) or a dash of Worcestershire or hot sauce, but I prefer my michelada pure, because for me, this is one of the most refreshing drinks I know. It immediately makes me feel more relaxed—maybe because I always drink them at the beach.

———————

Spread the salt on a saucer. Rub the rim of a well-chilled beer stein or similar-size glass with the lime quarter and then dip the rim of the glass in the salt to coat.

Pour the lime juice into the bottom of the prepared glass and fill to the rim with ice cold beer.

SANGRITA SPICY TOMATO-CITRUS DRINK

MAKES 4 ½ CUPS /
1L PLUS 65ML

13 oz / 390ml tomato juice (this is a
    bit more than 1½ cups / 360ml)
13 oz / 390ml Clamato
3 oz / 90ml freshly squeezed
    lime juice
3 oz / 90ml freshly squeezed
    orange juice
4 oz / 120ml ketchup
1 Tbsp minced onion
1 Tbsp minced serrano chile
1 Tbsp minced cilantro leaves
1 Tbsp minced celery

Sangrita is a fiery red accompaniment to tequila, to be enjoyed alongside it, served in its own caballito, which is like a shot glass. But don't throw back your tequila like a shot! Only gringos do that. Good tequila should be sipped and appreciated. The sangrita cleanses the palate between sips of tequila, allowing you to savor the taste. In Mexico, it's actually common to serve three glasses per person: one with lime juice, one with white tequila, and one with sangrita. This is called a bandera, or a "flag," for reasons you can probably guess.

———————

In a large serving pitcher that you can chill, combine the tomato juice, Clamato, lime juice, orange juice, ketchup, onion, chile, cilantro, and celery. Refrigerate until cold. Store in the pitcher in the refrigerator for up to 2 days.

Pictured in glasses (from top left, counterclockwise): Carajillo (page 359), mezcal, Sangrita (page 352), Michelada (page 352), Margarita con Mezcal (page 355), Pepino Mezcal (page 356), and Paloma (page 357).

MARGARITA CON MEZCAL MEZCAL MARGARITA

The margarita is the drink that most people associate with Mexico, so it's fitting to update the margarita (pictured on page 353) using mezcal instead of tequila. What people love about a margarita is the balance of flavors that hit the mouth at once: sweet, sour, salty. Mezcal adds smoky to the mix, making an already pleasurably complex cocktail a little more so.

—————

To make the simple syrup: Place the sugar and water in a saucepan with the orange peel and lemon peel and bring to a boil. Decrease the heat and simmer for 10 minutes. Cool completely. Discard the peels. Transfer the syrup to a jar with a tight-fitting lid and refrigerate until ready to use or for up to 1 month.

Spread the salt on a saucer. Rub the rim of a highball glass with the lime quarter and then dip the rim of the glass in the salt to coat. Fill the glass with ice.

In a cocktail shaker, add the mezcal, ¼ cup / 60 ml of the syrup, lime juice, and bitters with 1 cup / 130g ice. Shake and then pour over the ice in the glass.

MAKES 1 COCKTAIL

Simple Syrup
1 cup / 200g granulated sugar
1 cup / 240ml water
1 large swath of orange peel
1 large swath of lemon peel

1 Tbsp kosher salt
¼ lime
2 oz / 60ml mezcal
1 oz / 30ml freshly squeezed lime juice
2 dashes of orange bitters

PEPINO MEZCAL CUCUMBER-LIME COCKTAIL

MAKES 1 COCKTAIL

Honey Simple Syrup
1 cup / 340g honey
½ cup / 120ml hot water

1 English cucumber, peel on, cut
    into pieces
0.75 oz / 22.5ml freshly squeezed
    lime juice
1.5 oz / 45ml mezcal
2 sprigs fresh mint

Cucumber automatically makes a drink refreshing. Just think spa water. But the smokiness of the mezcal in this cocktail (pictured on page 353) complicates that freshness in the best possible way. Also, the simple syrup made from honey instead of sugar isn't quite so simple. None of these things tastes as if they should work together necessarily, but, oh, they do.

_____

To make the syrup: Combine the honey and water in a small saucepan over medium-high heat. Bring the liquid to a boil, then turn off the heat. Stir to combine completely. Transfer to a jar with a tight-fitting lid and chill before using. Store in the jar in the refrigerator for up to 1 month.

To make the cucumber juice, place the cucumber into the jar of a blender and puree it, adding a tablespoon of water or so if needed. Pour the puree through a fine-mesh strainer to catch only the juices, pressing the pulp against the mesh.

In a cocktail shaker filled with ice, combine 0.5 oz / 15ml of the honey syrup, 1 oz / 30ml of the cucumber juice, the lime juice, mezcal, and 1 mint sprig and shake vigorously. Fill a short glass with ice cubes. Pour the drink into the glass, garnish with the remaining mint sprig, and serve.

PALOMA GRAPEFRUIT AND TEQUILA COCKTAIL

The Paloma (pictured on page 353) is a super-popular drink in Mexico, typically made with tequila, lime, and Squirt or Jarritos, which are grapefruit-flavored sodas. Often, it's served in clay cups, and people toss some salt in with the ice, which makes it stay extra cold. This cocktail has been made in lots of forms, and these days it's often updated with freshly squeezed grapefruit juice, club soda, and simple syrup. To be honest, the result is never as good as when you make it the classic way, with grapefruit soda. So we use the best grapefruit soda we can get, so that it still has a natural fruity flavor, and a splash of Aperol for a bitter orange taste that complements the sweet soda.

_____

Spread the salt on a saucer. Rub the rim of a highball glass with the lime quarter and then dip the rim of the glass in the salt to coat.

Fill the glass with ice cubes. Add the tequila, Aperol, and lime juice to the glass. Fill it to the rim with the grapefruit soda, stir briefly to mix, and serve.

MAKES 1 COCKTAIL

1 Tbsp kosher salt
¼ lime
1.5 oz / 45ml tequila
0.5 oz / 15ml Aperol
1 oz / 30ml freshly squeezed
   lime juice
Grapefruit soda (preferably
   Q brand)

SANGRIA AÑEJA FRUITY TEQUILA PUNCH

MAKES 1 DRINK

Red Wine Reduction
1 cup / 240ml wine
1 cup / 200g granulated sugar
1 cinnamon stick

Hibiscus Reduction
1 qt / 960ml water
1½ oz / 40g whole organic dried
  hibiscus flowers
1½ cups / 300g granulated sugar

1.5 oz / 45ml tequila añejo
0.75 oz / 22.5ml freshly squeezed
  lime juice
0.75 oz / 22.5ml freshly squeezed
  orange juice
1 swath of orange peel

You can make sangria—a fruity alcoholic punch—from all kinds of ingredients. But this one is special, thanks in part to the use of tequila añejo, tequila that has been aged in wooden barrels for at least eighteen months, giving it some of the same taste as an aged bourbon. This special sangria also includes both a red wine reduction syrup and a hibiscus reduction syrup, both of which are vibrantly red in color and intensely flavored. It's a bit of work to make the two reductions, so I've given the instructions for making enough so you can easily "batch-up" to make a pitcher of sangria. After all, sangria really belongs in a pitcher. It's a party drink, nothing to be sipped in solitude. Multiply the quantities by the number of drinks you want to make. Since it's equal parts lime juice, orange juice, hibiscus syrup, and red wine syrup, you should be able to do the recalculation even if you've already had a glass of sangria—just to test the recipe and make sure it's good, you know?

_____

To make the red wine reduction: Combine the wine and sugar in a saucepan over low heat and simmer for 20 minutes. Add the cinnamon stick for the last 10 minutes so that it infuses the syrup without overwhelming it. Discard the cinnamon. Transfer the reduction to a jar with a tight-fitting lid and refrigerate to chill. Store in the jar in the refrigerator for up to 1 month.

To make the hibiscus reduction: Combine the water, hibiscus flowers, and sugar in a stockpot over low heat and simmer for 20 minutes. Place a fine-mesh strainer over a bowl. Pour the reduction through the strainer. Reserve the flowers to garnish the drink if you like. Transfer the reduction to a jar with a tight-fitting lid and refrigerate to chill. Store in the jar in the refrigerator for up to 1 month.

To make a single cocktail, fill a highball glass with ice cubes. Fill a cocktail shaker with ice and then pour in the tequila, lime juice, orange juice, 0.75 oz / 22.5ml of the hibiscus syrup, and 0.75 oz / 22.5ml of the red wine syrup.

Shake vigorously and pour into the glass. Garnish with the orange peel.

If you're "batching up," make this directly in a large pitcher filled with ice, adjusting the quantities based on how many drinks you want it to make and stirring (instead of shaking) to mix the ingredients.

CARAJILLO COFFEE COCKTAIL

The original Spanish incarnation of the carajillo (pictured on apge 353) was a hot coffee drink, spiked with brandy or another liqueur. In Mexico, we always drink it cold and served on the rocks, and we use Lícor 43, a sweet vanilla-and-citrus liqueur. Shake it up well for the foamy cap that will have you licking your lips with delight after every sip.

MAKES 1 COCKTAIL

2 oz / 60ml Lícor 43
1 oz / 30ml freshly brewed
    espresso, cooled
4 large ice cubes

Combine the cocktail Lícor 43, espresso, and ice cubes in a cocktail shaker. Shake until frothy.

Pour the cocktail into a Cognac glass and serve.

ACKNOWLEDGMENTS

This book is the result of a lot of work and the support of a group of extraordinary people who believe in me and what I do.

First of all, I want to thank my parents, Clara and Gabriel, and Carlos, my brother, for their endless trust and help every step of the way. Having that has made everything possible for me from the beginning.

To Nonna and Doña Concha, and those before them, I am eternally indebted. The abundance of love and caring for others through nourishment and delicious food, lives on. They are my north stars.

I thank my aunts, uncles, cousins, and family everywhere, from Mexico to Italy to the US, for the complex but very true and deep sense of belonging that eating and sharing have given me. Thank you for those long breakfasts in Tepoztlán, which turn into lunches and eventually into dinners. Those meals are the genesis of what has become my career. I need to thank Carlos Pellicer López for everything, but particularly for being the artist and poet in residence at Contramar from day one.

To my restaurant teams and partners, past and present, I thank you every day. You are my teachers. It has been challenging at times but, thankfully, mostly fun and a truly extraordinary experience getting to know each and every one of you. It's an honor to share our lives, to be inspired by you, and to have become a family along the way. I appreciate and love you all. Infinite thanks to our divine providence, CT Outis.

For their help with this book, I especially want to thank the entire teams both at Contramar and Cala; nothing would be possible without all of them. Thank you to Kenny Curran for the always inspiring dialogue on flavor and recipes; to Magdalena Vélez for the grace with which she has walked by my side all these years; to Maritza Velázquez for her infinite brightness and loyalty through everything; to Emma Rosenbush for her complicity and belief in that it is all possible; to Andrés Barragán for his stoicism and example; to Wilberth Itza for his ancestral wiseness; to Christian Becker, Ana Paola Rivas, and Isabella de Hoyos for the recipe testing and enthusiasm; and to Isabel Velázquez and Mónica Fernández for keeping things rolling. I am eternally grateful for my personal magic ninjas, Mao Bravo and Armando Camacho, whose leadership at Contramar and Entremar is beyond anything I could have ever dreamed of. Thank you to Rigoberto Fernández, who led their way.

Thank you to Lorena Jones for being the best possible editor and pulling this book along through my crazy schedule. Thank you to the whole Ten Speed team: Ten Speed Publisher Aaron Wehner, Publishing Director Hannah Rahill, Marketing and Publicity Director Windy Dorresteyn, Assistant Publicity Director David Hawk, managing editors Lisa Regul and Doug Ogan, Senior Production Designer Mari Gill, Production Manager Jane Chinn, Creative Director Emma Campion, former Associate Creative Director Kara Plikaitis, production designer Mara Gendell, copyeditor Dolores York, proofreader Ivy McFadden, and indexer Ken DellaPenta.

Thank you to literary agent Katherine Cowles, for having the tenacity to get this project going and the continued support, and for reintroducing me to writer Malena Watrous, whose intelligence and friendship made this project fun at every step and whose loving support, great writing, and precise recipe testing made this book what it is now.

Of course, I need to thank designer James Casey for having always wanted me to make a book, for his smart and beautiful advice and work, and for introducing me many years ago to photographer Marcus Nilsson, who is a joy to work and spend time with and whose extraordinary eye and energy make every shoot exciting.

I want to thank the owners and teams of Bar Montejo, Casa Merlos, El Sella, El Churchill's, Tacos Don Juan, Tacos Hola, El Danubio, El Jarocho, El Bajío de Atzcapotzalco, El Círculo del Sureste, and El Covadonga for having some of my favorite establishments in Mexico City and for letting us shoot at them. Thank you also to Armando Vega and the "El Navegante" team for the friendship and partnership of so many years, and to all the people who provide us with their finest produce daily.

Thank you to the one and only Diana Kennedy, for the love and friendship and for teaching me so much about plants, food, and life. You are my family and constant reference.

Thank you, Alice Waters, for the inspiration and generosity, and for trusting that the world can be a better place.

To Gilbert Pilgram, thanks for lighting the way so many times, and for reminding us all that laughing and enjoying life is as nurturing as food.

Thank you to Ignacio Mattos for sharing so much about life and food, and for introducing me to Fernando Aciar.

Thanks to Fernando Mesta and Pepe Rojas, for being my family and for opening Gaga every day.

Thank you to Christian de León for the daily inspiration and infinite love.

Thank you also to friends who have helped so much in different ways through the years: Federico Shott, for all the conversations about life and book titles; Eduardo González, for the laughs and support throughout; and to Azikiwee Anderson for the recipe testing, but mostly for the friendship.

And thanks to all the friends from the notable Bay Area community of cooks, bakers, food producers, and farmers, and to the community of teachers and parents at the San Francisco Friends school. You have all shown us a home outside of Mexico City.

Last, to all our guests in the restaurants who have trusted us and make it possible to go on doing what we love day after day, thank you.

INDEX

Text copyright ©2019 by Gabriela Cámara
Photographs copyright ©2019 by Marcus Nilsson

Published in the United States by Lorena Jones Books,
an imprint of Crown Publishing Group, a division of
Penguin Random House LLC, New York.
www.crownpublishing.com
www.tenspeed.com

Lorena Jones Books and the Lorena Jones Books colophon
are trademarks of Penguin Random House, LLC.

Library of Congress Cataloging-in-Publication Data
on file with publisher

Hardcover ISBN: 978-0-399-58057-4
Ebook ISBN: 978-0-399-58058-1

Design and art direction by James Casey.

Printed in China

This book was set in Neutraface and Neutraface 2,
by House Industries.

10 9 8 7 6 5 4 3 2 1

First Edition